# THE HAGUE TRIBUNAL, SREBRENICA AND THE MISCARRIAGE OF JUSTICE

# THE HAGUE TRIBUNAL, SREBRENICA AND THE MISCARRIAGE OF JUSTICE

## FOUR ESSAYS

### BY

Christopher Black
Stephen Karganović
Višeslav Simić
Jovan Milojevich

FOREWORD BY
James Bissett,
Canadian Ambassador to Yugoslavia (1990–1992)

AFTERWORD BY
Peter Brock

POST SCRIPT BY
Jean Toschi Marazzani Visconti

Unwritten History, Inc.
Chicago, Illinois

# CONTENTS

PREFACE by Stephen Karganović ........................ vii

FOREWORD by Ambassador James Bisset ................... xi

THE ICTY'S OPEN CONTEMPT FOR JUSTICE by Christopher Black .... 17

THE ICTY AND SREBRENICA by Stephen Karganović ........... 45
1. The Theoretical Framework ........................ 45
2. The Nature of Proof ............................. 47
3. Case Study I: The Branjevo/Pilica Execution Site ........... 50
   *I.* .......................................... *51*
   *II.* .......................................... *52*
   *III.* ......................................... *54*
   *IV.* .......................................... *66*
   *V.* ........................................... *71*
   *VI.* .......................................... *74*
4. Case Study II: The Kravica Execution Site ............... 77
5. ICTY radio intercept evidence ...................... 96
6. Genocide ..................................... 115
7. Conclusions ................................... 126
ANNEX I: DRAŽEN ERDEMOVIĆ'S ARMY
   OF REPUBLIKA SRPSKA CONTRACT WITH
   SIGNATURES OF GENERAL MLADIĆ (VERSION A)
   AND GENERAL DE GAULLE (VERSION B) ............... 129
ANNEX II: MODEL WITH HANDS
   TIED IN THE BACK AND LYING FACE
   DOWN AS DESCRIBED BY WITNESS "Q" ............... 133
ANNEX III: INTERPRETATION OF
   FORENSIC EVIDENCE RELATED TO THE
   KRAVICA WAREHOUSE IN ICTY JUDGMENTS ........... 134
   *POPOVIĆ ET AL., TRIAL JUDGMENT* .................. *134*
   *KARADŽIĆ TRIAL JUDGMENT* ...................... *135*
ANNEX IV: FORENSIC SITUATION AT MASS BURIAL
   SITES LINKED TO THE KRAVICA WAREHOUSE ......... 138
   *RAVNICE* ..................................... *138*
   *GLOGOVA* .................................... *139*
   *ZELENI JADAR* ................................. *140*
ANNEX V: MUSLIM MILITARY AGE
   MALES CAPTURED BUT NOT EXECUTED BY
   SERB FORCES BETWEEN 11 AND 17 JULY 1995 ......... 141
PERCEPTIONS OF INJUSTICE: THE ICTY HAS PLANTED
THE SEEDS OF FUTURE BALKAN WARS by Višeslav Simić ....... 145

Introduction.............................................................. 146
Unexpected Agreement on the
  Need for a War Crimes Tribunal............................ 150
Many Former Yugoslavs, Particularly Serbs,
  Believe the ICTY Is an Illegitimate Institution........ 155
The ICTY as a Western Political Tool......................... 161
Problems with the Rules of
  Procedure and Evidence at the ICTY...................... 166
The Problem of Biased and Selective Indictments........ 169
The Deaths of Accused Persons *en Route* to
  The Hague as well as of Those in Its Custody.......... 176
The Disparity in Acquittals and Length of Sentencing
  with Respect to the Nationality and Religion of Those
  Who Have Been Detained, Accused, and Convicted... 178
Racism as a Perceived Basis
  for the Establishment of the Tribunal.................... 179
Conclusions............................................................ 180
WHEN JUSTICE FAILS by Jovan Milojevich................. 185
Critics Versus Supporters of the ICTY....................... 189
Method.................................................................. 196
  *Sample*............................................................. *196*
  *Coding*.............................................................. *196*
Results................................................................... 198
  *Preliminary Analyses*......................................... *198*
Sample Characterization........................................ 200
Ethnicity of Victims................................................ 202
Ethnicity of Defendants.......................................... 204
Discussion............................................................. 211
Ethnicity Versus Other Factors................................ 211
Bosnian Croatians Versus "Croatian Croatians"......... 213
Limitations and Future Directions............................ 215
Conclusion............................................................ 216
References............................................................. 218
AFTERWORD: CARICATURE by Peter Brock............... 221
'Justice Delayed Is Justice Denied'........................... 224
What Price? What Costs?......................................... 226
'Out of Africa' by 'Moonlight'.................................. 228
POST SCRIPT by Jean Toschi Marazzani Visconti....... 233
NOTE ON THE AUTHORS......................................... 240

# PREFACE

The Bologna-based *Yugoslav Coordination* (*Coordinamento Nazionale per la Jugoslavia*) may take credit for inspiring this volume. Two essays in this book, *The ICTY and Srebrenica* (as it was originally titled) and *When Justice Fails: Re-raising the Question of Ethnic Bias at the International Criminal Tribunal for the Former Yugoslavia* (ICTY), shared the 2018 Giuseppe Torre Award, which was established by the group's Secretary Andrea Martocchia.

The young American scholar Jovan Milojevich investigates the possibility of bias in ICTY verdicts in *When Justice Fails*. His meticulously documented study reaches the unfortunate conclusion that "the only factors that predicted verdict and sentencing were defendant ethnicity and victim ethnicity." If correct, it's a far cry from the traditional representation of blind justice.

In *The ICTY's Open Contempt for Justice*, the distinguished international lawyer Christopher Black dissects the inner workings of The Hague and Rwanda *ad hoc* tribunals, before both of which he has appeared. His conclusions, if upheld by time, the sternest judge of all, are skeptical of the future of international justice.

Political scientist Višeslav Simić asks pertinent questions about the impact of The Hague Tribunal on local co-existence and reconciliation in his amply documented essay *Perceptions of Injustice: The ICTY Has Planted the Seeds of Future Balkan Wars*.

The International Criminal Tribunal for the Former Yugoslavia ("the ICTY" or "the Hague Tribunal") is a peculiar institution. It was illegally established in 1993 in contravention of the UN Charter. The Tribunal's creation also bore strong traces of the involvement of intelligence agencies.[1] The Hague Tribunal has violated elementary principles of judicial independence by allowing itself to be largely staffed and financed by the very states that hold a political interest in the outcome of its proceedings. Consequently, the Tribunal has dutifully produced boiler plate verdicts often devoid of substantive evidence and it has relied heavily upon "conventional wisdom."[2] More than twenty years after its creation, the Hague Tribunal remains an institution that merely simulates a proper international court but surprisingly it still manages to find a credulous audience to take its verdicts seriously.

This conflict between judicial independence and "conventional wisdom" is blatant in the case of Srebrenica. The ICTY is the single greatest proponent of the bankrupt conventional narrative about the events that took place in Srebrenica, which consists essentially of two tirelessly repeated refrains of wartime propaganda: "genocide" and "8,000 executed men and boys." Once a war is over, the propaganda which accompanied it normally recedes into oblivion. No one today takes seriously the allegation, common during World War I, that German soldiers were eating Belgian babies for breakfast. Once it was no longer necessary to generate outrage and rouse the fighting spirit, this one was quietly shelved like many similarly outlandish allegations.

Whatever tactical purposes Srebrenica may have served at its inception in July 1995 (such as overshadowing the NATO-orchestrated Croat ethnic cleansing and murder rampage in Kraj-

---

1  *See* DCI Interagency Task Force, February 1, 1993, p. 7, policy recommendations addressed to CIA director, including "Establish a War Crimes Tribunal," CIA Historical Balkan Task Force Collections Division document #C05916707.

2  The phrase is gratefully borrowed from: Jokić, A. "Conventional Wisdom About Yugoslavia and Rwanda: Methodological Perils and Moral Implications," Journal of Philosophy of International Law, (2013) v.4(1).

ina which began three weeks later, as freely admitted by U.S. ambassador in Zagreb at the time, Peter Galbraith, or preventing hardline Bosnian Serb leaders from participating in the Dayton peace conference, as confirmed by Galbraith's diplomatic colleague, Richard Holbrooke), shortly thereafter, Srebrenica was assigned some strategic political tasks as well.

To name a few, Srebrenica soon evolved into the founding myth of the Bosnian Muslim ethnicity. It emerged also as the generator of a seemingly permanent rift between Muslim and Orthodox communities in Bosnia, the two largest, which necessitated in turn the permanent presence of imperialist forces supposedly to ensure stability and maintain peace between the opposing factions. And last, but not least, it was transfigured into a handy rationale for the imperialist doctrine of R2P, Right to Protect. In its practical application — inspired by the slogan "never another Srebrenica" — the doctrine has led to several destructive and illegal Western military interventions motivated by narrow geopolitical interests and plain plunder. These "humanitarian" wars have so far cost several million — paradoxically mostly Muslim — lives.

Without the quasi-judicial veneer provided by The Hague Tribunal's mercenary treatment of Srebrenica, arguably much of the above would not have happened or at least could not have been as easily accomplished. Nor could — in the eyes of many superficially informed laymen — the "conventional wisdom" of the Srebrenica wartime propaganda narrative have been ostensibly validated by what is misleadingly packaged to appear as a serious international judicial institution.

Stephen Karganović
*President, Srebrenica Historical Project*

# FOREWORD

by

Ambassador James Bissett
Canadian Ambassador to Yugoslavia (1990–1992)

*The evil that men do lives after them.*

William Shakespeare

The wars in the Balkans in the early 1990s were the first indications that despite the collapse of the Soviet Union, and the triumph of the United States as the supreme global power, the expected *Pax Americana* was not going to usher in a new world order of peace, security, and happiness ever-after. Instead, what we saw was the emergence of a "New World Order" of a different kind. One that was prepared to use any means — legal or illegal; fair or foul; military force, or economic pressure — to ensure that no other power might arise that could challenge American world dominance.

The eventual recovery of Russia presented the only possible rival at the time. Despite suffering the shock of the collapse of the Soviet Union, Russia still possessed nuclear weapons and powerful economic potential. The American leadership lost no time in taking steps to ensure that this did not happen. One of the first targets was the Socialist Federal Republic of Yugoslavia. During the Cold War, Yugoslavia had played an important role as a buffer between the West and the USSR, but it had now become an obstacle to the geopolitical plans of the United States as well as of the self-interest of newly united Germany.

The dissolution of Yugoslavia and the subsequent armed conflict that followed among the religious and ethnic factions was a direct result of the determination of the U.S. and German leaderships to ensure that what had been a peaceful and relatively successful non-aligned nation was broken up into its component parts.

xi

The break-up thus removed a possible impediment to the long-range plan of using NATO as the primary instrument to encircle and isolate Russia. The plan was successful but at terrible costs.

The costs are to be measured not only by the dreadful loss of life and the displacement of thousands of people from their Balkan homelands; not only by the horrific nature of the many atrocities committed by all sides in this unnecessary conflict; not only because of the lies, duplicity, and hypocrisy manifested by the United States and its strongest NATO allies; but also by their actions which were from beginning to end in violation of international law and the United Nations Charter. Although the leaders of these nations were professing to be interventionists in the name of human rights, they were in fact guilty of the most serious of all war crimes — waging aggressive war.

Of the many crimes committed, clearly one of the most egregious was the manner in which U.S. President Bill Clinton turned the NATO treaty upside down and transformed what had been a purely defensive organization into an aggressive and powerful war machine. The purely defensive nature of the 1949 treaty was anchored in the wording of its first article — that NATO would never "... use, or threaten to use force, in the resolution of international disputes, and would always act in accordance with the United Nations Charter." Article 1, of the NATO treaty was simply ignored when the U.S. President, during the illegal bombing of Serbia in March 1999, announced at NATO's fiftieth birthday party in Washington that NATO would henceforth intervene militarily whenever and wherever it decided to do so. So much for the rule of law.

During that same month, the U.S. President also announced that Poland, the Czech Republic, and Hungary would be joining NATO, and he thus broke the promise made to Russian President Mikhail Gorbachev that if Russia allowed a united Germany to join NATO, then NATO would never expand eastward. So much for promises kept. Since then we have seen Russia completely surrounded by NATO countries. As a German member of the Bundestag has warned: "Germans Wake Up! Do you realize that German panzers are once again within a few hundred kilometers of 'Leningrad'?" The irony of his warning was not lost on his fellow countrymen.

One of the most (among a number of) disturbing features of the Balkan disaster is the ease with which our so-called democratic leaders were able to get away with the most blatant crimes without even a murmur or suggestion that what they were doing was in utter contempt and a serious violation of everything their citizens had so recently fought for against the threat of world domination by Hitler's Nazis. The illegal bombing of Serbia shattered the framework of international peace and security that had existed since the end of World War II, yet the NATO leaders, with the exception of Greece, uttered not a note of concern.

During the Balkan wars, Western politicians, the mainstream media, and the rank and file of most of the NATO countries sheepishly fell in line and accepted the simplistic notion that everything that was going wrong in the Balkans was the fault of the Serbs. All the atrocities, all the killing, all the ethnic cleansing, all the ceasefire violations — it was only the Serbian leaders who were responsible. No one questioned why Croatia was able to "cleanse" over the course of five days in August 1995 a quarter of a million ethnic Serbs who had lived in the country for hundreds of years. Again, not a note of concern because it was unworthy of western media attention.

No one questioned how it was possible in the closing months of the twentieth century that NATO aircraft would rain down bombs and missiles for seventy-eight days and nights on a small country in Europe that was no threat to its neighbors; that possessed no weapons of mass destruction; that had valiantly fought at the side of Britain and France in two world wars; and that was simply attempting lawfully to suppress an armed rebellion against an acknowledged terrorist organization. Those few who did protest this outrage were regarded at best as naive or at worst disloyal.

The dissolution of Yugoslavia was a premeditated and well-planned strategy based on a formula that was later used to bring down a succession of other countries targeted by the United States and that was frequently supported either by some or all its NATO allies. The formula involved first: destabilizing the chosen country by cutting off aid and other financial instruments, thus creating economic difficulties and social unrest. This was followed by establishing and supporting NGOs to work against the ruling power and by providing financial assistance to opposition politicians and anti-government media outlets. Street demonstrations and protests designed to provoke retaliation and obtain foreign news coverage were organized and financed, which added to the image of a nation in revolt against its dictatorial leaders.

The next step was to demonize the leaders by portraying them as power-mad and evil tyrants who were guilty of crimes against human rights as well as atrocities. These charges were then used to indict individuals before a judicial body that was organized and controlled by their accusers. In the case of Yugoslavia, the International Criminal Tribunal for the Former Yugoslavia (IC-TY) was given this role. This tribunal was inaugurated by the Americans in 1993 during the fighting in Bosnia and Croatia allegedly to bring war criminals to justice, but in reality to serve as an instrument that would do as it was told by its political masters. Its judicial image draped it in the robes of impartiality and distinction. It was a high-profile court with dignified and impartial judges, all of whom were chosen with care; were flattered to be so chosen; and they were well paid.

The Hague Tribunal is the subject of these essays. The four authors (two attorneys and two political scientists) have chosen to examine and analyze the Tribunal. After having followed its deliberations, its procedures, and its judgments, they concluded that among all the other crimes committed by the US-led NATO powers during the Balkan wars, the role of The Hague Tribunal stands out as the single crime that has had the most damaging impact on future attempts to realize a truly genuine system of international justice.

The Tribunal and its final judgments are assumed by its creators as having achieved a major triumph. They boast that the Tribunal has finally brought to justice some of the most deadly international war criminals since the Nuremberg Trials. They boast that the Tribunal helped set the stage for the creation in 2005 of the International Criminal Court. These claims have been accepted by world public opinion partly because the day-to-day proceedings of the Tribunal received little publicity or coverage by the international media, and the Tribunal itself of course carefully controlled any news releases or press conferences it fed to the compliant media.

However, as the authors of this book disclose in graphic detail, The Hague Tribunal in fact violated almost all of the fundamental and basic principles of the law. From the dubious legality of its origins to its obvious and shameless bias against Serbian military and political leaders, the Tribunal has performed more like a Star Chamber than a respected legal body empowered to judicially administer the law. Time and again the Tribunal violated the cherished principle of prosecutorial impartiality. One of its most disturbing judgments involved its adjudication of the so-called Srebrenica massacre. As this book points out, there is little hard evidence that would justify any normal court to reach the conclusion that genocide took place there. Yet this was the ruling of the Tribunal. Attempts made to review this decision have as yet failed.

To their credit, these essays unequivocally destroy the methods used by the Tribunal to justify what went on in Srebrenica after it fell to Bosnian Serb forces. The Tribunal itself was unable to agree on the number of victims alleged to have been executed by Serbian forces. It accepted second-hand evidence from witnesses who were not subject to cross-examination. It accepted without question a video of unknown origin of the apparent executions of six or seven young men miles away from Srebrenica as proof of genocide. It was, in truth, a verdict reeking of political interference and motive. It was a verdict that yet may prove to discredit and undermine any hope of gaining wholehearted public confidence or trust in any International Criminal Court.

If further evidence were needed to illustrate that the Tribunal was acting throughout its existence as an apologist and collaborator of the United States and NATO, it is the outright refusal of the Tribunal to entertain any request to examine whether NATO itself had committed the supreme war crime of waging aggressive war. The facts are obviously clear — NATO's bombing of Serbia was an act of aggressive war in violation of the United Nations Charter. By any standard of legality, NATO should answer for it. The response of some NATO apologists that the bombing, although perhaps illegal, was nevertheless "legitimate," is a cynical and offensive excuse.

This extremely important book is also a terribly sad disclosure of the failure of American foreign policy to accept the fall of the Berlin Wall and the collapse of the Soviet empire as the overture to a new twenty-first century of peace and reconciliation between the United States and Russia. A new century that would dedicate itself to the rejection of Great Power rivalry and the promotion of peace and security, so that for the first time military might and brute force would not dominate the world.

# THE ICTY'S OPEN CONTEMPT FOR JUSTICE

by

Christopher Black

The indictment of President Slobodan Milošević for alleged war crimes drew the public's attention to the International Criminal Tribunal for the Former Yugoslavia at The Hague ("ICTY" or "The Hague Tribunal") and raised important questions about its impartiality and, ultimately, its purpose. For centuries, the independence of judicial bodies has been considered one of the fundamental precepts of the quest for justice. As Lord Hewart stated in 1924, it is "... of fundamental importance that justice should not only be done but should manifestly and undoubtedly be seen to be done." There is nothing more important than the public administration of justice, but, in the case of the Tribunal, a compelling argument can be made that private justice has replaced public justice, and that even the appearance of fundamental justice has been replaced by an outright contempt for justice.

It is clear that American, British, French, and German interests facilitated the creation of The Hague Tribunal from the outset, and that they worked ceaselessly behind the scenes in order to establish it. They first considered the creation of such a Tribunal during the Gulf War in order to prosecute Iraq and its leader, Saddam Hussein. The idea apparently originated with the U.S. Department of the Army, which alone should reveal much about its true purpose. The public relations campaign used to justify such a body to the general public was, of course, heavily seasoned with concerns for "human rights," the "dignity of the individual," "genocide," and "democracy."

The creators of the Tribunal, however, faced a problem. It was generally agreed that no tribunal could be created without the mechanism of a treaty ratified by all the parties affected by it. There was no time to draft such a treaty with respect to Iraq and Saddam Hussein, so other methods were used to pressure the Government of Iraq. Between 1991 and 1993, American, British, French, and German interests continually advocated the idea of an international criminal court as a means of effecting policy, a court which would be created by the members of the Security Council instead of by treaty.

Yugoslavia presented the next opportunity for such an experiment. It was first necessary to discredit its leaders in order to accelerate the break-up of this country into quasi-independent colonies, principally of Germany and the United States. Next, a tribunal was necessary, one with an international character which the general public would accept as a neutral organ of the administration of justice; but the Tribunal would also, in fact, serve as an effective propaganda weapon because it would be, of course, controlled to achieve certain political ends.

The Tribunal was created through Resolutions 808 and 827 of the Security Council in 1993. Both resolutions stated that the situation in Bosnia at that time constituted a threat to international peace and security, and that a tribunal to prosecute war criminals would help to restore peace. There was no basis for the characterization of the situation in Bosnia as a threat to international peace because it was a civil war partly controlled by the very countries that wanted to create the Tribunal. But the members of the Security Council had to characterize the civil as a threat to international peace, otherwise the Security Council would have no jurisdiction to act. The set-up for this characterization was a prior Resolution 688 of 1991, in which the Security Council stated that disregard for human rights constituted a threat to international security, so the civil war could no longer be treated as an internal matter. This reinterpretation or revision of the UN Charter, which in fact undermined the very basis of the Charter, was forcefully advocated by Mr. Genscher, the German Foreign Minister at the time, in speeches he delivered to the German Parliament; likewise, British, French and of course American ministers advocated this approach in speeches and memorandums to each other, as well as to the Canadian Parliament in Ottawa.

Chapter VII of the UN Charter requires that there be a threat to the peace or an act of aggression before the Security Council may make use of special powers available to it under this Charter. This provision has always been understood to mean a threat to international peace — not to national peace. The members of the Security Council recognized this, so they chose to redefine a national problem as an international one. Yet in all those speeches and memoranda devoted to the subject, not one compelling reason was given to support the internationalization of the conflict other than vague references to the collapse of the socialist bloc as well as to the imperative of establishing a new world order. In fact, Mr. Genscher in his speech before the Canadian Parliament stated unequivocally that no nation would any longer be allowed to ignore the decisions of the Security Council. Even if this redefinition were a legitimate interpretation of the UN Charter — which it is not — the UN Charter only provides first for economic and then military measures, but it provides for neither judicial nor criminal measures.

Chapter VII of the UN Charter must be read in context with Chapter I of the Charter which addresses international cooperation in solving international problems of an economic, social, cultural, or humanitarian character. It says nothing of humanitarian problems arising from crises of a domestic character. It states that the UN is based on the principle of the sovereign equality of its members, a fundamental principle of international law, and that the UN is the primary guarantor of the right to self-determination of the world's peoples. If a people do not possess

19

sovereignty, then the right to self-determination is a sham. The creation of the Tribunal has completely negated this principle.

Lastly, the Charter states that nothing contained in it shall authorize the UN to intervene in matters which are essentially within the domestic jurisdiction of any state. This fundamental principle, put in the Charter so that the UN could not be used by some members to bully others, has also been fatally undermined by the creation of the Tribunal. The members of the Security Council — more precisely, the permanent members — now hold the opposite position. I submit that they have done so for reasons connected more to imperialism and less, if any at all, to humanitarianism.

In light of these facts, the Security Council's authority to create such a tribunal is more than questionable. Its creation may be credited to Madeleine Albright, who persuaded the Russian and Chinese members to vote in favor of its creation in return for economic considerations as well as for the ability to control smaller states within their own spheres of interest.

Yugoslavia was the first experiment in using a quasi-judicial international body to attack the principle of national sovereignty. As U.S. politicians have learned so well, the best way to gain support from the domestic population as its political leaders destroy another country's economy before they intervene militarily, is to condition the domestic population to hate the leadership of the target country by demonizing their leaders. The Serbian leadership was thus targeted and transformed into cartoon villains. They were compared to Adolf Hitler, a comparison which was used with alarming frequency by the United States against the long list of nations it has attacked over the last fifty years, though sometimes these leaders were just condemned as either common criminals, as Manuel Noriega was, or simply insane, as Muammar Ghadaffi was, when the nation was too small to make the Hitler comparison credible. I think Saddam Hussein was the first leader to be compared to Hitler, and declared a common criminal as well as a madman all at the same time.

Judge Antonio Cassese made the Tribunal's political character quite clear in a statement to the Secretary-General of the United Nation, Mr. Boutros-Boutros Ghali, on January 21, 1994 when he said of the role of the Tribunal: "The political and diplomatic response [to the Balkan conflict] takes into account the exigencies and the tempo of the international community. The military response will come at the appropriate time." In other words, the Tribunal was considered a political response. He went on to state: "Our tribunal will not be simply 'window dressing' but a decisive step in the construction of a new world order."

Article 16 of the governing statute of the Tribunal states that: "the Prosecutor shall act independently and shall not seek or receive instruction from any government or any other source." Article 32 states that the expenses of the Tribunal shall be borne by the regular budget of the United Nations. Both of these provisions were openly and continually violated.

Senior officials of the Tribunal openly stated, if not bragged, about its particularly close ties to the Government of the United States. In her remarks to the United States Supreme Court in Washington, D.C., on April 5, 1999, Judge Gabrielle Kirk McDonald, President of the Tribunal and an American as well, stated: "We benefited from the strong support of concerned governments and dedicated individuals such as Secretary Albright. As the permanent representative to the United Nations, she had worked with unceasing resolve to establish the Tribunal. Indeed, we often refer to her as the 'mother of the Tribunal'."[3] If she is the mother, then paternity may be ascribed to Bill Clinton, as

---

3  Tariq Ali [ed.]: *Masters of the Universe? NATO's Balkan Crusade* (Verso, 2000), pp. 164-165

Louise Arbour confirmed by her action of reporting to the President of the United States the decision to indict President Milošević two days before she announced it to the rest of the world, which was in blatant violation of her duty to remain independent. Furthermore, she and her successors in the position of prosecutor have made public appearances with U.S officials, including Madeleine Albright, and openly stated that they relied on NATO governments, which were keenly interested in undermining the Yugoslavian leadership, for investigations.

In 1996, the Prosecutor met with the Secretary-General of NATO and the Supreme Allied Commander in Europe to "establish contacts and begin discussing modalities of cooperation and assistance." On May 9, 1996, a memorandum of understanding between the Office of the Prosecutor and Supreme Headquarters Allied Powers Europe (SHAPE) was signed by both parties. Further meetings took place, including one between the President of the Tribunal and General Wesley Clark. The memorandum of May 9 detailed the practical arrangements for U.S. support for the Tribunal as well as for the transfer of indicted persons to it. In other words, NATO forces became the gendarmes of the Tribunal — not UN forces — and the Tribunal placed itself at the disposal of NATO. This relationship has continued despite the Tribunal's mandate to be independent of any national government and, therefore, any group of national governments.

The Tribunal received substantial funds from individual states, private foundations, and corporations in violation of Article 32 of its Charter. Much of its funding came from the U.S. government directly in cash and donations of computer equipment. The United States provided $700,000 in cash and $2,300,000 worth of equipment for the initial phase of its operation in the years 1993–1995 when it was being set up. During that same period, the Open Society Institute, a foundation established by George Soros, the American billionaire financier, to bring "openness" to the former east bloc countries, contributed $150,000; the Rockefeller family, through the Rockefeller Foundation, contributed $50,000; and U.S. corporations such as Time-Warner and Discovery Products made significant donations. It is also important to note that Mr. Soros' foundation not only funded the Tribunal but it also funded the main Kosovo Liberation Army ("KLA") newspaper in Pristina, an obvious conflict of interest that has not once been mentioned in the Western press.

The Tribunal also received funding from the United States Institute for Peace for its Outreach project, the public relations arm of the Tribunal set up to squelch opposition to its work in the former Yugoslav republics as well as to deflect the constant criticisms of its selective prosecution and its application of double standards. These objections, which have obvious merit, were never addressed either by the Tribunal or by any of its sponsors. The Institute for Peace is described as "an independent, nonpartisan federal institution created and funded by Congress to strengthen the nation's capacity to promote the peaceful resolution of international conflict." The Institute was established in 1984 under Ronald Reagan, and its Board of Directors is appointed by the President of the United States.

The Tribunal also received support from the Coalition for International Justice, whose purpose was to enhance the standing of the Tribunal in public opinion. The CIJ was founded and is funded by, once again, George Soros' Open Society Institute and something called CEELI, the Central and East European Law Institute, which was created by the American Bar Association and by lawyers close to the U.S. government to replace of socialist legal systems with free market ones.

Furthermore, these groups have supplied the Tribunal with much of its legal staff. In her speech to the Supreme Court, Judge McDonald said: "The Tribunal has been well served by the tremendous work of a number of lawyers who have come to the Tribunal through the CIJ and CEELI . . . ." It is also interesting to note that the occasion of Judge McDonald's speech was her acceptance of an award from the American Bar Association and CEELI. In the same speech she also said, "We are now seeking funding from states and foundations to carry out this critical effort."

The Tribunal Prosecutor Carla Del Ponte thanked the Director of the FBI at a press conference for assisting the Tribunal, and she stated: "I am very appreciative of the important support that the U.S government has provided the Tribunal. I look forward to their continued support." In response to a question as to whether the Tribunal would be investigating crimes committed by others (meaning NATO) in the Yugoslav theatre of operations, she said: "The primary focus of the Office of the Prosecutor must be on the investigation and prosecution of the five leaders of the Federal Republic of Yugoslavia and Serbia who have already been indicted." Why "must"? It was not explained. Why, if the Tribunal were impartial, wouldn't it focus equally on NATO war crimes, and the war crimes of Clinton, Schroeder, Chirac, Chretien, among others?

We can only speculate as to why. When Louise Arbour was asked by a group of Canadian lawyers led by Professor Michael Mandel to investigate all NATO leaders for war crimes in 1999, she refused to do so and later accepted, from the Prime Minister of Canada, Jean Chretien, the position of a justice of the Supreme Court of Canada, a lifetime appointment, her reward for bringing before the Tribunal the indictment against Mr. Milosevic, despite the lack of evidence against him. Since then, she has been appointed to "prestigious" positions, first on the UN Human Rights Committee, then as Director of a CIA front group, the International Crisis Group, and currently the Special Representative of the UN Secretary General for International Migration.

From the outset, the Office of the Prosecutor conducted meetings with NGOs that were eager to "cooperate with and assist the tribunal." Many of these were linked to George Soros through his Open Society Foundation. All these monies flowed through a special UN account which was financed by assessed contributions from member states as well as by voluntary contributions from states and corporations, once again in violation of its own statutes. Incidentally, it's interesting to note that the role of the Tribunal as a propaganda vehicle was indirectly acknowledged by its own staff when they failed to provide for either a courtroom or holding cells in their first budget, which amounted to approximately US$32 million. The Security Council returned the draft budget to the staff so that they could include these items, because, after all, this was supposed to be a criminal tribunal! The staff did as they were instructed. The added expense was $500,000, a mere 1.5% increase. It's also interesting to note that three of the Tribunal's first four court rooms in the Peace Palace in The Hague were loaned to it by the Carnegie Foundation.

In order to give itself the appearance of a judicial body, the Tribunal appointed judges, prosecutors, clerks, investigators, and set up its own rules of procedure and evidence as well as its own prison system. The Tribunal claimed to apply the presumption of innocence; however, unlike criminal courts with which we are familiar, the court itself is involved in laying charges against defendants. When a charge was laid, the approval of one of the trial judges had to be obtained. Yet, despite this close relationship between the prosecutor and the judges, not to mention the commitment to the charges the judges made by signing the indictment, the Tribunal rules insist on the presumption of innocence, which has been compromised in other ways, as well. The most egregious is detention, which is automatic upon arrest. There is no bail, no form of release pending trial, unless the prisoner is able to prove "exceptional circumstances." Loss of job, loss of contact with friends, family, indeed country, were not sufficient circumstances. Even ill health was deemed insufficient to obtain bail. Prisoners were treated as if they had already been convicted. They were kept in cells and had to obey prison rules; they were subjected to discipline if they did not; they were subjected to constant surveillance; their mail was censored; their family visits were restricted; they were permitted to communicate with family members only at their own expense; and there were restrictions on what defendants could see or hear on radio or television. Prisoners had to wait many months — sometimes years — before a trial took place. Yet, the Tribunal still insisted that these men were presumed innocent.

The rules of evidence of the Tribunal were relaxed to such a degree that restrictions on the admission of hearsay evidence, which had been developed over the centuries in all national courts, were pushed aside and replaced by an anything-is-admissible-if-deemed-relevant approach, even if it was third-hand hearsay. There was no jury. Witnesses were allowed to either testify by written statement or under code names. In the Tribunal's yearbook for 1994, this statement appears: "The Tribunal does not need to shackle itself with restrictive rules which have developed out of the ancient trial-by-jury system." There are provisions in the rules, in circumstances which are vaguely defined, for closed hearings — in other words, for secret trials — which is not only the very essence of injustice but it is also the *modus operandi* of political courts. The Tribunal used sealed indictments so that no one could know whether he had been charged until the military police swept him off the street. Suspects could be detained for up to ninety days without charge. We all know from newspaper accounts what prisoners may be liable to undergo in a day or two when they are being held by the police.

Rule 92 is perhaps the most dangerous. It states that confessions shall be presumed to be free and voluntary unless the contrary is established by the prisoner. Imagine that a confession may be presumed to be free and voluntary after ninety days of incarceration during which the prisoner is at the mercy of military police and prosecutors. Almost every other court in the world presumes the opposite or, because of the notorious unreliability of confessions made in police custody, is moving to prohibit such confessions entirely. This Tribunal went back to the days of Star Chamber and resorted to the justice of the thirteenth century. Finally, those who have been sentenced and convicted are imprisoned in foreign countries, with the result that they are imprisoned and exiled at the same time.

There is even a special provision for the obtaining of evidence from NGOs such as George Soros Open Society Foundation, whose conflict of interest has already been demonstrated. Those who stand accused have the right to choose counsel — on paper, at least — but in reality this right is infringed by the Registrar, who may disqualify counsel for many reasons, including unfriendliness to the Tribunal. In fact, this writer and a Russian colleague, Prof. Alexander Mezyaev, were prohibited from representing General Mladić on the grounds that we were unfriendly to the Tribunal and that we had been critical of it.

Among the many ironies of the NATO war against Yugoslavia, one was the role of the Tribunal's Chief Prosecutor, Louise Arbour, who was elevated by Canadian Prime Minister Jean Chretien to Canada's highest court in 1999. Although this nomination was entirely justified on the grounds of political service to the NATO powers, it was in fact a monumental travesty when the question of the proper administration of justice entered into consideration. In fact, since both Arbour and the Tribunal played a key role in expediting NATO's war crimes, an excellent case could have been made that in a just world she would be wearing a ball and chain instead of judicial robes.

The moment of truth for Arbour and the Tribunal came in the midst of NATO's seventy-eight-day bombing campaign against Yugoslavia in 1999. Arbour appeared at an April 20 press conference with British Foreign Secretary Robin Cook to receive from him documentation on alleged Serbian war crimes. Then on May 27, Arbour announced the indictment of Serbian President Slobodan Milošević and four of his associates for war crimes. The inappropriateness of a putative judicial body taking such steps in the midst of the war, when Germany, Russia, and other powers were trying to find a diplomatic resolution to the conflict, was staggering.

At Arbour's April 20 appearance with Cook, she stated that: "It is inconceivable . . . that we would in fact agree to be guided by the political will of those who may want to advance an agenda." But her appearance with Cook and the follow-up indictments perfectly fitted the agenda of the NATO leadership. There was growing criticism of NATO's increasingly intense bombardment of civilian infrastructure in Serbia. Meanwhile, Blair and Cook were lashing out at critics in the British media for insufficient enthusiasm for the war. Arbour and the Tribunal's intervention, which declared the Serbian leadership guilty of war crimes, was a public relations coup that helped justify NATO policies and permitted the bombardment to escalate. Madeleine Albright, among other NATO leaders and propagandists, noted that the indictments "make very clear to the world and the publics in our countries that this [NATO policy] is justified because of the crimes committed, and I think also will enable us to keep moving all these processes [i.e., bombardment] forward" (CNN, May 27) U.S. State Department spokesperson James Rubin said that "this unprecedented step . . . justifies in the clearest possible way what we have been doing these past months." (CNN "Morning News," May 27)

Although the Tribunal had been established in May 1993, and the most serious atrocities in the Yugoslav wars occurred as the old Federation disintegrated from June 1991 to the Dayton peace talks in late 1995, no indictment was ever brought against Milošević for any of those atrocities. The aforementioned indictment of Milošević on May 27 referred only to a reported 241 deaths in the early months of 1999. Thus, this indictment bears the hallmarks of having been hastily prepared to meet an urgent need. Arbour even mentioned on April 20 that she had "visited NATO" to "dialogue with potential information providers in order to generate unprecedented support that the Tribunal needs if it will perform its mandate in a time frame that will make it relevant to the resolution of conflict . . . of a magnitude of what is currently unfolding in Kosovo." Even though her indictment of Milošević impeded a negotiated resolution, it did help expedite a resolution by intensifying the bombing campaign. Arbour noted that: "I am mindful of the impact that this indictment may have on the peace process," and she said that although indicted individuals are "entitled to the presumption of innocence until they are convicted, the evidence upon which this indictment was confirmed raises serious questions about their suitability to be guarantors of any deal, let alone a peace agreement." (CNN "Live Event," Special, May 27) So, not only did Arbour admit awareness of the political significance of her indictment, but she also suggested that her possible interference with any diplomatic efforts was justified because the indicted individuals, though not yet found guilty, were unsuitable negotiating partners.[4] This

---

4　The identical agenda was articulated by one-time ICTY President Antonio Cassese, to the effect that, "The indictment [of Milošević and Karadžić] means that these gentlemen will not be able to participate in peace negotiations . . . . The politicians may not give a damn, but I'm relying on the pressure of public opinion." Quoted in "Karadžić A Pariah, Says War Crimes Tribunal Chief," ANP English News Bulletin, July 27, 1995.

spectacularly contra-judicial political judgment, along with the convenient timing of the indictments, points up Arbour and the Tribunal's highly-charged political role.

The NATO powers focused almost exclusively on alleged Serbian misdeeds during the entire course of the breakup of Yugoslavia, and the Tribunal has followed suit in the wake of NATO. A great majority of the Tribunal's indictments have been of Serbs, but those few indictments against Croats and Muslims often seemed to have been timed to counter claims of anti-Serbian bias (*e.g.*, the first indictment of a non-Serb (Ivica Rajić)) was announced during the peace talks held in Geneva while NATO was still bombing the Bosnian Serbs in September 1995).

Arbour did state on April 20, 1999 that: "the real danger is whether we would fall into that [*i.e.*, following a certain political agenda] inadvertently by being in the hands of information-providers who might have an agenda that we would not be able to discern." But even an imbecile could discern that NATO had an agenda, and that by simply accepting the flood of documents proffered by Cook and Albright, advertently, the Tribunal necessarily followed that agenda. Arbour even acknowledged her voluntary and almost exclusive "dependencies . . . on the goodwill of states" to provide information that "will guide our analysis of the crime base." Her April 20, 1999, reference to the "morality of the [NATO's] enterprise" and her remarks on Milošević's possible lack of character which disqualified him from negotiations, as well as her eagerness to support NATO with his indictment, point quite clearly to her understanding of rendering political service to NATO.

In a dramatic illustration of Arbour-Tribunal bias, a 150-page Tribunal report entitled "The Indictment of Operation Storm: A Prima Facie Case" describes war crimes committed by the Croatian armed forces in their expulsion of more than 200,000 Serbs from Krajina in August 1995, during which "at least 150 Serbs were summarily executed, and many hundreds disappeared." This report, leaked to *The New York Times* (to the dismay of Tribunal officials), found that the Croatian murders and other inhumane acts were "widespread and systematic," and that "sufficient material" was available to make the three named Croatian generals accountable under international law.[5] But the article also reported that the United States, which supported the Croats' ethnic cleansing of Serbs in Krajina, not only defended the Croats in the Tribunal but also refused to supply requested satellite photos of areas of Krajina that had been attacked by the Croats. The U.S. failed to provide other requested information. The result was that the Croat generals named in the report on Operation Storm were never indicted. Even though the number of Serbs who had been executed or who simply disappeared over the course of a mere four days was at least equal to the 241 victims of Serbian named in the indictment of Milošević, no corresponding indictment of Croatian President Tuđman was ever issued by the Tribunal. But this was not a failure of data collection — the United States opposed indictments of its allies: thus, the Tribunal did not produce any.

As for President Milošević, it is this writer's position that he raised a successful defense against the false charges against him, and that this resulted in his murder at the hands of the Tribunal.

On March 11, 2006, President Slobodan Milošević died in the NATO prison at Schevenignen. No one has yet been held accountable for his death. In the years since the end of his lonely struggle to defend himself and his country against the false charges fabricated by the NATO powers, the only country to demand a public inquiry into the circumstances of his death was

---

5 Raymond Bonner, "War Crimes Panel Finds Croat Troops 'Cleansed' the Serbs," NYT, March 21, 1999.

Russia, when Foreign Minister Sergey Lavrov, who stated that Russia did not accept The Hague Tribunal's denial of responsibility, demanded an impartial international investigation be conducted. Instead, the NATO tribunal conducted its own investigation, known as the Parker Report, which, as one might expect, exonerated itself of all blame.

But Milošević's death cannot go unexamined, the questions unanswered, the guilty unpunished. The world cannot continue to accept war and brutality in place of peace and diplomacy. The world cannot continue to tolerate governments that hold peace, humanity, national sovereignty, the self-determination of peoples, and the rule of law in contempt.

The death of Slobodan Milošević was clearly the only way out of the dilemma the NATO powers had brought upon themselves by charging him before the Tribunal. The propaganda against him was on an unprecedented scale. His trial was portrayed in the press as one of the world's great dramas, as world theatre in which an evil man would be made to answer for his crimes. But, of course, there had been no crimes, except those committed by the NATO alliance, and the attempt to fabricate a case against him collapsed into farce.

The trial was necessary from NATO's point of view in order to justify the aggression against Yugoslavia. The trial also attempted to justify the putsch by the pro-Western forces in Belgrade, which were supported by NATO and through which democracy in Yugoslavia was finally destroyed and Serbia reduced to a NATO protectorate under a quisling regime. Milošević's illegal arrest by NATO forces in Belgrade, his illegal detention in the Belgrade Central Prison, his illegal rendition to the former Gestapo prison at Scheveningen near The Hague, and the show trial that followed were all part of the melodrama scripted for the edification of global public opinion, and it could only end with the conviction — or death — of the cardboard villain, President Milošević.

Since the conviction of President Milošević was clearly not possible after all the evidence had been heard, his death became the only way out for the NATO powers. His acquittal would have brought down the entire structure of the propaganda framework of the NATO war machine and the western interests that use NATO as their armed fist.

NATO clearly did not expect President Milošević to defend himself with such courage and determination. The media coverage of the beginning of the trial was constant and front-page. It was touted as the trial of the century. Yet soon after it began, the media coverage evaporated and coverage of the trial was relegated to the back pages. Things had gone terribly wrong for NATO right from the very start. The key to the problem was expressed by the following statement President Milošević made to the Tribunal judges during the trial:

"This is a political trial. What is at issue here is not at all whether I committed a crime. What is at issue is that certain intentions are ascribed to me from which consequences are later derived that are beyond the expertise of any conceivable lawyer. The point here is that the truth about the events in the former Yugoslavia has to be told here. It is that which is at issue, not the procedural questions, because I'm not sitting here because I was accused of a specific crime. I'm sitting here because I am accused of conducting a policy against the interests of this or another party."

The Prosecution, *i.e.*, the United States and its allies, were not expecting a real defense. This is clear from the inept indictments and confused charges, as well as the complete failure to bring any evidence that could withstand even the most rudimentary scrutiny. The Prosecution case began falling apart as soon as the trial began. But once started, it had to continue. NATO was locked into a box of its own making. If the Tribunal had dropped the charges — or if Milošević had been acquitted — then the political and geostrategic ramifications were would have been enormous. NATO would have to explain the real reasons for the aggression against Yugoslavia. NATO leaders would themselves have to face war crimes charges. The loss of prestige would have been incalculable and irreversible. President Milošević would once again have enjoyed the status of a popular political figure — if not a hero — in the Balkans. The only way out for NATO was to end the trial but without either releasing Milošević or admitting the truth about the real motives for the war. This logic required his death in prison and the subsequent abandonment of the trial.

The Parker Report contains facts indicating that, at minimum, the NATO Tribunal engaged in criminal conduct with respect to Milošević's failing health by withholding medical treatment during his detention, which resulted in his death. The Tribunal was told time and again that he was gravely ill; that he was suffering from heart problems that needed proper diagnosis and treatment. Milošević needed complete rest before engaging in a lengthy trial. The Tribunal, however, continually ignored the advice of the doctors and pushed him to keep going with the trial, because the Tribunal knew full well that the stress of the trial would eventually kill him.

Thus, the Tribunal refused to allow Milošević to undergo prescribed medical treatment in Russia for apparently political reasons, and it once again favored its own political interests instead of Milošević's health-care requirements. In other words, they deliberately withheld necessary medical treatment that could have led to his recuperation. This is a form of homicide. It is manslaughter in common law jurisdictions.

Several unexplained facts contained in the Parker Report need further investigation before ruling out poisoning, namely, the presence of the drugs Rifampicin and Droperidol in his system. No proper investigation was conducted as to how these drugs had been introduced into his body. The Report gave no consideration to their effect. The presence of these drugs combined with the long unexplained delay in performing an autopsy raised serious questions which today still remain unanswered.

The Parker Report, despite its illogical conclusions exonerating the NATO tribunal, provides the basis to call for a public inquiry into the causes of the death of President Milosevic. This is reinforced by the fact that the Commandant of the UN prison where President Milošević was held, a certain Mr. McFadden according to documents published by WikiLeaks, was supplying information to U.S. authorities about Milošević throughout his detention and trial. The call for a public inquiry is further reinforced by the fact that Milošević wrote a handwritten letter to Sergei Lavrov in care of the Russian Embassy just a few days before his death which stated that he believed he was being poisoned. Unfortunately, Milošević died before the letter could be delivered in time for a response.

Taken together, these facts as well as others demand that a public international inquiry be held to thoroughly investigate the circumstances surrounding President Milošević's death, not only for his sake and for his widow and son's sake, but for the sake of all of us who face the relentless aggression and propaganda of the NATO powers. Justice requires it. International peace and security demand it.

### *"All that is a lie. This is a NATO-style trial."*

The defiant words of General Mladić to the judges of the Tribunal rang out loud and clear the day they pretended to convict him. He could have added "but history will absolve me" and much more, but he was thrown out of the courtroom by the chief judge, Alphons M.M. Orie, in his condescending manner as if he were dealing with a delinquent schoolboy instead of a man who had been falsely accused of crimes he did not commit.

Maria Zakharova, the Russian Foreign Ministry spokeswoman, echoed General Mladić's words on November 23, 2017:

> We have again to state that the guilty verdict, delivered by the International Criminal Tribunal for the former Yugoslavia against Mladić, is the continuation of the politicized and biased line [of thinking], which has initially dominated the ICTY's work.

Both General Mladić and the Russian government are correct. The document, referred to as a "judgement," proves it, for it reads like a propaganda tract instead of a legal judgement. In just over 2,500 pages, the trio of "judges" recite the prosecution version of events from the first to the last paragraph. The Defense is mentioned only in passing.

The Tribunal rejects claims that it was a biased court — "a NATO court" — but it proved it with the very first witnesses called to set the stage for the travesty of justice that was to follow. Richard Butler was called to testify on general military matters as well as on the political structure in Bosnia and the Republika Srpska. He was presented as an expert witness, a "military analyst," which he is, but not an independent one. No, at the time of his testimony he was a member of the United States National Security Agency who had been seconded to the Tribunal as a staffer. So, the first witness against General Mladić was biased on two counts. He worked for the American intelligence services that supported the enemies of General Mladić and Yugoslavia, and he was a member of the prosecution staff. It is as if the NSA and the Prosecutor had, at the same time, stepped into the box to testify against the accused. Butler's testimony played a large role in the trial; the same role he had played in the trial of General Krstić.

Another military expert, Reynaud Theunens, who is also working on the staff of the Prosecution, then appears. Expert witnesses in criminal trials are supposed to be completely neutral. But not only was Mr. Theunens acting on behalf of the Prosecutor, he was at the same time a Belgian Army intelligence officer. So there we have it right at the opening of the trial. The stage was set. NATO was in charge of the case. NATO officers were on the payroll of the Tribunal. It *was* a NATO tribunal masquerading as a UN tribunal. Accordingly, throughout the judgement, NATO crimes and the crimes of the opposing Bosnian forces are never referred to. The context is deliberately constricted in order to present a narrow and distorted picture of events which favors the NATO alliance.

The Mladić judgement continues with detailed recitations of Prosecution witness testimony. Defense witnesses, on the few occasions in which they appear, never had their testimony set out in like detail. One line perhaps was devoted to a witness and all of them are dismissed as biased if their testimony conflicted with the testimony of the Prosecution witnesses.

And of what does the Prosecution evidence consist? It consists of some oral testimony of NATO military officers involved in the events in question and who were also working in with UN forces against General Mladić as well as the troops under his command; it consists of the testimony of opposing Bosnian Army soldiers and their families; and it consists of witness statements and "adjudicated facts," that is "facts" held to be so by another set of judges in another ICTY case, no matter whether true or false. On a number of occasions, the judges state something to the effect that "the Defense claims X did not happen and relied on certain evidence to support that claim. Where this evidence conflicts with the adjudicated facts, we reject it."

There are numerous instances of reliance on hearsay evidence. Time and again, a paragraph in the judgment begins with the words, "The witness was told . . . ." Thanks to corrupt jurists like former Canadian Prosecutor Louise Arbour, the use of hearsay evidence — even double hearsay — was admitted as evidence in these trials even though it is forbidden in the rest of the world, because hearsay testimony cannot be verified for reliability and accuracy.

I was not able to personally observe much of the trial. I only followed it intermittently by video, so I am unable to comment on all the factual findings the trial judges determined in the voluminous judgement in which they condemned, on page after tedious page, General Mladić and his government. Those who are aware of the real history of events will realize that each paragraph of condemnation was neither more nor less than the same NATO propaganda put out during the conflict, but made to resemble a judgement.

Because it is not a judgement. A true judgement in a criminal trial should contain the evidence presented by the Prosecution, the evidence presented by the Defense, and the arguments of both sides about the evidence. It must contain references to witness testimony both as witnesses testified in chief and under cross-examination. Then there must be a reasoned decision by the judges on the merits of each party's case and their reasoned conclusions. But one will be hard pressed to find any trace of the Defense evidence in this document. I could find none, except for a few references in a handful of paragraphs and some footnotes, in both of which testimony of a Defense witness was briefly referred to simply in order to dismiss it because it did not support the Prosecution version of events.

Even more shocking is paucity of reference to oral testimony, that is, witness testimony. Instead there are references to "experts" connected to the CIA or the U.S. State Department or other NATO intelligence agencies that set forth their version of history, which the judges accept without question. There is no reference to any Defense experts.

Consequently, there are no reasoned conclusions from the judges as to why they decided to accept the Prosecution evidence but not the Defense evidence. After having read this document, one would be led to believe that the Defense presented no evidence at all or perhaps made only a token effort. This is not a judgement.

But there is something even more troubling about this "judgement." It is not possible to make out whether many of the witnesses referred to in the judgment testified in person because there are few references to actual testimony. Instead there are countless references to documents of various kinds and "witness statements."

This is an important factor in these trials because the witness statements referred to are statements made — or alleged to have been made — by alleged witnesses to investigators and lawyers working for the Prosecution. We know from experience in other trials that in fact these statements are often drafted by Prosecution lawyers as well as by investigators, and then presented to the "witnesses" to learn by rote. We also know that the "witnesses" often came to the attention of the Prosecution via routes that indicate the witnesses were presenting fabricated testimony and were recruited for that purpose.

At the Rwanda tribunal (which was established and controlled by the same forces and for the same reasons as the ICTY), we made a point in our trial of aggressively cross-examining these "witnesses." They invariably fell apart on the witness stand, because they could not remember the scripts that had been assigned to them. Furthermore, we made a point of asking these "witnesses" how they came to meet with the Prosecution staff as well as how their interviews were conducted and how these statements were created.

The results embarrassed the Prosecution because it became clear that the Prosecution had colluded with investigators to manipulate, pressure, and influence "witnesses." The Prosecution was complicit in inventing testimony.

Furthermore, it is important for anyone who reads this "judgement" to be able to refer to the transcript pages of the witness testimony in order to read the testimony, and read what the witness said under cross-examination. In contrast, a witness statement is not testimony. It is just an unverified statement.

A statement cannot be used as evidence. That requires the witness to get in the box and to state under oath what they observed. Then they can be questioned as to their reliability as observers, their bias, if any, their credibility, and so on. But in this case we see hundreds of references to "witness statements." This indicates that the judges based their "judgement" not on the oral testimony of the witnesses (if they were called to testify) but on their written statements prepared by the Prosecution and without facing any cross-examination by the Defense.

It is not clear at all from this judgement that any of the witnesses referred to in the statements actually testified or not. If they had, then their testimony should be cited — not their statements. The only valid purpose the statements have is to notify the lawyers of what a witness is likely to say in the trial, and to disclose the Prosecution's case to the Defense so it can prepare its case and then use the statements in the trial to cross-examine the witness by comparing the prior statement with the witness' testimony under oath on the stand.

The formula is a simple one. The Prosecution witness gets in the witness box, is asked to state what he observed about an event, and then the Defense questions the witness:

> Mr. Witness, in your statement dated x date, you said this, but today you say that.... Let's explore the discrepancy.

That's how it is supposed to go. But where is the cross-examination in this case? It is nowhere to be found.

It would require a book to recite all the problems with the Mladić "trial" as exhibited by this judgement. But there is one example which highlights the rest. It relates to Srebrenica and concerns a famous meeting that took place at the Fontana Hotel on the evening of July 11, 1995 at which General Mladić met with a Dutch peacekeeper, a colonel, in order to arrange the evacuation of civilians from the Srebrenica area and to arrange the possible laying down of arms by the 28th Division of the Bosnian Army Division. There is a video recording of this meeting available on YouTube.[6] I paraphrase, but the video shows General Mladić asking why NATO planes were bombing his positions and killing his men. He asks why the UN forces were smuggling weapons to the Bosnian military. He asks why UN forces tried to murder him personally. To each question General Mladić receives an apology from the Dutch colonel. He then asks the Dutch colonel whether he wants to die and he says no. Mladic replies: "nor do my men want to die, so why are you shooting at them?" The colonel does not answer.

The rest of the video records the discussion of a plan to evacuate the town during which Mladić offers the UN men cigarettes and offers them wine to ease the tension. For me, as a Defense lawyer, this video is a crucial element for the Defense case concerning the charges made against General Mladić with respect to Srebrenica. But there is no reference to this video in the judgement. Instead, the judges refer to the testimony of several UN-NATO officers who were at the meeting in which they totally distort and twist what was said. There is no clue as to whether the Defense ever cross-examined those liars using the video:

---

6   https://www.youtube.com/watch?v=idf_sdeVpO4

Christopher Black

"Sir, you state that this was said, but here in the video it shows that you are wrong. What do you say?" Such an exchange is nowhere to be found. Was it used and ignored by the judges or not used? I am informed that in fact the video recording was not used as evidence, which the Defense counsel on that case needs to explain. But it is clear that the Prosecution chose not to use this video recording because it would have meant the collapse of their entire case. For even the Prosecution's evidence makes it clear that the men of the Bosnian 28th Division refused to lay down their arms and that they fought their way to Tuzla. Most of the deaths resulted from fighting along the way. Many were taken prisoner. A handful of Bosnian witnesses claim these prisoners were massacred. But their testimony is of the "I-was-the-lone-miraculous-survivor-of-the-massacre" variety they tend to use in these trials.

I won't enter into the heavy use of the bogus legal concept of a "joint criminal enterprise" in order to impute criminal liability to General Mladić. It is guilt by association, and it eliminates the legal requirement of intent. That they used it shows they know they had no case against him.

In summary, the Mladić "judgment" contains within it little sense of the Defense case or even what facts were presented by the Defense, or what the Defense arguments were on the facts, nor their full legal arguments. But most importantly, we have no idea what the testimony was of most of the Prosecution witnesses, and no idea what the testimony was of Defense witnesses. It is as if there were no trial, and the judges just sat in a room sifting through Prosecution documents writing the judgement as they went along. We must suppose that this is not far from the truth.

This "judgement" and the trial are another humiliation of Yugoslavia and Serbia by the NATO alliance, since it is clear from its creation, financing, staffing, and methods that the Tribunal is

42

a NATO-controlled tribunal. This is confirmed by the statement made by the NATO Secretary-General, who said:

> I welcome the ruling . . . the Western Balkans are of strategic importance for our Alliance....[7]

In other words, General Mladić's conviction helps NATO to consolidate its hold on the Balkans by keeping the Serbs down and out. General Mladić has been made a scapegoat for the war crimes that the NATO alliance committed in Yugoslavia, which the Tribunal covers up, and thus assists NATO in committing yet more war crimes, as we have since seen.

The Tribunal has proven to be just what we expected it to be, a kangaroo court, using fascist methods of justice that engaged in selective prosecution in order to advance the NATO agenda of conquest of the Balkans as a necessary prelude to aggression against Russia. NATO uses the Tribunal as a propaganda weapon to broadcast a false history of the events in Yugoslavia, to cover up its own crimes, to keep the former republics of Yugoslavia under its thumb, and to justify NATO aggression and its occupation of former Yugoslav territory. It is a stain on the face civilization: the open contempt for justice.

---

7 Comment of NATO Secretary-General Jens Stoltenberg, 22 November 2017, https://www.nato.int/cps/en/natohq/news_149054.htm

# THE ICTY AND SREBRENICA

by

Stephen Karganović

## 1. The Theoretical Framework

The word "tribunal" originally referred to the podium, or dais, in the Roman Forum where the *praetor*[1] was seated to hear cases and render judgment in disputes brought before him. In antiquity, a tribunal dispensed justice in a way that closely corresponded to what we today call a court. Over the course of time, the practice of law began to diverge in letter and spirit from the procedures of the ancient tribunal. In more recent times, "tribunal" has acquired, whether rightly or wrongly, a decidedly more somber and peremptory — if not sinister — connotation. During the French Revolution, the *Tribunal revolutionnaire* operated as a special court tasked with trying enemies of the Revolution. It was largely unencumbered by procedural niceties. More recently, after World War II, it reappeared in the form of Military Tribunals convened by the victorious Allied Powers, one in Europe, the other in the Far East, to try the leadership of the vanquished enemies. The latest incarnation of this judicial phenomenon is the International Criminal Tribunal for the Former Yugoslavia ("ICTY") at The Hague, which was established in 1993 to judge malefactors in the Balkan conflicts of the 1990s.[2]

---

1 A Roman magistrate who ranked below consul.

2 An analogous and also *ad hoc* institution (ICTR) was established in 1994 to handle issues of criminal responsibility arising from the conflict and massacres in Rwanda earlier that year, but here its performance will not be the subject of consideration.

For the most part, The Hague Tribunal has been spared the wide-ranging as well as the close critical scrutiny that such a conceptually new (and *ad hoc*) institution — with pretensions of dealing with critical contemporary legal issues — should have been subjected to. This is not to imply that the ICTY has enjoyed universal acclaim; that a critical analysis of its performance has been entirely lacking. Yet the ICTY was obviously designed to serve as a legal laboratory to test innovative procedures and principles in anticipation of the establishment of a permanent international organ founded on similar principles, as ultimately took place with the founding of the International Criminal Court (ICC) in 2002. It is therefore regrettable that the ICTY's practices have generally received uncritical endorsement despite the fact that sporadic reservations have been expressed about certain aspects of its work.

Unlike the ICTY, whose jurisdiction is limited to the Former Yugoslavia, the ICC, for better or for worse, enjoys global jurisdiction. Its approach to dispensing international criminal justice will necessarily be influenced by its precursor. The creation of the ICC sends the implicit message that the ICTY has acquitted itself in exemplary fashion; therefore, the ICC may now legitimately benefit from the ICTY's experience, emulate its performance, and advance the cause of universal justice in a similar fashion. This conclusion is presented so vehemently that it discourages any re-examination of the dubious aspects of the ICTY's performance. Consequently, the results of the ICTY's activities have now been incorporated at a "higher level" by globalizing ICC's scope, but at the same time these same results gravely imperil the integrity of international justice.

This paper will focus on aspects of the ICTY's practice that pertain to its fact-finding mission as well as to the legal conclusions it rendered in relation to the "Srebrenica massacre," which took place in July 1995. In general, we will consider a number of illustrative examples of how various chambers of the ICTY have treated evidence in Srebrenica-related cases tried before them. More narrowly, we will examine how evidence purporting to prove the two fundamental claims made by the standard Srebrenica narrative, to wit, "8,000 executed men and boys"[3] and "genocide" — which have now been adopted by the ICTY — were received and interpreted by ICTY chambers.

How did the evidence presented to the ICTY correspond to the conclusions drawn by its chambers? How professional have its chambers been in analyzing such evidence and in applying commonly accepted legal tests of proof? Last, but not least, have the principles of the presumption of innocence and *in dubio pro reo* been properly applied in ICTY proceedings?

## 2. The Nature of Proof

In the Western legal tradition,[4] the elements that compose probative evidence and the proper standards for evaluating it are

---

3    The standard 7,000 to 8,000 figure for the number of Srebrenica victims emerged initially as a media construct, but ultimately it found judicial validation in the *Krstić* judgment (par. 487) in 2001. After several permutations in succeeding judgements, the figure settled back in the 8,000 range in the *Mladić* trial judgment (2018). But between the first and the last Srebrenica trial, ICTY chambers put forth a wide array of disparate execution figures, all based on evidence that hardly varied from one case to another. In the case of Bosnian Serb colonel Vujadin Popović, the ICTY judgment states: "The Trial Chamber has found that, from 12 July until late July 1995, several thousand Bosnian Muslim men were executed" (Trial Judgment, par. 793). The Chamber elaborated that it "found that at least 5,336 identified individuals were killed in the executions following the fall of Srebrenica, and this number could well be as high as 7,826" (Trial Judgment, footnote 2862). In the ICTY judgment in the case of Bosnian Serb general Zdravko Tolimir, the figure of "4,970 victims" is given (Appeals Judgment, par. 426). In the *Karadžić* judgment (par. 5519) the Chamber determined that "at least 5,115 men were killed by members of the Bosnian Serb Forces in July 1995 in Srebrenica."

4    That may not have been true in the past, as in ancient Athens where "the speeches the Greek orators constructed and presented in the Athenian

(Footnote continued on next page)

indisputable, so a detailed theoretical introduction is unnecessary; nevertheless, a brief outline of the fundamental principles of evidence is called for.

Probative evidence is generally described as follows:

> When a legal controversy goes to trial, the parties seek to prove their cases by the introduction of evidence. All courts are governed by RULES OF EVIDENCE that describe what types of evidence are admissible. One key element for the admission of evidence is whether it proves or helps prove a fact or issue. If so, the evidence is deemed probative. Probative evidence establishes or contributes to proof.[5]

Furthermore,

> Probative facts are data that have the effect of proving an issue or other information. Probative facts establish the existence of other facts. They are matters of evidence that make the existence of something more probable or less probable than it would be without them. They are admissible as evidence and

---

(Footnote continued from previous page)

courts of the fifth and fourth centuries BC indicate that in classical Greek law, trials were what we might call "at large," meaning that nothing was irrelevant. In a case on a contract, a litigant might remind the jury of how bravely he had fought against the Persians in the great victory at Salamis. We would say that the war record of the plaintiff or the defendant in a contract action was not relevant and could not be introduced into evidence." *See* Stephen Wexler, *Six Basic Ideas About Legal Proof: Lectures and Aphorisms*, p. 13, http://faculty.law.ubc.ca/wexler/legal_proof.html Oddly, the ICTY, as demonstrated by its practice, may be returning to some form of the "at large" approach in the admission of evidence.

5   http://legal-dictionary.thefreedictionary.com/probative. Let note be taken that the main source of *The Free Dictionary*'s legal dictionary is West's Encyclopedia of American Law, Edition 2.

aid the court in the final resolution of a disputed issue.[6]

Evidence is said to have probative value when it "is sufficiently useful to prove something important in a trial."[7]

It is also a settled principle of law that probative evidence "that is otherwise admissible may still be excluded if its probative value is substantially outweighed by the danger of unfair prejudice, confusion of the issues, or misleading the jury"[8] — *a fortiori*, we might add, if it is evidence characterized by dubious probative quality. The point about "unfair prejudice, confusion of the issues, or misleading the jury" is particularly pertinent to The Hague Tribunal. It operates with a panel of judges, of course, not a jury, but international public opinion acts informally as a jury in a figurative manner in ICTY's proceedings. So, in that sense, the issues of unfair prejudice and confusion that result from the airing of improper evidence before a conventional jury may still be considered. The Tribunal takes a position not unlike the one taken by ancient Greek courts, which conducted their trials "at large." These courts were reluctant to exclude as irrelevant anything that could remotely be deemed evidence. It is the view of The Hague Tribunal that any hearsay — twice, even thrice removed — any scrap of paper with virtually anything written on it with the remotest bearing on some aspect of a case, any copy of any purported document even if there is no original to back it up, may be admissible without impairing the administration of justice because the Chamber is composed of experienced professionals who, presumably unlike an Athenian mob,

---

6   *Ibid.*

7   http://legal-dictionary.thefreedictionary.com/probative+value

8   http://definitions.uslegal.com/p/probative-force/

are superbly qualified to separate the wheat from the chaff and make a proper assessment of the matters at hand.

Finally, the closely related but somewhat broader concept of PROOF refers to:

> [T]he establishment of a fact by the use of evidence. Anything that can make a person believe that a fact or proposition is true or false. It is distinguishable from evidence in that proof is a broad term comprehending everything that may be adduced at a trial, whereas evidence is a narrow term describing certain types of proof that can be admitted at trial.[9]

There may be sufficient proof that an event took place; nevertheless, the evidence could be found insufficient to show that the event in question occurred in a specific way or that criminal liability for it may be imputed to a specific party.

The concept of evidence, as applied by The Hague Tribunal in practice, requires far more discussion and analysis than has so far been accorded to it. The way evidence is defined, presented, and handled is fundamental to court procedures. In criminal cases it is a matter of particular significance. If a judicial system labors under an erroneous concept of evidence, then this is not an ordinary or easily remedied error but a fundamental deficiency that ultimately sabotages the machinery of justice. If evidence is improperly received and assessed, confidence in the integrity of the entire judicial process — including its final outcome, the verdict — will be substantially undermined.

### 3. Case Study I: The Branjevo/Pilica Execution Site

How does ICTY get away with proving mass murder ascending to the level of genocide when the bulk of the evidence does

---

9  http://legal-dictionary.thefreedictionary.com/proof

not support many of its factual conclusions? We can try to answer this question by reviewing the evidence which various ICTY chambers used to reach their conclusions. We will first review and test the evidence for the Pilica/Branjevo massacre site narrative, then the evidence for the alleged events that took place at Kravica, also the site of a massacre. Both episodes of mass murder occurred within the larger context of the execution of Muslim prisoners of war captured by Serbian forces following the takeover of Srebrenica on July 11, 1995. The evidentiary basis will be tested to assess the degree of correspondence between the evidence presented (or ignored) in open court and the conclusions that the chamber ultimately reached.

## I.

Our first case study will test the way in which evidence, broadly understood, was treated by The Hague Tribunal by focusing on the massacre at Pilica/Branjevo.

The prisoners were initially quartered at a facility in Pilica. They were then taken to a nearby field in Branjevo, where they were shot. This massacre was one of a series of similar episodes which occurred over a week's time in the final stages of the Bosnian war and after the fall of Srebrenica on 11 July 1995. The ICTY maintains that these episodes collectively constituted the Srebrenica massacre.[10]

The focus on Pilica/Branjevo (generally referred to as "Pilica" because that was where prisoners were assembled prior to execution, while nearby Branjevo is the location of the field where the killings took place) is deliberate because of its para-

---

10  Be it noted that the Srebrenica massacre has been ruled a genocide in the *Krstić, Popović, Tolimir, Mladić,* and *Kardžić* cases before various chambers of ICTY.

digmatic character. The principal witness, Dražen Erdemović, ultimately signed a plea-bargaining agreement with the ICTY Prosecution. This agreement obligated him to testify at all Srebrenica-related trials, where he retold his story with greater or lesser consistency and persuasiveness. There are also two alleged survivors of the massacre who have also given evidence.

## II.

What happened in Pilica? Here follows a brief and relatively uncontroversial recital of the basic facts.

On 11 July 1995, Serbian forces completed a successful offensive and shut down the then-protected enclave of Srebrenica. Under an agreement signed in April 1993, the enclave was supposed to have been demilitarized in exchange for the Serbs halting their military operation, which had threatened to defeat the forces within Srebrenica that were loyal to the Sarajevo authorities. Prior to April 1993, forces from Srebrenica conducted a widespread and systematic campaign against Serbian villages and settlements in the area. The 2002 Dutch Government NIOD Report estimated that between "1,000 and 1,200 Serbs died in these attacks, while about 3,000 of them were wounded.... Ultimately, of the original 9,390 Serbian inhabitants of the Srebrenica district, only 860 remained..."[11] After the April 1993 truce which declared Srebrenica to be "a safe area," Srebrenica forces loyal to Sarajevo openly ignored the demilitarisation provision; the fully armed 28th Division of the Army of Bosnia and Herzegovina remained in control of the enclave; attacks, ambushes,

---

11  NIOD Report, Part I: *The Yugoslavian problem and the role of the West 1991–1994*; Chapter 10: Srebrenica under siege.

and provocations from the Srebrenica "safe area" against surrounding Serbian settlements continued unabated.[12]

Serbian forces, motivated to avenge their civilian losses, occupied the Srebrenica enclave in July 1995, whence they safely
evacuated[13] about 20,000 inhabitants, mostly women, children,
and the elderly, to Muslim-held territory about 50 kilometers
away. Serbian forces engaged in armed clashes on numerous
occasions with a mixed Muslim military/civilian column, which
was estimated to number between 12,000 and 15,000 men, and
which was conducting an armed breakthrough from Srebrenica
and was heading toward Muslim lines near Tuzla. During the
numerous clashes, many members of the column were killed in
combat; others were captured. Of those captured, some were
transferred to a prisoner-of-war camp and ultimately exchanged;
others were summarily executed by a possibly rogue outfit called
10th Sabotage Detachment, to which Prosecution witness Dražen
Erdemović had once belonged.

Erdemović's account of events states that on 16 July 1995
some of the Muslim prisoners, alleged by Erdemović to have
numbered about 1,200, were transported from a detention center
in Pilica to a field on a farm in nearby Branjevo. Between approximately 11:00 a.m. and 3:00 p.m., a firing squad of eight
men, one of whom was Erdemović, executed these prisoners.
Another 500 prisoners who were being held at a different location in Pilica were executed later that afternoon by another firing
squad.

In March 1996, Erdemović contacted the media as well as the
ICTY. He claimed that he was suffering pangs of conscience for

---

12  Debriefing on Srebrenica (October 1995), pars. 2.20, 2.30, 2.34, 2.35,
    2.38, and 2.43.

13  In the view of several ICTY Chambers, they were forcibly expelled.

his actions, yet he also expressed the hope that in exchange for his cooperation as a witness for the ICTY Prosecution he would be granted immunity from prosecution and would be accorded resettlement — along with his family and under a new identity — in a Western country.[14]

The other allegedly percipient witnesses to the Pilica massacre were Protected Witness Q and Ahmo Hasić, who has testified with and without protective measures. Both claim to have luckily escaped from the execution site on 16 July 1995.

It is time now to turn our attention to both the witness and the forensic evidence to determine what it indicates about the events that took place in Branjevo.

### III.

*The Dražen Erdemović narrative.*[15] The Prosecution of the Hague Tribunal has frankly acknowledged that before Erdemović's transfer to the ICTY by Yugoslav authorities on 30 March 1996 (that is to say, nine months after the fall of Srebrenica) it knew nothing important about the Pilica massacre,[16] which eventually became the best documented episode in a series of mass prisoner executions that compose the alleged Srebrenica genocide. At Erdemović's trial in The Hague on 19 November 1996 (a year and four months after the events in Srebrenica charged in the indictment), Jean-René Ruez, the ICTY Chief In-

---

14  Renaud Girard, « Bosnie: la confession d'un criminel de guerre, » *Le Figaro* (Paris), 8 March 1996.

15  For an exhaustive analysis of Erdemović's evidence, *see* Germinal Čivikov, *Srebrenica: The Star Witness* [Translated by John Laughland], Belgrade 2010.

16  Erdemović, T. 150.

vestigator in charge of Srebrenica, said that even at this late stage Erdemović was still the Prosecution's only source for information about the major killing operation that allegedly took place in Pilica.[17] So, presumably he must have had important and probative evidence to give. His evidence, therefore, should have been crucial to sorting out one major episode in an interconnected series of crimes which are said to amount to — genocide.

Erdemović's alleged personal involvement may have been a good starting point, but the obligation of proper conduct on the Prosecution's part included a good faith effort to verify allegations intended to be used as evidence, and likewise excluded the use of any uncorroborated assertion just because it happened to support the Prosecution's case. In the adversarial system of justice,[18] the Prosecutor's obligation as an "officer of the court" is to check the facts before presenting them to the Chamber to ensure that the version of events is internally consistent and credible — or at least appears that way. To what degree have these requirements been met in the case of Dražen Erdemović, the star witness who is cooperating with the Prosecution?

To start with, the manner in which he burst on the scene in the Srebrenica controversy should have set off alarm bells for any dispassionate observer. On 3 March 1996, while recuperating in Serbia from wounds he sustained in a shoot-out with another member of his unit — possibly over the division of spoils from the alleged massacre[19] — Erdemović invited French jour-

---

17 Erdemović, T. 150-151

18 The fiction at the Hague Tribunal is that it operates on a fusion of the Common Law and Continental legal traditions. It is hardly disputed, however, that in reality it is the adversarial approach of the Common Law system that predominates.

19 Erdemović, testifying at the trial of Radovan Karadžić, admitted under cross-examination that he sustained serious injuries in a bar room brawl,

(Footnote continued on next page)

nalist Arnaud Girard and his American colleague Vanessa Vasić-Jenek/ić to hear his dramatic revelations. The interview resulted in a long article that appeared in *Le Figaro* on 8 March 1996. The key portion of the interview, which bears on Erdemović's motives and which should have aroused critical examination by the present journalists as well as by the ICTY Prosecutor and Chamber, is this:

> The former soldier who has reported these facts has been negotiating with the Tribunal in The Hague. In return for the promise of immunity and the possibility of resettling in the West with his family, he is ready to tell all.[20]

So, it should have been clear right at the outset to all the interested parties that Erdemović's motives were, if not completely corrupt, then at least mixed. In addition to salving his conscience (if we are to give him the benefit of the doubt), he clearly presented as his motive the desire to start a new life elsewhere, far from the reach of his querulous co-perpetrators and, even more importantly, with immunity from prosecution for the horrendous crimes he was describing and in which he was also admitting participation. *Quid pro quo* was obviously on his mind, and he signalled it from the start. So, the first logical question that any careful investigator and trier of fact would ask is: to what extent might these motives have colored, influenced, or enhanced his

---

(Footnote continued from previous page)

which was the context of the shoot-out. <u>See</u> *Karadžić* Transcript, 28 February 2012, pp. 25390-25391.

20 *Le Figaro*, op. cit. « L'ancien soldat qui rapporte ces faits a négocié avec le tribunal de La Haye. Contre la promesse d'une immunité et la possibilité de s'installer en Occident avec sa famille, il était prêt à tout dire. »

narrative to fit the expectations of the Prosecution, from whom he was expecting not only refuge but also immunity?

The general picture of the executions at Branjevo has been largely consistent to the extent that witness Erdemović has repeatedly testified in several trials that the process began around 10:00 a.m. or 11:00 a.m. on 16 July and was over by about 3 p.m. the same day, and that the prisoners were shot in groups of ten.[21] The central claim which makes his evidence vitally important to the Prosecution is his estimate that in that time period — about five hours — Dražen Erdemović and seven other members of an execution squad drawn from the Tenth Sabotage Detachment shot, by his estimate, between 1,000 and 1,200 Muslim men who had been captured by Serbian forces after the fall of Srebrenica a few days earlier.[22] It is clear that demonstrating that as many as 1,200 Srebrenica victims were shot at a single location over the course of five hours would put the Prosecution well on its way to proving the cold blooded murder of 8,000 prisoners of war; however, if the ICTY chambers who accepted Erdemović's testimony had critically examined the mathematical feasibility of his claim from a time-study engineering standpoint, some serious questions would immediately have been raised. And perhaps some hasty conclusions might have been avoided.

Five hours is 300 minutes, and 1,200 prisoners come to 120 groups of ten. Dividing 300 minutes (the period of time the executions lasted according to this witness) by 120 (the number of groups), we get about 2.5 minutes per group of ten men (as he claimed) to walk the 100–200 meters from the bus to the execu-

---

21    The latest iteration of this scenario was made at the *Karadžić* Trial, T. 25374 – 25375.

22    *See* evidence at the *Popović et al.* Trial, T. 10983: "According to my estimate, between 1,000 and 1,200."

tion site, throw their IDs and valuables into a pile, to be shot —
and finally for a Serbian soldier to check for survivors and finish
them off before the next group of ten was brought to go through
the same routine. How likely is this scenario in the time frame
indicated by Erdemović? For comparison, a similar massacre
said to have taken place in nearby Orahovac[23] involved the execution of 1,000 prisoners, somewhat less than the top figure alleged by Erdemović. Oddly, the Chamber there concluded that
the Orahovac executions started on 14 July 1995 in the afternoon
and continued all evening and into the morning of the following
day, 15 July, and finally ended at 5:00 a.m. While the same
*Blagojević* and *Jokić* Chamber validated Erdemović's chronolog-
ically tight Branjevo narrative,[24] it apparently failed to notice the
incongruity of this story with its other findings in the same
judgment about analogous events that took place in Orahovac.
Nevertheless, the Chamber sensibly gave the Orahovac executioners three times as much time to perform a task of similar
magnitude and complexity as the one in Branjevo. In Branjevo,
the firing squad must have been really quick on the draw.

But mathematical computation (for the length of time required to perform these acts) is not the only questionable aspect
of witness Erdemović's report about what happened in Branjevo.
Apparently, Erdemović had taken care to portray his role in the
killings in a light that he thought would most likely minimize his
own criminal responsibility. He testified on various occasions
that he held the rank of sergeant in the Tenth Sabotage Detachment, the unit from which the executioners were drawn, and he
testified that in 1994 he joined the outfit with the rank of ser-

---

23  According to the finding of the ICTY Chamber in *Blagojević* and *Jokić*,
    Trial Verdict, Par. 763.

24  *Ibid.*, Par. 349-350.

geant. But he claimed that in April 1995, just months before the July massacre in which he admitted to having taken part, he was demoted by his superiors to the rank of private for an infraction he had committed. One marvels at the convenient timing. The demotion is of some importance in his narrative[25] because he constructed an image of himself as an unwilling executioner, verging on a conscientious objector, who grudgingly went along and — by his own admission — executed 70 to 100 prisoners in Branjevo because, being a mere private, he was himself threatened with execution if he had refused. Ever since the Nuremberg Trials, "following orders" has not been a valid excuse for participating in atrocities; however, Erdemović is not a lawyer but an unemployed locksmith, so, being a layman, he may have been uninformed on this point. He just tried to do what he thought was best to minimize his own liability, though an alert Prosecution and Chamber would have questioned how this comports with his insistent proclamations of repentance.

The Prosecution and Chamber had plenty of evidence to make them question the veracity of Erdemović's testimony. For one thing, the 10 July 1995 Order issued by the detachment commander Milorad Pelemiš for the unit to join battle in Srebrenica unambiguously lists Erdemović as a "sergeant"[26] at a time he claimed he was a simple soldier. Moreover, his immediate superior in the chain of command, Col. Petar Salapura, flatly contradicted Erdemović's claim of demotion in his own testimo-

---

25  The Chamber accepts the demotion as a proven fact in its judgment of 29 November 1996, Pars. 79 and 92. Erdemović was initially sentenced to ten years in prison on a plea-bargaining agreement, but after he successfully challenged the basis for the agreement, is sentence was reduced to five years. He served a total of three years and a half in prison.

26  *See* document OTP file number 04230390, *Order to Deploy of the Command of the Tenth Sabotage Detachment*, 10 July 1995.

ny.[27] This claim was also debunked by Dragan Todorović, the unit's logistics officer, who was very well acquainted with Erdemović as well as with his status.[28] These credible denials of Erdemović's claim that he was a lowly private at the time he participated in the massacre assume additional weight in light of his further claim — which strains credulity — that another simple soldier, Brano Gojković, was actually in charge of the execution squad in Branjevo even though one of the Tenth Sabotage officers, Lt. Franc Kos, was also present among the executioners and was presumably taking orders from Private Gojković.[29]

Erdemović also reported that when the killing was over in the afternoon, the same lieutenant-colonel who had brought them there that morning and who had then left, now reappeared and announced to Private Gojković, whom as we have already noted was supposed to be in charge, that there were an additional 500 prisoners in another facility in Pilica who also needed to be executed. Gojković then conveyed this order to Erdemović. Erdemović replied that he had by then tired of executions and refused the order despite the fact that he was a mere foot soldier. He no longer claimed that he was threatened with death for insubordination. The high-ranking officer and Gojković then ordered another group of soldiers to carry out the further execution of pris-

---

27  *Blagojević* and *Jokić*, T. 10526.

28  *Popović et al.*, T. 14041.

29  The *Tolimir* Chamber held unambiguously that soldier Brano Gojković was in command, Par. 493. Gojković was arrested by Serbian authorities and sentenced to a ten-year prison term after concluding a plea-bargain with the prosecution (*Balkan Insight*, 4 February 2016, https://balkaninsight.com/2016/02/04/serbia-jails-bosnian-serb-soldier-for-srebrenica-02-04-2016/ ). The underlying circumstances of the apprehension and, most importantly, the factual admissions supporting his guilt remain confidential. Thus, the role of one of the more intriguing protagonists in the Srebrenica controversy remains shrouded in mystery.

oners. They ignored the presence of Lt. Kos, who presumably would have been more suitable as the lieutenant-colonel's interlocutor, if one takes the normal chain of military command into consideration.

The confusion about who was in charge at the execution site is compounded by the ICTY Prosecution's manifest desire to link the Serbian Supreme Military Commander, General Ratko Mladić, as directly as possible to the commission of a crime. From the prosecutorial point of view, this is perfectly understandable and it is a legitimate way to proceed. One would think, however, that the concept of Command Responsibility, long settled by the Tribunal, would serve as the legal mechanism to achieve this. But apparently, in the Prosecution's view, it was insufficient. So, at the Milošević Trial the Prosecution produced a document purporting to be the Enlistment Contract Dražen Erdemović had signed when he joined the Tenth Sabotage Detachment.[30] The main feature of this otherwise unremarkable document is what appears to be the signature of "Colonel-General Ratko Mladić" in the lower right hand corner on p. 2 of the Contract. Underneath Mladić's purported handwriting is the signature of Platoon Commander Milorad Pelemiš, who would presumably be expected to sign off on such a document. [See Annex I.]

The controversy, if there is one at all, obviously centers on Mladić's signature. The Prosecution has a strong interest in validating this document judicially, even though it has been circulated exclusively in the form of photocopies, of which the original has never been produced — it has never even been requested in court. Nor has its provenance, in other words, the chain of custody of this document, ever been presented in court. The latter

---

30   OTP file number 00399985-6.

point (without minimizing the former) is important because of the specific history surrounding this document. Erdemović presumably brought it with him to Serbia in early 1996 when he arrived from Bosnia to receive medical treatment after having been injured in the aforementioned shootout with his firing squad companions in Bijeljina. On the evening of 3 March, Yugoslav State Security arrested Erdemović after he had given his interview to the French journalist Arnaud Girard, and it also seized his personal documents as well as his belongings. Yugoslav State Security kept his personal effects after extraditing him to the ICTY on 30 March 1996. His personal items were not sent to the Tribunal until 12 November 1996, shortly before Erdemović's trial was scheduled to begin. No itemized list of personal belongings, presumably forwarded by the Yugoslav authorities to the Tribunal, has ever been presented in court; one is simply compelled to assume, without any particular evidence, that this is how the Enlistment Contract came into the Prosecution's possession. It popped up at the Milošević trial and, predictably, it appeared again at the trial of General Ratko Mladić.[31] The chain of custody of the Shroud of Turin is clearer than the chain of custody of this key piece of Prosecution evidence that links — with compelling directness — Supreme Commander Mladić to a lowly sergeant assigned to an obscure detachment. This conveniently results in a nexus where the evil deeds to which Erdemović confessed can be neatly imputed to Gen. Mladić as well, without the tedious business of going through the chain of command, even as a mere formality.

To return to the first point, the widespread — more correctly, exclusive — use of photocopies as evidence at the Tribunal must be highlighted. Defense teams routinely fail to request original

---

31 *Prosecutor v. Ratko Mladić*, Transcript, 2 July 2013, p. 13704.

copies, as they would in ordinary criminal cases before domestic U.S. courts, in order to demand vigorously, if necessary, that the best possible evidence be made available for proper forensic analysis. At the ICTY, there is a tacit understanding by and among the Prosecution, the Defense, and the Chamber that requesting originals, whether they be documents or radio intercepts, is simply not done. This unspoken convention has a chilling effect on any attempt to authenticate key evidence. This point requires no further elaboration.

This aspect of The Hague Tribunal's practice lends itself well to *reductio ad absurdum*. Instead of contesting the validity of Erdemović's enlistment documents, which bear Gen. Mladić's signature, since absent the original this is a futile undertaking, we decided to resort to Photoshop in exactly the same way that we suspect the Prosecution has done. It was no technical challenge at all to substitute the signature of General Charles de Gaulle for that of General Ratko Mladić in the document. [*See* Annex I.] If photocopies are the best available evidence in this case, then both versions of Erdemović's Contract must be deemed equally authentic. How General de Gaulle, who passed away in 1970, could have signed an Enlistment Contract dated 1 February 1995 is a puzzle we leave to the Chambers of The Hague Tribunal to sort out.

The confused chain of command is just one of the problems found in Erdemović's evidence. The figure of 500 additional prisoners allegedly slain in Pilica later that same afternoon is also of material importance. Added to the alleged total in Branjevo, that makes about 1,700 Srebrenica victims, which constitutes about 20%, of the aggregate total of 8,000. So, it is important to establish the authenticity of the figure of 500 prisoners allegedly killed during the final act of the execution drama in the Cultural Centre in Pilica, as described by Erdemović.

It turns out to be a case of double hearsay. Erdemović reported what Brano Gojković said to him about the number of those prisoners, while Brano Gojković in turn had heard it from the unidentified high-ranking officer.[32] After refusing to carry out these additional executions, Erdemović and several of his now weary firing squad companions went to a café across the street from the Cultural Centre, where the on-going shooting was still clearly audible. Once again, there is no percipient evidence about the act itself or the number of victims.

Despite the multiple hearsay in the evidence of "crown witness" Dražen Erdemović, the Prosecution at the Karadžić trial decided to enhance the impact of Erdemović's assertions, but it was done in a manner so comical that it lowered the Court's problematic reputation even further to the level of *opéra bouffe*.

In the *Popović* case, the Prosecution introduced witness Jevto Bogdanović[33] to confirm the basic outline of Erdemović's story about the alleged execution of 500 prisoners in Pilica — but what was the actual testimony this witness gave? Footnote 18643 in the *Karadžić* judgment approvingly directs us to p. 11333 of the transcript in the *Popović* case. This is Bogdanović's testimony as it appears in the *Karadžić* judgment:

---

32 On 4 February 2016, the Serbian media reported that Brano Gojković had been apprehended and "admitted guilt for the murder in July of 1995 of several hundred persons from Srebrenica" and that as a result, "following his admission of guilt, the High Court in Belgrade sentenced him to ten years of imprisonment" (http://ba.n1info.com/a80448/Vijesti/Brano-Gojkovic-osudjen-na-10-godina.html). No information whatsoever was provided about the location or the circumstances of Gojković's apprehension. As one of the key figures in Srebrenica events, Gojković undoubtedly could have revealed much in an open trial; however, due to the application of the plea-bargain principle, he was quietly and discretely placed *ad acta*.

33 The day after the executions, Bogdanović with other soldiers allegedly took part in the clean-up operation at the Pilica Cultural Center. See *Popović at al.*, Transcript, 10 May 2007, p. 11329.

Q. When you were drinking that day, could you say what it was you were drinking?

A. Rakija brandy.

Q. Where did you get that?

A. Neighbours, the locals, brought that to us. We drank for courage, to be able to sustain looking at the blood and the bodies, and the brains of the people.

Q. During the course of that day, did you hear anybody mention a number of how many bodies were in the dom[34]?

A. I heard somebody on the road saying that there were 550, but we ourselves did not count.

Q. But based on your work that day, does that number seem a reasonable number to you?

A. Well, it does. It should.[35]

How did the ICTY transform mere hearsay into a reputable finding of fact? It's very simple: The Hague Tribunal considers multiple hearsay to be a legitimate evidentiary tool. Hence, the ICTY is receptive to the testimony of a witness who admits to having been drunk while taking part in the post-execution removal of bodies at the Pilica Cultural Center (see *Popović et al.*, Transcript, 10. May 2007, p. 11329). Then this witness passes on to the Chamber remarks made to him in passing by an unidentified individual, while the witness' judgment, and perhaps recollection of events, could have been impaired by excessive consumption of alcohol during the period of time in question. In several ICTY judgments, the number of prisoners alleged at one

---

34  *dom* (Serbian) Cultural Center.

35  *See* Transcript in *Popović et al.*, 10 May 2007, p. 11332-11333.

time by Erdemović, and then by Bogdanović at another, to have been executed in Pilica, which is about five hundred, was declared established and is now, presumably, written in stone: it is history. No reliable witness has ever testified under oath, in any court, to seeing 500 or 550 prisoners at the Pilica Cultural Center prior to the alleged execution, nor has anyone ever testified under oath about the later collection and accounting for the number of corpses. This narrative, which verges on pulp fiction, is unsupported by a shred of objective evidence, yet it has been solemnly enshrined in four separate judgments[36] as a judicially established fact by The Hague Tribunal.

Is there another court anywhere in the entire world where such a thing would be possible?

## IV

So much for the alleged witness-perpetrator Dražen Erdemović and his evidence. There are also two alleged survivors who have equally interesting narratives: Protected Witness Q[37] and Ahmo Hasić, who testified variously under pseudonyms as well as *in propria persona*. In order not to violate ICTY rules, we will focus here only on the evidence that Mr. Hasić gave under his real name.

*Witness Q.* This witness' evidence encompasses several different episodes of the events that took place at Srebrenica. We will discuss only the portion relevant to Pilica/Branjevo. In essence, Q has claimed that on 14 July he was bused with a number of other prisoners from the town of Bratunac, near Srebreni-

---

36   *See* trial judgments in *Blagojević* and *Jokić*, par. 355; Popović et al., footnote 1927; *Perišić*, par. 715; and *Tolimir*, par. 500.

37   He testified in various trials under different pseudonyms, but here we will use here the pseudonym assigned to him in the *Krstić* case.

THE ICTY AND SREBRENICA

ca, to the schoolhouse in Pilica, about 60 km to the north. There he spent two nights under unpleasant conditions. On 16 July, busloads of prisoners were driven from Pilica to a field on a farm in Branjevo, about a ten-minute ride from there, to be executed. This is where the first significant anomalies in his evidence occur. In different trials, Q testified variously that he and his group arrived at the execution site at: 7:45 that morning:[38] between 9:00 and 9:30 a.m. that morning;[39] and "after 4:00 p.m."[40] that day, with the executions in this version lasting into the night. The third time frame seriously conflicts with Erdemović's account, according to which it was all over by 3:00 to 4:00 p.m., depending on the trial Erdemović testified in. The commencement of the executions on the morning of 16 July also diverges considerably from Erdemović's testimony. The discrepancies do not simply concern the time, but also the condition of the field, which, on the one hand, according to Erdemović's testimony, was empty when he and his group arrived at the field; while witness Q, on the other hand, claims that there were already a number of corpses there. Even so, the spectacularly problematic aspects of Q's narrative are yet to come.

The most intriguing question, of course, is how Q managed to survive and tell his story. Briefly, it happened as follows. Q claims that the executioners simply began shooting after he and his group had been lined up in the field without the usual order of *ready, aim, fire*. Miraculously, Q fell face down to the ground

---

38  Witness statement to the *State Commission for the Compilation of Facts about War Crimes*, Tuzla, 20 July 1996, p. 3. OTP file number 00950186-00950191.

39  Witness statement to ICTY Office of the Prosecutor, 23 May 1996, p. 4. OTP file number 00798704 -00798712.

40  *Karadžić*, T. 24158.

with his hands tied behind his back faster than his executioners' shots travelled, so he dodged their bullets before they could strike him.[41]

Q's hands were still tied behind his back as he lay on the ground pretending to be dead. He heard Serbian soldiers approaching the recently executed lot and heard one of them comment to the other, as they were getting nearer to him, that shots to the head were messy and that it was better to stop administering the *coup de grâce* to the head, and to shoot the victims in the back instead because brain matter tended to splatter all over the executioner's clothing.[42] But this grotesque flourish to the narrative makes no sense. The laws of kinetics dictate that, in a situation such as Q is describing, brain matter would splatter not from the bullet's point of entry upwards toward the shooter, but through the exit point and downward to the ground. There was in fact no risk of an executioner soiling his clothing in this fashion. These are the hallmarks of a make-believe horror story.

According to the chronology of his narrative, just minutes later Witness Q luckily cheated a bullet intended for him a second time. The fastidious administrators of the *coup de grâce* did not want to soil their uniforms, so, as they were standing above witness Q, they agreed to avoid shooting the victims in the head. But they were bad shots, so they missed Q's back and the bullet instead passed just beneath his armpit, between his arm and torso, without grazing him.

This is truly amazing when one considers that Q testified that his arms had been tied behind his back, which means that they must have been pressing tightly against the sides of the body,

---

41  Statement to the BiH War Crimes Commission, 20 July 1996, p. 4.

42  *Tolimir, T.* 30419.

thus leaving no gap for the errant bullet to pass through without damaging soft body tissue before harmlessly hitting the ground. This analysis is strongly supported by an examination of the picture in Annex II, which depicts a model whose hands have been tied behind his back and who was positioned face down on the ground, just as Q had claimed he was. But Q's astonishing testimony was accepted as authentic and his narrative was incorporated in all the Srebrenica ICTY judgments, with the exception of the *Tolimir* case. Even though Q gave evidence in that case, as well, the *Tolimir* Chamber did not mention him at all in its judgment. Perhaps the chamber found his story absurd; yet it did not want to break ranks with the other trial chambers by publicly saying so.

The gist of Q's account of the massacre of Pilica is supposed to corroborate executioner Erdemović's account. Q then waits for night to fall, and then he sneaks away from the killing field, as it is usually done in the movies.

*Ahmo Hasić.* There are two main points of interest in Hasić's evidence. The first, and most glaring, is of a statistical character. It may be recalled that Erdemović referred to 1,200 execution victims in Branjevo and another potential 500 victims at the Cultural Centre in Pilica. While giving evidence in the *Popović* case, it seems that Hasić was inadequately rehearsed for his part because he let the cat out of the bag. He said that as the Serbs were bussing him to the detention facility in Pilica, he disobeyed orders to keep his head down, snuck a peek, and noticed that his group was being taken to the execution site in a convoy of seven buses,[43] which would hardly have been enough vehicles to accommodate the 1,200 to 1,700 execution victims alleged to have been taken on their final journey. Asked to estimate the capacity

---

43  *Popović* et al, T. 1190.

of each bus, Hasić put it at "50 or so."[44] This would suggest a maximum capacity of 350 to 400 persons, which falls considerably short of the number asserted in the narrative that Hasić was enlisted by the Prosecution to corroborate.

Like Q, Hasić says that bursts of gunfire began suddenly before any command had been given, and it is not entirely clear how he managed to fall faster than the bullet flies, but he fortunately survived.[45] Then, as Hasić describes it, an extraordinary thing happened. Instead of administering the *coup de grâce* indiscriminately to one and all, the Serbian soldiers decided to do it the easy way: "[w]hen the bursts of fire died down, one of them asked, 'Are there any survivors?' 'I survived, kill me,'" Hasić quoted one victim as saying. "So they ... would go from one survivor to another and fired a single bullet to the head." This time they were apparently unconcerned with the risk of soiling their uniforms. At that moment, Hasić says that even he toyed with the idea: "I thought about notifying them that I was alive."[46] Luckily for him, as well as for the Tribunal, he resisted the temptation.

There seems to be no need to attempt an in-depth critique of Ahmo Hasić's evidence concerning the execution site. It speaks for itself, and it has been quoted merely to demonstrate the kind of material that passes for evidence at The Hague Tribunal.

## V

Finally, a brief review of the forensic data and its treatment by the Tribunal is in order to complete the picture.

---

44  *Ibid.*, T. 1198.

45  *Ibid.*, T. 1202-1203.

46  *Ibid.*, T. 1203.

The forensic record pertaining to the execution site in the farming field in Branjevo is straightforward. In 1996 and 1997, an international team of experts conducted exhumations on behalf of the Office of the Prosecutor of the ICTY.

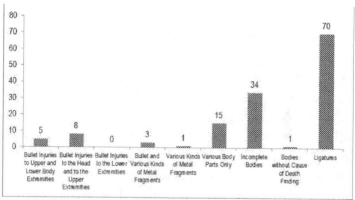

A breakdown of the contents of the Pilica/Branjevo mass grave[47]

The Pilica/Branjevo farm is notable for the number of bodies with blindfolds and/or ligatures. They number 70, or 51 % of the total number of cases examined here. That at least confirms that prisoners must have been executed there. The remainder is either body fragments or incomplete bodies. With regard to the incomplete bodies from this mass grave, it may be noted from the graph that, in addition to bullet fragments, various other metal fragments were found, as well; another portion had only bullet-related injuries; and the rest did not exhibit any injuries at all, so no cause of death could be determined. Of the fifteen cases

---

47  S. Karganović [ed.]. *Deconstruction of a Virtual Genocide: An Intelligent Person's Guide to Srebrenica.* Den Haag – Belgrade 2011. Chapter VI, Ljubiša Simić: "Presentation and interpretation of forensic data (Pattern of injury breakdown" p. 101. Den Haag – Belgrade 2011.

where only a small body fragment or a few bones existed, the cause of death could not be determined in twelve.

There was a total of 137 "cases" in this mass grave, which, following the classification methodology of Prosecution forensic experts, are not the equivalent of 137 bodies. As shown in the breakdown, based on an analysis of the forensic team's autopsy reports from this locale, forty-nine "cases" fall outside the category of complete bodies and consist of fragments or body parts. To give a precise answer to the question of how many individuals are buried in this mass grave is not an easy task. But if we take a conservative approach and deduct the fifteen cases in the "various body parts category" from the 137 "cases", then we obtain an approximation of 122 bodies; if we rely on pairs of femur bones as the criterion, then there would be 115.

To this number we should perhaps add thirty-two cases from other mass graves that were found to be DNA-linked to Pilica/Branjevo.[48] The procedure of separately counting disarticulated body parts found in another grave may be questionable, because it could be argued that such body parts belong to the same person, most of whose remains would be found at the original burial site. But since this methodology has been accepted by the ICTY in practice, and since the addition scarcely makes material difference, we can avoid unnecessary contention by just accepting it provisionally.

Adding up 122 bodies found in the Branjevo mass grave and 32 bodies presumably also originating from Branjevo, we have material evidence pointing to at most 154 murders at that location.

---

48  These are: Kamenica 4, 1 body; Kamenica 9, 26 bodies; Čančari Road 11, 3 bodies; and Čančari Road 12, 2 bodies, for a total of 32.

Interestingly, during Radovan Karadžić's cross examination of Erdemović, information turned up indicating that an earlier mass grave, possibly going back to World War II, may have overlapped with the Branjevo execution site.[49] This suggestion is corroborated to a limited extent by the fact that fourteen autopsy reports[50] from the 1996 exhumation demonstrate the existence of remains that have been completely skeletonized. Since the disintegration of soft tissue generally takes four to five years, it is unlikely that victims of a murder that took place a year and a half before such exhumation would have been skeletonized so quickly.

The resulting forensic picture of Pilica/Branjevo is complex. It requires an analytical approach taking into account a variety of factors. There are strong suggestions that a crime did take place there, and that, given the great number of ligatures found there, the crime probably did involve prisoners; however, these findings do not lend much specific support to the narratives put forward by either Dražen Erdemović or by the two purported execution survivors. Those narratives have been received sympathetically by all the ICTY trial chambers that heard them; were treated as factual evidence; and were incorporated into judgments which purport to give a true and accurate representation of what actually happened at the Branjevo/Pilica location.

## VI

To summarize the results obtained so far: the primary objective is not to polemicize against the The Hague Tribunal's man-

---

49  *Karadžić*, T. 25387-8.

50  The following are the official ICTY designations of Pilica Autopsy Reports (1996) which are completely skeletonized: PLC-59-BP; PLC-61-BP; PLC-82-BP; PLC-106-BP; PLC-119-BP; PLC-123-BP; PLC-125-BP; PLC-127-BP; PLC-129-BP; PLC-131-BP; PLC-132-BP; PLC-134-BP; PLC-136-BP; PLC-138-BP.

ner of dealing with evidence but to illustrate it, and, in a few selected cases, to test its efficacy in empirically quantifiable terms. In a judicial setting, "efficacy" is a determination of whether a procedure assists or hinders the fact-finding process, which, therefore, either advances or impedes the administration of justice. The Pilica/Branjevo massacre was selected as a test case because it is probably the best documented of the several episodes, occurring immediately after the fall of Srebrenica, in which Muslim prisoners of war were extrajudicially executed by elements said to be associated with Serbian forces.[51] "Empirically quantifiable terms" refers to the availability of physical evidence (in this specific case, exhumed human remains and corresponding autopsy reports that describe their condition) as opposed to statements and impressions of witnesses. The latter are also potentially valuable fact-finding tools; provided, however, that the sources are credible witnesses. Even so, witness evidence is known to be fraught with the subjectivities inherent to human nature. Its reliability is strengthened by the degree to which it conforms to the material evidence. That is why a synopsis of the empirical findings resulting from exhumations conducted in the field has been presented for comparative analysis. This makes it possible to compare key foreground points in the various witness statements to a background of objective facts in order to test the former's reliability.

Viewing the picture as a whole, it clearly cannot be said that evidence indicating a massacre had taken place in Pilica/Branjevo is entirely fabricated. It would be more accurate to say that it was manipulated, primarily in order to affect the perception of the massacre's scale and — in conjunction with simi-

---

51  Regular or rogue is an issue we can set aside for the moment.

lar manipulations of other post-July 11 events that took place in and around Srebrenica — its legal characterization.

The principal percipient informant about the events that took place in Branjevo on 16 July and their scale is Dražen Erdemović. Messrs. Q and Hasić were introduced by the Prosecution merely for atmosphere, to convey from their limited personal perspectives the horror of what had taken place. Erdemović evidently is not a witness of truth, although he may have been present and some of the details he recounts might be accurate. But he had an ulterior motive: to get off with the lightest possible sentence and to be awarded various perquisites by the Tribunal in exchange for his cooperation as a witness. He inflated the number of prisoners, as well as the death toll, and he adjusted his account to serve prosecutorial requirements and expectations. The two "supporting actors," witnesses Q and Hasić, simply overacted their parts. If all three of them had stuck to what they had actually seen and experienced, instead of adding such transparent melodramatic flourishes and outright lies that make even a basically accurate story fall apart, we might now be in a better position to sort out what actually happened in Branjevo.

We are thus facing the enormous disparity between witness evidence, routinely given precedence by ICTY Chambers, which alleges in this case 1,200 to 1,700 murder victims in Branjevo, while evidence of *corpora delicti* in the field indicates a number of about 154. This yields an impressive 10:1 ratio of disproportion in the number of victims between witness testimony allegations and forensic evidence. Should Tribunal sceptics really be reproached for exercising caution in evaluating the ICTY's findings under these circumstances?

Needless to say, the assertions made by these corrupt witnesses would have had little or no impact on the proceedings if only the Prosecution had faithfully executed its obligation to test the integrity of its evidence before presenting it in court. And even if in its overzealousness the Prosecution failed to meet its obligation, the vaunted Chamber of experienced professionals should have been sufficiently alert to detect the absurdities in the witness testimony, to exercise its prerogative to ask probing questions, and ultimately to assign it the low credibility rating that it merits.

The Defense's duty to act with integrity when presenting evidence is clearly spelled out in the *ICTY Code of Professional Conduct for Counsel Appearing before the International Tribunal* (the "ICTY Code"). In Article 23, <u>Candour Toward the Tribunal</u>, it states:

    (B) Counsel shall not knowingly:

        (i) make an incorrect statement of material fact or law to the Tribunal; or

        (ii) offer evidence which counsel knows to be incorrect.[52]

The same rules apply equally to the Prosecution. It so happens that The ICTY Code [Draft version] in Article [7] (5) contains an analogous provision. Prosecution counsel are enjoined to "[N]ever knowingly make a false or misleading statement of material fact to the Court or offer evidence which he or she knows to be incorrect..."[53]

So, with the benefit of hindsight, the Prosecution and the Chamber are the main points where the system of evidence breaks down at the ICTY. Under a doctrine that treats the judges as discerning professionals who cannot be fooled by most kinds of trickery — which is tantamount to an attribute of infallibility

---

52  http://www.icty.org/x/file/Legal%20Library/Defence/defence_code_of_conduct_july2009_en.pdf

53  http://www.amicc.org/docs/prosecutor.pdf

— the Prosecution's duty to act with integrity when presenting evidence has been essentially suspended. The Prosecution enjoys *carte blanche* to use the courtroom as a stage to introduce a large cast of charlatans as witnesses who are then permitted to recite their incoherent stories — steeped in horror and replete with wild misrepresentations — for the benefit of a global audience, which is far wider than the Chamber itself. Uncritical media reporting of these improbable courtroom narratives engineers public perceptions. The media-generated pressure is also reflected in the judges' reluctance to challenge defective evidence either during the proceedings or later in their judgments. The Court's misguided preference for flawed evidence, and its arrogant disdain for establishing facts by using time-tested judicial techniques for distinguishing fact from fiction, have been the hallmarks of Tribunal's jurisprudence. For the ICTY, never calling the Prosecution to account for presenting evidence that verges on misrepresentation and is often plainly beyond the pale of credibility, results in a bitter harvest of widely disputed factual findings and dubious legal conclusions.

## 4. Case Study II: The Kravica Execution Site

The other major execution site worthy of examination is Kravica, and not just from the quantitative standpoint, although that certainly is a factor because over 1,000 victims are claimed to have been killed and buried there. It is also interesting from an analytical standpoint largely because — unlike many other similar locations of alleged Srebrenica executions — there is also a fair amount of material evidence associated with it, as was the case with Branjevo/Pilica.

Kravica is a Serbian village located about 10 kilometers from Srebrenica, which was under the control of the 28th Division of the Army of Bosnia and Herzegovina (ARBiH) from the summer of 1992 to July 1995. In Kravica, the execution of captured prisoners from the Muslim 28th Division took place on July 13, 1995, on the premises of the Agricultural Cooperative Warehouse, where they were detained after having been captured. It is noteworthy that two and a half years earlier, this village had been attacked by Muslim forces from Srebrenica on January 7, 1993, Orthodox Christmas day. After this attack, the village was devastated and there were dozens of civilian casualties. The incident was prominently featured at the trial of Naser Orić, the military commander on the ARBiH side, who faced war crimes charges at the ICTY for his pre-July 1995 activities. The Orić Chamber had this to say about the January 1993 attack on Kravica:

> On 7 and 8 January 1993, Kravica, Šiljkovići and Ježestica were attacked by Bosnian Muslim fighters from Sućeska, Glogova, Biljeg, Mošići, Delići, Cerska, Skugrići, Jaglići, Šušnjari, Brezova Njiva, Osmače, Konjević Polje, Jagodnja, and Joševa. Also the Accused and members of his group of fighters participated in the attack. The fighters were followed by thousands of Bosnian Muslim civilians. At the time of the attack, there were relatively well-armed village guards and some Bosnian Serb civilians in Kravica, Šiljkovići and Ježestica. Evidence shows that there was also Bosnian Serb military presence in the area. The attack met with resistance. Bosnian Serbs fired artillery on the attacking Bosnian Muslims from houses and other buildings. Houses in the area were burning. In Ježestica, Bosnian Muslim fighters and civilians set many houses on fire, causing destruction on a large scale. In Kravica, property was also destroyed on a large scale. However, the evidence is unclear as to the number of houses that were wantonly destroyed by Bosnian Muslims, as opposed to other causes. As to Šiljkovići, there is in-

sufficient evidence to establish that property was destroyed on a large scale.[54]

In contrast to the Orić Chamber's circumspect description of the nature, consequences, and tactical purpose of the ARBiH's 1993 attack on Kravica, Serbian sources claim that the attackers killed several dozen civilians. ICTY Prosecution spokesperson at the time, Florence Hartman, stingily conceded only 13 victims.[55] In contrast, the ICTY Srebrenica chambers were unequivocal — even generous — in their estimate of the number of victims of the July 1995 massacre of ARBiH prisoners in trials involving Serbian defendants.

The ICTY chambers, when analyzing evidence of ARBiH victims in the Kravica Warehouse on July 13, 1995, were forthcoming to accommodate Prosecution claims of the number of victims, and they were not the least bit shy to clearly identify the perpetrators as Serbian forces that were guarding the prisoners.

---

54  *Prosecutor* v. *Naser Orić*, Trial Judgment Summary, p. 9, http://www.icty.org/x/cases/oric/tjug/en/060630_Oric_summary_en.pdf

55  In relation to Serbian casualties in the 1993 attack, Ms. Hartman was quite reserved: "First of all, the OTP is always very careful in the use of the word 'victim' (...) I would comment on the various figures circulating around the Kravica attack of January 1993. The figures circulating of hundreds of victims or claiming that all 353 inhabitants were 'virtually completely destroyed' do not reflect the reality. During the attack by the BH army on Kravica, Jezestica, Opravdici, Mandici and the surrounding villages (the larger area of Kravica), on the 7th & 8th January 1993, 43 people were killed, according to our information. Our investigation shows that 13 of the 43 were obviously civilians. Our findings are matching with the Bratunac Brigade military reports of battle casualties which are believed in the OTP to be very reliable because they are internal VRS reports," ICTY Weekly Press Briefing, 06.07.2005. Little of this admirable restraint was evident when the ICTY estimated the number of victims of Serbian conduct in July 1995.

Naser Orić was acquitted,[56] yet Serbian military and political leaders have been held sternly to account for nothing less than genocide.

While ICTY Prosecution officials such as Ms. Hartman were ready to publicly haggle about the number of Serbian victims, the number of ARBiH victims was set at about 1,000 in a succession of judgments. Depending on the judgment, the number was a bit smaller in one case and a bit larger in another. Remarkably, none of the chambers ever bothered to verify the number of people who could fit in the space, even when filled beyond capacity.[57] The dimensions of the Warehouse are well established. The measurements were in fact made and properly documented by Prosecution investigators.[58] Yet no empirical test, which could easily have been done, was ever conducted to determine the maximum number of individuals the Warehouse could hold — even when tightly packed.[59] Instead, ICTY chambers based

---

56  Orić was acquitted on the spurious grounds that he did not have "effective control" over ARBIH forces in Srebrenica during the period covered by the indictment. See Orić Appellate Judgment, Par. 90–93 and 160.

57  In the Karadžić Trial Judgment the Chamber in fact found this to be the case: "Around 5 p.m. the warehouse became so tightly packed that the detainees almost suffocated." (Par. 5227) See also Tolimir Trial Judgment, par. 355.

58  For Warehouse dimensions, see Popović et al., Footnote 1507 Ex. P04529, "Sketch with measurements of Kravica Warehouse, with marked copy of Ex. P01563 and attached declaration of Tomasz Blaszczyk, 4 May 2009.

59  Andy Wilcoxon has suggested the following solution, which is based on the Warehouse dimensions as well as on evidence of the number of prisoners brought to Kravica: "The Kravica Warehouse is a finite space. The total floor space of the two rooms of Kravica warehouse where the prisoners were held is 589.5 square meters; 262.5 square meters in the west room, and 327 square meters in the east room. Therefore, we can estimate that the number of prisoners who could have been seated on the floor of Kravica warehouse is somewhere in the region of 600 or 700 men if the warehouse were empty, which it wasn't. The warehouse was in use at the time of the massacre and part of the floor space was occupied by the mate-

(Footnote continued on next page)

their figures of the number of Kravica Warehouse victims on mere speculation,[60] a mixture of eyeball estimates[61] and often convoluted extrapolations from the forensic evidence.[62] [*See* Annex III.]

---

(Footnote continued from previous page)

rial being stored inside of the warehouse. One of the men who survived the massacre testified that inside the room of the warehouse where he was sitting there were containers, an old wire fence, and a dilapidated old car that were all being stored inside of the warehouse." See: *Srebrenica: The Ugly Truth*, 21 July 2014, http://www.slobodanmilosevic.org/news/srebrenica071114.htm

60  Prosecution expert witness Dusko Janc was of the view that "it is impossible to provide the exact number of [Kravica] victims." (See *Mladić* Trial Judgment, par. 2706)

61  See *Tolimir* Trial Judgment, par. 376. Also, *Karadžić* Trial Judgment, par. 5277.

62  The hodgepodge nature of the forensic evidence relied on by the *Karadžić* Chamber in arriving at its Kravica victim estimate is evident in pars. 5257–5258 of the Trial Judgement: "The Accused argues in his final brief that the Glogova gravesite was a "mixed grave" which contained not only victims from the Kravica Warehouse incident but from other killing incidents related to the fall of Srebrenica, as well as victims who had died years earlier. The Prosecution acknowledges that a number of bodies found in the Glogova gravesites were brought from places other than the Kravica Warehouse. The Prosecution explains that this number includes at least 80 victims executed in Bratunac, including at the Vuk Karadžić School, plus approximately 100 individuals who cannot be determined beyond reasonable doubt to have been executed (...) As of 13 January 2012, DNA analysis led to the identification of 226 bodies from Glogova 1 and 171 from Glogova 2, as persons listed as missing following the take-over of Srebrenica. However, Dušan Janc clarified that not all of these 397 individuals can be linked to the killings at the Kravica Warehouse, since bodies which cannot be linked to this execution site were brought to Glogova, namely at least 80 victims executed in Bratunac, plus approximately 100 bodies brought from other locations..." See also *Popović et al.* Trial Judgment, par. 443.

Each of the various ICTY chambers that heard a Srebrenica case determined a different figure for the number of Kravica victims:

*Krstić*: "Between 1,000 and 1,500 Bosnian Muslim men."[63]

*Blagojević and Jokić*: "On the evening of 13 July, at least 1,000 Bosnian Muslim men were killed in the Kravica Warehouse."[64]

*Popović et al.*: "Taking the evidence outlined above into account, the Trial Chamber concludes that at least 1,000 people were killed in Kravica Warehouse."[65]

*Tolimir*: "[T]he Chamber finds beyond reasonable doubt that members of the Bosnian Serb Forces killed between 600–1,000 Bosnian Muslims at Kravica Warehouse on 13 and 14 July 1995."[66]

*Karadžić*: "[T]he Chamber finds that, on 13 July 1995, between 755 and 1,016 Bosnian Muslim men were killed by members of the Bosnian Serb Forces at the Kravica Warehouse."[67]

*Mladić*: "[T]he Trial Chamber finds that from 13 to 14 July 1995 [Serbian forces] killed approximately 1,000 Bosnian-Muslim males, including minors and elderly, who were detained in Kravica Warehouse."[68]

---

63  *Krstić* Trial Judgment, par. 205

64  *Blagojević and Jokić* Trial Judgment, par. 296

65  *Popović et al.* Trial Judgment, par. 443.

66  *Tolimir* Trial Judgment, par. 376.

67  *Karadžić* Trial Judgment, par. 5286.

68  *Mladić* Trial Judgment, par. 2707.

These varying conclusions of the death toll at the Kravica Warehouse pose several significant problems.

(1)     First of all, the glaring imprecision of the victim count, coupled with the tendency of the trier of fact to maximize the statistical dimension of the criminal act, is meant to enhance the psychological impact of the crime. The Kravica death toll fluctuates around the 1,000 mark, but the range of "possible" figures varies between 600 and 1,500. Doesn't a 900-victim margin of error strain credibility? The ICTY Srebrenica chambers betray an inherent incentive to maximize the number of victims at each separate execution site in order to facilitate reaching the preordained overall total of about 8,000 victims. The circumstances which make it difficult to determine the precise number of a large concentration of victims also make it easier to inflate the number of victims.

(2)     Srebrenica-related judgments exhibit a general pattern of downplaying the number of combat deaths in favor of inflating the number of execution deaths. The *Krstić* judgment, the first in this series, dismissed with a few casual remarks the huge issue of legitimate combat deaths suffered by the ARBiH column.[69] Over time, evidence accumulated of the staggering casualties experienced by the 12,000- to 15,000-man mixed military/civilian column that was conducting a breakout from Srebrenica to Tuzla. Since the introduction of this evidence in various trials,[70] it was no longer possible for the chamber to

---

69    *Krstić* Trial Judgment, par. 77.

70    ICTY Prosecution military expert witness admitted in the *Popović* trial the mixed nature of the column as well as its legitimacy as a target, Transcript, p. 20244, lines 19–25 and 20245, line 1. Chief Prosecution Investigator Jean-René Ruez acknowledged that "a significant number [of Mus-

(Footnote continued on next page)

minimize or conceal these facts. It had to be admitted that the column was a legitimate military target for Serbian forces and that inflicting losses on the column was not a war crime.[71] As the series of Srebrenica trials drew to a close, the Defense began presenting evidence — particularly statements given by several dozen column survivors upon their arrival in territory controlled by the Sarajevo government — depicting an enormous number of legitimate combat casualties that were occurring simultaneously with extrajudicial executions of prisoners, both of which were taking place in the same small operational area.

Therefore, simply counting corpses is unsatisfactory. To attribute criminal liability correctly, it is necessary to identify and then distinguish two different categories of soldiers: those who were captured and then executed; and those who were killed in action. This distinction is particularly crucial with respect to Kravica, because, the day before the Warehouse massacre, the column exiting Srebrenica passed within a few kilometers of Kravica, where it clashed with the Serbian military forces. Six known survivor statements exist that were given to debriefers in Tuzla. These statements confirm the clashes and detail considerable ARBiH casualties.[72] Even though these statements originate from Prosecution discovery ma-

---

lims] were killed in combat." *Monitor*, April 19, 2001, EDS number 06038344.

71  It is significant to note that no one was ever prosecuted for attacking this column either at The Hague or before the War Crimes Court in Sarajevo.

72  These witnesses are: Behudin Muminović, EDS no. 00464352; Ševal Ademović, EDS no. 01008095; Ramiz Husić, EDS no. 00813498; Midhat Kadrić, EDS no. 00371768; Nurif Memišević, EDS no. 00396028; and Husejn Mustafić, EDS no. 00401647.

terial, neither the Prosecution nor any of the chambers have taken them into account, nor did they make an effort to distinguish between two legally different causes of death that were occurring within a short distance of one another and only a few hours apart.[73] The ICTY's failure to discuss a factor of such magnitude, and its attribution of almost all exhumed human remains found in the vicinity of Kravica to the Warehouse massacre, seriously skews its analysis of this event.

(3)     The statement of column survivor Behudin Muminović is revealing in connection with the possible composition of burial sites in the proximity of Kravica. It is designated in the ICTY Electronic Disclosure System (EDS) as document no. 00464352. Muminović stated that he left Srebrenica with other males on July 11, 1995; that *en route* he witnessed combat with Serbian forces at Sandići[74] and Kamenica; that the principal type of ammunition to which he and other members of the column were exposed was artillery shelling; that at Kravica he saw six corpses

---

73   The column's engagement in combat in the evening hours of July 12 in the general area, including Kravica, is confirmed in the *Popović* Trial Judgment, par. 381. In the *Karadžić* Trial Judgment, par. 5162, reference is made to the fact that "during the night of 12 July and the morning of 13 July, there was an exchange of fire between the Bosnian Serb Forces and members of the column, resulting in many Bosnian Muslim deaths" in the general area of Kravica. Heavy fighting and column casualties around Kravica are also confirmed in the NIOD Report on Srebrenica prepared in 2002 for the Dutch Parliament: "The rearmost section of the column thus came to suffer serious losses. The delays also hampered the column in passing Kamenica, as the VRS had been given the opportunity of laying ambushes which would form an insurmountable obstacle for the larger part of the column. The assaults on the column in the area around Kravica, Konjević Polje and Nova Kasaba were therefore responsible for the heaviest death toll," *Part IV, Chapter 1, The Journey from Srebrenica to Tuzla.*

74   Village in close proximity to Kravica.

and that on July 12 in passing with others in the column he saw a mass burial of an estimated 500 bodies being conducted by the Serbs. Muminović was later captured by Serbian forces, taken to a prisoner of war camp, and then exchanged on 24 December 1995. If one so wishes, Muminović's visual sighting of "500 bodies" may be interpreted figuratively instead of being taken literally as meaning "many" without diminishing the point of his account. Most of the human remains attributed to the Warehouse massacre were exhumed from the Glogova burial sites in the village of Sandići, where this witness saw a mass burial taking place a day before the Warehouse events (13 July) — and at least two days before the burial of Warehouse victims had begun. All these remains were, as a matter of course, indiscriminately attributed to the Kravica Warehouse killings.[75] Neither the Prosecution nor the Chamber addressed this anomaly; it is not known whether this issue of confounded victim counts was ever raised by any of the defense teams.

(4)     It turned out that, perhaps inadvertently, Prosecution expert witness, pathologist Richard Wright, in his evidence at the *Karadžić* trial was most helpful in clarifying some of the Kravica burial issues. Regarding several of the burial sites at the Glogova location,[76] the expert asserted that in the reburial operation conducted in October 1995 the contents of some of the sites were moved, but not of oth-

---

75  See *Popović et al.* Trial Judgment, par. 439; *Tolimir* Trial Judgment, par. 376; *Karadžić* Trial Judgment, par. 5258 and 5282; and *Mladić* Trial Judgment, par. 2706.

76  Primary burial location associated by the Tribunal with the Kravica massacre.

ers.[77] It may logically be assumed that the purpose of the reburial operation — if there was one — would have been to conceal traces of the crime. The question, therefore, naturally arises why the perpetrators, who may be assumed to have had precise knowledge of the location of all the primary graves where they had buried their victims, left any of the compromising evidence in place at all when in October they decided to cover up their tracks? At the other well-known execution site, Pilica/Branjevo, we find inexplicably a similar odd pattern of behaviour. Some of the bodies buried there were also allegedly moved, and for the same reason, but curiously about 120 bodies were left behind in the primary grave. That was just enough to be discovered later and for that discovery to lend general credence to the allegations of "crown witness" Dražen Erdemović. The defense failed to highlight this unusual mode of conduct and did not point out the suspicious analogy.

Further on, in response to a question put to him by the Prosecutor, expert witness Wright confirmed that in his report he mentioned finding in the Glogova mass graves he examined numerous bodies disjointed as a consequence of so-called "blast injuries."[78] This is an important detail because it helps explain numerous injuries described in Srebrenica autopsy reports (of which there are about 150),[79] the implications of which are steadfastly ignored. Blast injuries inflicted by high-velocity projectiles exclude execution as a possible manner of death. Furthermore, infliction of

---

77  *Prosecutor* v. *Karadžić*, Transcript, p. 22269 and 22301.

78  *Ibid.*, p. 22273.

79  This is from a cohort of about 1,920 individuals whose body parts make up the 3,658 "cases" in ICTY autopsy reports.

blast injuries was one of the characteristic ways in which opposing forces were neutralized in the Srebrenica theater. Their presence points to combat as the likeliest explanation for at least some of the AR-BiH casualties that in Glogova and elsewhere were found intermingled with possible execution victims.

Describing a shattered skull, expert witness Wright concedes that it was probably fragmented by an exploding grenade, which suggests that the deceased was a combat casualty rather than an execution victim. He goes on to describe hand grenade fragments found nearby, which also suggest a similar conclusion.[80] The witness added that in the Glogova 1 gravesite he found remnants of explosive devices in the form of grenades and shrapnel.[81] Given the fact that Glogova is located in close proximity to the Kravica Agricultural Cooperative, where on July 13 1995 the incident resulting in the massacre of prisoners took place, the legal strategy behind the Prosecution's determination to link all human remains in the area to the Kravica massacre and to place the massacre itself firmly within the larger context of "Srebrenica genocide" is perfectly understandable. The problem, however — as stated elsewhere in this chapter — is that on the previous day, July 12, the 28th Division column passed nearby as it was breaking out of Srebrenica on its way to Tuzla. A significant engagement in combat occurred between the column and ambushing Serbian forces, which resulted in hundreds of ARBiH casualties. This, arguably, is the reason why numerous casualties buried in the Glogova gravesites during the ground-clearing opera-

---

80   *Ibid.*, p. 22271-2.

81   *Ibid.*, p. 22273.

tion that followed the clash show a pattern of injury pointing to death in combat.

There are at least six column survivors' statements in ICTY files confirming the battle and its lethal consequences. This version of facts is also accepted in the Dutch War Institute's 2002 report about Srebrenica.

Significantly, under cross-examination Prosecution expert witness Richard Wright agreed that it is not possible to discount the possibility that Glogova burial site bodies were in fact collected at other locations, where combat deaths had occurred, and were subsequently brought from there to Glogova for interment.[82]

(5)   The forensic evidence is murky when it comes to corroborating the statistical aspect of the now-established Kravica narrative, that about 1,000 prisoners were summarily executed there, which constitutes a large chunk of the presumed total of about 8,000 Srebrenica victims. Without going into excessive detail, autopsy reports from the exhumations at the burial sites considered to be related to the July 1995 events around Kravica[83] tell a complex and heterogeneous story. This is important to point out because when mass death is attributable to a single cause and set of circumstances, it is reasonable to expect a mostly uniform pattern of injury. In this case, however, there are human remains without a determinable cause or time of death, or with causes of death attributable to artillery fire and other weaponry not known to be used in executions, and their num-

---

82   *Ibid.*, p. 22305-6.

83   Burial sites Glogova 2-9, Blječeva 1, as well as Zeleni Jadar 5 and 6, see *Mladić* Trial Judgment, par. 2706, and Ravnice, see *Karadžić* Trial Judgment, par. 5285.

bers are statistically significant.[84] This raises serious evidentiary issues that were, once again, systematically ignored by the Chambers, the Prosecution, and the Defense in ICTY proceedings.

(6)     Equally important, there is a credible alternative version of events leading up to the Warehouse killings that undermines the view of the Kravica episode as part of a broader Joint Criminal Enterprise ("JCE")[85] to execute such a large number of ARBiH prisoners that it rises to the level of genocide. Evidence was presented in several Srebrenica trials that the killings at the Warehouse occurred spontaneously and were sparked by an incident during which one of the prisoners seized a guard's weapon, then shot and killed the guard.[86] The remaining fifteen to twenty guards panicked and overreacted by opening fire on the prisoners. It is difficult to reliably reconstruct this sequence of events because the ICTY chambers rely preferentially on the two "surviving witnesses." (When physical evidence is lacking, such witnesses tend to pop up conveniently to fill the gaps in the Prosecution's case; two of them testified pseudony-

---

84   See Annex IV, *Forensic Situation at Mass Burial Sites Linked to Kravica Warehouse in ICTY Judgments.*

85   "Joint Criminal Enterprise" is a mode of criminal liability that is not mentioned in the ICTY Statute. It was made up entirely out of whole cloth by ICTY judges. A person charged under this form of liability could not possibly have known that conduct for which he is being be punished was illegal at the time he allegedly engaged in it.

86   Information about this incident is acknowledged in the *Popović* Trial Judgment, par. 444. It is accepted as confirmed in the *Tolimir* Trial Judgment, par. 359 ["The Chamber finds that a Bosnian Muslim prisoner killed Krsto Dragičević which led to Čuturić sustaining burns to his hand and that this incident caused the Bosnian Serb guards to become agitated and angry and led to the shooting of many Bosnian Muslim prisoners in front of the warehouse as described by PW-006."]. An oblique reference is made to it in the *Karadžić* Trial Judgment, par. 5230.

mously in various trials about what happened in the Kravica Warehouse, just as Q and Ahmo Hasić played a similar role in the preceding Branjevo/Pilica case study.) In the *Popović, Tolimir,* and *Karadžić* judgments, the chambers at least made passing mention or allusion to the existence of this alternative account, without, however, granting it any serious consideration. Jurists would argue that this was surely an error on the part of the chambers. A spontaneously erupting slaughter, regardless of how catastrophic the consequences may be, cannot be made to fit the Prosecution model of a JCE to commit genocide, which in general requires some prior planning, and in particular *dolus specialis.* At least one ICTY chamber showed signs of being aware of this difficulty when it nonchalantly ruled that if the prisoners in the Warehouse had not been killed under such circumstances, then they would have been properly executed later, anyway.[87] Jurists not beholden to the ICTY or its sponsors will surely cite this prescient ruling as an example of judicial speculation at its most outrageous.

(7)     Finally, there is the role of Prosecution's omnipresent cooperating witness Momir Nikolić,

---

87  The *Popović* chamber's refined reasoning to this effect is articulated in par. 444 of its judgment: "The Trial Chamber is of the view that the only reasonable inference is that the full-scale execution of the Bosnian Muslim men at Kravica Warehouse was part of the common plan to murder the able-bodied males of Srebrenica and of the genocidal plan. The Trial Chamber is also satisfied that the prisoners were detained there temporarily, most likely to be moved to another detention site, as was the pattern throughout, to ultimately be killed. However, as a reaction to the unexpected 'burnt-hands' incident, the Trial Chamber finds that the plan to murder the Bosnian Muslim prisoners detained in Kravica Warehouse was moved forward and they were killed on the spot." The chamber cites no evidence presented during the trial upon which this "view" of the prospective course of events could have been based.

provided some of the key details. Nikolić was a security officer for the Bratunac Brigade, a Serbian military unit that played a prominent role in Srebrenica-related events in July 1995. Nikolić was eventually arrested and brought to The Hague to face a litany of the usual charges, including genocide. A short time before his trial was scheduled to start, he entered into a plea-bargaining agreement with the ICTY Prosecution in which he agreed to admit guilt to some charges in exchange for a reduced sentence that was ultimately fixed at twenty years' imprisonment. He agreed to act as a Prosecution witness in subsequent Srebrenica trials as part of the arrangement. One peculiarity in Nikolić's case should be noted. In order to impress the prosecution with his cooperativeness, Nikolić even lied by taking responsibility for several murders that, as was eventually established by a diligent Defense attorney, he did not commit.[88] Liu Daqun, the sentencing judge, initially rejected Nikolić's dishonest guilty plea only to later reverse himself and accept it, but in the judgment, Nikolić's evidence was excoriated for its "lack of candor,"[89] while in its submission to the *Popović* Chamber it was the Prosecution that proposed that Nikolić's "evidence should be relied on only when corroborated."[90] That wise stipulation was ignored in Nikolić's subsequent appearances as Prosecution witness. At

---

88 *See* IWPR ICTY, 3 October, 2003, Sporan kredibilitet svedoka maskara u Srebrenici [Credibility of Srebrenica Massacre witness disputed], https://iwpr.net/sr/global-voices/sporan-kredibilitet-svedoka-maskara-u-srebrenici

89 See *Momir Nikolić*, Trial Judgment, Par. 156.

90 See *Popović* Sentencing Judgment, Par 49. In assessing this witness' credibility, the *Popović* Chamber took the further unusual step of advising a "cautious and careful approach when considering the evidence of Momir Nikolić" (*ibid.*, Par. 51).

the ICTY, apparently, the ancient adage *falsus in uno, falsus in omnibus* ("false in one thing, false in everything") never entered its judicial practice.

Momir Nikolić rendered uniquely valuable services as a witness for the ICTY Prosecution: he seemed to pop up anywhere an evidentiary gap needed to be filled. For the Prosecution, he is the principal source of evidence for the alleged reburial of executed prisoners in secondary and tertiary mass graves, which was allegedly undertaken by Serbian forces to conceal evidence of the mass crime.[91] Nikolić was in Potočari, so he could apprise the court of the details of the Serbian "ethnic cleansing operation" during which about 20,000 Srebrenica residents — women, children, and the elderly — were evacuated by Serbian authorities by busses away from the combat zone to safety in Kladovo, the nearest town controlled by the ARBiH.[92] Nikolić also just happened to be in the company of General Ratko Mladić in Konjević Polje. He testified in Mladić's trial that Mladić ran a finger across his neck in a throat-slitting gesture in response to Nikolić's question of what fate was awaiting the prisoners. This gesture supposedly left no doubt about the General's intentions.[93] Predictably, Nikolić, a natural Johnny on the Spot, was also in the proximity of the Kravica Warehouse at just the right time to offer his first-hand observations to the court of what

---

91   See Momir Nikolić, *Statement of Facts and Acceptance of Responsibility*, https://www.legal-tools.org/uploads/tx_ltpdb/NikolicM._ICTYTCPleaAgreement_Statement offacts_06-05-2003_E_05.htm

92   *Ibid.*

93   See *Nezavisne Novine* (Banja Luka), 3 June 2013, *http://www.nezavisne.com/novosti/bih/Momir-Nikolic-Mladic-nagovijestio-ubijanje-zarobljenika-u-Srebrenici/194724*

Stephen Karganović

had happened there. Interestingly, Nikolić actually went above and beyond the call of duty in his 2003 confession to affirm "that he had ordered the executions at Kravica Warehouse."[94] He later recanted this confession, which was never corroborated by any other evidence but, in the view of ICTY chambers, this tenuous connection apparently sufficed to validate this bearer of false witness to testify on other aspects of the Kravica affair.

By accepting Kravica details furnished by Nikolić and by incorporating them into its judgment as credible evidence, the *Karadžić* Chamber went out of its way to be empathetic and lenient:

"The Chamber examined his explanation for this untruth, wherein he stated *inter alia*, in relation to his plea agreement '[...] we'd been working on [it] for a long time and I did not want it to fall through. I wanted this agreement to be reached'. In this situation, Nikolić was prepared to sacrifice himself and assume responsibility for something he had not in fact done. The Chamber reviewed his evidence and is satisfied that, unfortunate as it might have been, Nikolić's inconsistency was not the result of any oblique motive to lead the Chamber into error. It was extremely important to him that the agreement did not turn out to be an abysmal failure and he was willing to compromise the veracity of his statement in order to ensure that outcome. The Chamber was also mindful of the fact that Nikolić voluntarily corrected his inconsistency at the first available opportunity."[95]

---

94  *Popović et al.*, Trial Judgment, Footnote 72.

95  *Karadžić* Trial Judgment, par. 5058. The Chamber went on to cite another one of Nikolić's overzealous lies but concluded reassuringly that the witness' credibility remained intact: "The Chamber also notes the false identification Nikolić made of himself in a photograph that had been shown to

(Footnote continued on next page)

What general conclusions may now be drawn about the IC-TY's account and evaluation of events that took place on 13 July 1995? The first fundamental conclusion we may draw is that, even after half a dozen trials where evidence about Kravica was heard over an almost twenty-year period, we are today none the wiser about the number of prisoners who had been killed in the incident. There is, moreover, a credible account that the incident was provoked by a spontaneous outburst. Without calling into question that a crime had been committed, this incident makes it difficult to fit Kravica into either a JCE or a genocidal scenario, whatever may be said in this regard of other episodes in the Srebrenica chain of events. One could argue that the *in dubio pro reo* principle requires the court to at least duly consider this alternative account and, even if it is found wanting, the court should at least offer reasoned grounds for rejecting it, along with its obvious implications. Secondly, the forensic evidence is at best muddled because human remains deriving from heterogene-

---

(Footnote continued from previous page)

him and the explanation he advanced for that falsity. He testified that he thought the individual in the photograph looked like him. He did not want to tell the Prosecution that he was not the person in the photograph; he stated, '[p]erhaps I had forgotten something. So I didn't want to exclude the possibility.' Nikolić then felt himself impaled on the horns of a dilemma when he was told that the photograph had been taken in Sandići because he knew that he was never in Sandići. As it turned out, the photograph was of another man. The Chamber holds the view that in his desperation to ensure that he did nothing to jeopardize his agreement with the Prosecution, Nikolić found himself in an intractable situation of his own creation. Accordingly, the Chamber is satisfied that his inconsistency was not inspired by any insidious desire to mislead the Chamber. In its final analysis, the Chamber is convinced that the aforementioned inconsistencies in no way affect Nikolić's overall credibility, nor do they justify a rejection of his evidence. In reaching this conclusion, the Chamber also paid particular attention to the fact tha the consistency of the witness remained undiminished throughout his various statements andtestimonies in respect of other matters." *Ibid.*, par. 5059.

Stephen Karganović

ous circumstances have clearly been intermingled, with no effort having been made to distinguish among them. As a result, the contention that as many as 1,000 prisoners were executed at the Kravica Warehouse, as part of a larger JCE to physically exterminate captured military-age males from the Srebrenica enclave, remains uncorroborated by the available evidence. Whatever actually happened in Kravica, the account articulated through ICTY judgments does not stand up to scrutiny.

**5. ICTY radio intercept evidence**

It is crucial to consider how radio intercept evidence has been treated by ICTY chambers, because it was used repeatedly to fill key gaps left by the unavailability of other types of evidence. How reliable are the intercepts that have been admitted into evidence by various ICTY chambers in Srebrenica-related trials? A brief review is in order. Already in the fourth paragraph of the *Krstić* Trial Judgment, the ICTY Chamber set the stage for welcoming every conceivable sort of purported evidence that elsewhere would be inadmissible:

"The Trial Chamber draws upon a mosaic of evidence that combines to paint a picture of what happened during those few days in July 1995."[96] In the specific context of the *Krstić* case, a concrete and vitally important application of that "mosaic" principle makes its appearance. The *Krstić* Chamber discusses how it reached the conclusion that the Bosnian Serb Army had in its custody the requisite number of prisoners from Srebrenica to commit the mass slaughter that was attributed to it:

> There are also fragments of information from VRS communications about the possible magnitude of the executions. An intercepted conversation at 1730

---

96   *Prosecutor v. Krstić*, Par. 4.

hours on 13 July 1995, indicates that about 6,000 men had been captured from the Bosnian Muslim column by that time... Other intercepted VRS conversations reveal that, on 15 July 1995, midway through the executions, at least 3,000–4,000 Bosnian Muslim prisoners were being detained by the VRS. Further, on 18 July 1995, two unidentified Bosnian Serbs were heard in an intercepted conversation reflecting on the recent events in Eastern Bosnia, including matters relating to the Bosnian Muslim column. One participant said that of the 10,000 military aged men who were in Srebrenica, '4,000–5,000 have certainly kicked the bucket.'[97]

This evidence — as the Chamber says — is based in great part on intercepted communications, which leads to a dramatic conclusion in the next paragraph:

The Trial Chamber is satisfied that, in July 1995, following the take-over of Srebrenica, Bosnian Serb forces executed several thousand Bosnian Muslim men. The total number is likely to be within the range of 7,000–8,000 men.[98]

The cumulative impact of this "mosaic," including its intercept component, is clearly demonstrated in a further paragraph of the *Krstić* Trial Judgment: "The Trial Chamber finds that, following the takeover of Srebrenica in July 1995, the Bosnian Serbs devised and implemented a plan to execute as many as possible of the military aged Bosnian Muslim men present in the enclave."[99] Of course, the *Krstić* Chamber was obliged to consider, *pro forma* at least, the reliability of the evidence in which

---

97   *Ibid.*, Par. 83.

98   *Ibid.*, Par. 84.

99   *Ibid.*, Par. 87.

it had invested so heavily to form its "picture mosaic." This is done in Pars. 105 *et passim* where the Chamber addresses the reliability of intercept evidence. To paraphrase the Chamber's exposition of its findings, intercept records were handed over to the Office of the Prosecutor ("OTP") by the Bosnian government. The VRS did have secure means of communication, but its use was cumbersome, so they often used unsecured lines for expediency. The resulting intercepts recorded by ARBiH listening posts were later passed on to the ICTY's Prosecution, which relied on them for key evidentiary elements of its case. After having attributed such great weight to intercept evidence in the presentation of the Prosecution case, the Chamber concluded reassuringly: "The Trial Chamber was told that all possible measures were taken to ensure the accuracy of the transcribed conversations."[100]

The *Krstić* Chamber, after having noted that defense expert General Radinović had expressed some misgivings about the reliability of this type of evidence, ruled that it "accepts that the OTP did in fact diligently check and cross-reference the intercept material as part of the 'intercept project,'"[101] which should of course be sufficient to allay the general's concerns. The *Krstić* Chamber goes on to say that:

---

100 *Ibid.*, Par. 109.

101 The "intercept project" was an ICTY Prosecution in-house operation for checking the provenance of intercepts and certifying their authenticity, see *ibid.*, par.114. Disregarding the adversarial nature of the proceedings, the Chamber gave this self-policing mechanism a clean bill of health: "Meticulous procedures were used by the OTP for tracking the dates of the intercepted conversations and the former OTP employee who appeared before the Trial Chamber testified with 'absolute certainty' that the dates ascribed to the individual conversations were accurate." It's a cozy arrangement which inspired absolute confidence.

The Trial Chamber accepts that the OTP did in fact diligently check and cross-reference the intercept material as part of the 'intercept project'. In order to determine whether the material was reliable and genuine, the OTP looked at the internal consistency between the notebooks and the printouts of each conversation. Transcripts of a single conversation, which were recorded by two or more interceptors, were also compared. The OTP also embarked on a process of 'corroborating the intercepts with information obtained from other sources, such as documents acquired from the VRS, the RS Ministry of Defence and UNPROFOR, as well as aerial images'.[102]

It is difficult to avoid the disagreeable impression that, when it comes to presenting such important evidence, the Chamber leaves it to the Prosecution to monitor itself and that the Chamber is more than satisfied with the results of this arrangement. Should there be any lingering doubts advanced by sceptics such as General Radinović, the Chamber draws its trump card:

A former OTP employee assigned to the 'intercept project' testified that, as a result of this corroboration process, she became convinced that the intercepts were 'absolutely reliable'... the former OTP employee [identified as a certain Mrs. Frease] testified before the Trial Chamber that the dates ascribed to the individual conversations were accurate.[103]

Mrs. Frease' testimony alone should suffice to quell any remaining doubts. Unsurprisingly, Richard Butler, the Prosecution's military expert, endorsed the Chamber's view.[104] To rein-

---

102 Ibid., Par. 114.

103 *Ibid.*, Par. 114.

104 *Ibid.*, Par. 115.

force this iron-clad conclusion, it was not just Prosecution personnel at the ICTY who took great pains to guarantee the integrity of the collection process for intercept evidence. It turns out that Bosnian Muslim recording technicians were equally professional and conscientious:

> All possible measures were taken by the Bosnian Muslim interceptors to ensure the accuracy of the recorded conversations, as would be expected in any prudent army. This fact was reinforced by the measures taken by the OTP to verify the reliability of the intercepted evidence as part of the 'intercept project'.[105]

We shall soon see to what degree this is really true when we review the statement given by one of those BiH Army intercept operators to the Office of the Prosecutor, which describes his *modus operandi*.

We find similar dicta in the *Blagojević and Jokić* case. Most notably, the Chamber there announced unequivocally that "the Trial Chamber is convinced that the intercept-related evidence admitted is a reliable source of information."[106] Defense objections to this conclusion were summarized, but they were promptly overridden:

> The Defence of Dragan Jokić argued that the intercept transcripts were taken down by unknown personnel or personnel with a history of unreliable transcriptions and lacking sufficient training, that substandard equipment was used, that by not providing original tape recordings the Prosecution was effec-

---

105 *Ibid.*, Par. 116.

106 *Prosecutor* v. *Blagojević and Jokić*, Par. 30.

tively submitting hearsay evidence, which ought not to be admissible.[107]

When the Chamber says:

> ...bearing in mind the testimonial evidence and the very large amount of documentary evidence, the Trial Chamber cannot find that it is necessary to have access to the original audio recordings of the intercepts,

it is important to recall that of the more than 100 intercepts used in the *Krstić* case, there was audio for only one intercept. In the *Popović et al.* Trial Judgment rendered in June 2010, the Chamber considered various factors affecting the 213 intercepts that had been admitted into evidence prior to concluding that: "The Trial Chamber has found the intercepts to be overall probative and reliable."[108] The Trial Chamber's procedure was to examine whether

> based on the totality of the evidence, a reasonable trier of fact could find the intercepts to be what the Prosecution purports them to be — a contemporaneous record of intercepted VRS communications.

The Trial Chamber said that in the process it had

> considered the testimony of several witnesses relating to the intercepts, such as intercept operators, an expert in radio relay communications, and a Prosecution analyst. It considered all challenges made by the Defense including the theory that the intercepts had been fabricated, evidence relating to the chain of custody, and the general lack of audio recordings. In sum, the Trial Chamber concluded that the Prosecu-

---

107 *Ibid.*, Footnote 72.

108 *Prosecutor* v. *Popović et al.*, Par. 66.

tion had established that the intercepts as a whole were *prima facie* relevant and probative.[109]

So, it appears that all those challenges turned out to be lacking foundation, after all, and that the record-keeping practices of the Bosnian Muslim intercept operators in besieged Srebrenica were meticulous and satisfactory in every way. In fact, the Chamber made its determination to view this evidence favorably "particularly in light of the evidence given by the intercept operators."[110]

Two examples highlight the issues raised by the high level of receptivity shown by various ICTY chambers to intercept evidence tendered by the Prosecution. They strongly suggest that the way this evidence was gathered would almost certainly be found questionable by non-political judges in routine criminal cases in most national jurisdictions.

The reference in Par. 383 to a key purported intercept that provided information that was vital to the construction of the factual underpinnings of the *Popović* judgment and, therefore, vital to the credibility of the judgment itself, is an apt illustration. It concerns a July 13, 1995 intercept indicating the capture by Serbian forces of about 6,000 Srebrenica Muslim POWs. It is the only clear reference to the number of POWs in custody at that moment. If the Prosecution had then failed to establish this fact, then the case against the defendants would have been seriously undermined — if it wouldn't have entirely collapsed — because without evidence of the prior capture of thousands of Muslim prisoners, executions on such a huge scale could not have occurred. This is the Trial Chamber's summary of the intercept's

---

109   *Ibid.*, Par. 64.

110   *Ibid.*, Par. 65.

content: "A conversation intercepted at 5:30 p.m. on 13 July indicates that approximately 6,000 Bosnian Muslim prisoners were detained in the Bratunac area at three locations, with about 1,500 to 2,000 men in each location. One of the locations appears to be the football field at Nova Kasaba, another was 'up there where the checkpoint at the intersection is,' and a third was 'halfway between the checkpoint and the loading place.' In this context, the Trial Chamber is of the view that one of the places referred to is Sandici Meadow and the other Nova Kasaba."[111]

But a review of the actual intercept, as presented by the Prosecution and available as a trial exhibit in the Tribunal data base,[112] raises serious concerns. The interlocutors are merely designated as X and Y, which means that they are anonymous. In fact, their very existence cannot be verified, which precludes the possibility of ever cross-examining individuals X and Y. Other than a sheet of paper with some writing on it, which purports to be an intercept of such conversation, no objective evidence exists from first-hand sources that these conversations ever took place or, if they had, that the participants were in a position to know what they were talking about. The latter point is of critical importance. A key conclusion about the number of prisoners was based exclusively on a conversation attributed to these two individuals. The gratuitous assumption was then made that they were competent reporters of the relevant facts. But even if we were to credit this piece of evidence, it is still susceptible to varying interpretations. According to the Prosecution, and the Chamber concurred, anonymous individuals X and Y had a conversation at 5:30 pm on July 13, 1995 where Y informs X that there were at

---

111    *Ibid.*, Par. 383.

112    EDS document 0104 3225.

each of three different locations "about 1,500 to 2,000" prisoners, or a total of "6,000." Even if we were to accept the authenticity of the conversation, it does not support "beyond a reasonable doubt" the Prosecution and the Chamber's interpretation regarding the total number of captured prisoners. For each location cited, a range of 1,500 to 2,000 captured prisoners is given. Assuming that the Chamber chose, for whatever reason, to lend credence to an intercept of a conversation with unidentified participants, the Chamber still had the option of choosing the lower total of about 4,500 POWs. The *in dubio pro reo* principle would strongly favor this approach.

Since the purported intercept makes no claim of an accurate headcount, the Chamber would have acted reasonably by erring on the side of caution. But no, four and a half thousand captured prisoners, though a considerable number, would not do because it falls far too short of the requisite total of 8,000 "victims of genocide." The court, therefore, simply added up the maximum figures generated by an unsubstantiated document and then used it as the basis for its calculation. Thus, mass murder of the necessary magnitude was finally rendered more plausible — on paper, at least. By relying on this and by applying a bit of evidentiary engineering, it's possible to demonstrate that the alleged executioners had approximately the projected number of victims in their custody. The rest is easy.

Another curious use of "intercept evidence" was put on display at the *Krstić* trial. The Prosecution's military expert Richard Butler drew equally momentous conclusions in his testimony about a July 18, 1995 intercept.[113] Butler, using an English translation, offered his interpretation of a July 18 intercept in which he claimed that the execution of several thousand Muslim pris-

---

113   See *Krstić* trial transcript, p. 5205,

oners was being described in coded language as having "kicked the bucket."

"I can only assume," Butler testified, "that this was a reference to Muslim men who were transferred to the Zvornik Brigade zone of responsibility, where they were executed."[114] The issue is important because the collocutors in the intercept refer to 4,000 to 5,000 persons. Two important preliminary observations are in order. First, Butler admitted that he is not a Serbo-Croatian speaker; therefore, he would have been unable to follow the conversation in the original language. Second, there is no record of the existence of a Serbo-Croatian original of this intercept in the ICTY data base, where there is only an English-language version. Butler's expert opinion was based on the version of this intercept that was shown to him by the Prosecution (and ultimately accepted as authentic by the Chamber in its Judgment). Butler opined that the phrase "kicked the bucket," which is used in the sole existing English version, signified violent death.

Serbo-Croatian as well as English speakers might question Butler's exegesis. First, there is no expression equivalent to "kick the bucket" that native Serbo-Croatian speakers might have used in the intercept or elsewhere. Since there is not even a Serbo-Croatian original of this key conversation — if indeed such a conversation ever took place — we will never know. Second, from the standpoint of the English language, in which Butler presumably is native speaker, "to kick the bucket" is not customarily used to describe violent death.[115] So, at a minimum,

---

114   *Ibid.*, Transcript, p. 5205.

115   *Cambridge Dictionary* defines "to kick the bucket" as simply "to die," without any further elaboration about the mode of death, https://dictionary.cambridge.org/dictionary/english/kick-the-bucket?a=british. *Oxford Dictionary* offers the same definition, coupled with an illustrative sentence which encapsulates the idiomatic meaning of

(Footnote continued on next page)

some serious questions can be raised not just about the authenticity of this intercept, but about Butler's interpretation, as well.

This brings us to the central issue: how reliable are the intercepts that have been accepted as evidence by the ICTY? A corollary question is: how trustworthy are the judicial conclusions based on such evidence? Dramatic — but completely ignored — answers to these questions were provided by Emir Osmić, one of the Bosnian Muslim Army's intercept operators who was monitoring Srebrenica radio traffic within the Army of the Republic of Srpska [VRS]. In a statement given to OTP investigators on May 6, 1999, Osmić described in detail his duties as a BH Army intercept operator and the working methods he and his colleagues used. This is how he depicts the process:

> When my shift on duty was over, I would hand my notebooks over to the commander who would then type them up and return them to the next shift to continue to use. When the notebooks were filled with notes the commander would take them and, I believe, carry them over to the division headquarters, after which they would send them to the archive or something like that. I had nothing to do with what went on with them after I turned them over to the commander. The tapes that we used we kept reusing because we did not have enough tapes. We used tape-recorder tapes and we would tape over the previously recorded material if during the shift the tape ran out. I am not sure if a single one of the tapes on which we recorded important conversations was preserved. The one

---

(Footnote continued from previous page)

the phrase in the English language which also would seem to exclude violent death: "Die. 'When the old girl finally kicked the bucket there was no mention of yours truly in the will.'"
https://en.oxforddictionaries.com/definition/kick_the_bucket

thing I do recall is that we had to use the same tapes over and over again because we did not have enough of them. I have no idea what happened to those tapes.[116]

The situation we have here, according to operator Osmić, is that in numerous instances no physical audio trace of the incriminating conversations of VRS officers and personnel is available. The same tapes were used repeatedly, and, with each use, the previous recording was erased. Written notes were presumably made of what was supposedly recorded before erasure, but they ended up in some black hole at headquarters, and in "the archive." Between the time of their archiving and their appearance in court at The Hague, there seems to be no verifiable chain of custody, and no assurance that they had not been tampered with by Bosnian Muslim authorities, who had the notes under their control and were not a neutral party in the ICTY proceedings. These facts should be assessed against the backdrop of pious protestations by some ICTY chambers about "authentication" that were cited earlier.

Furthermore, the transcription methods described by Osmić are implausible when they are compared to professional transcription practices. In the case of documentary television material, for instance, transcriptions are always made either immediately after production for the benefit of the editors or immediately after a program is finished for closed captioning. In fact, Mr. Osmic's description of the working methods used by the ARBiH are, in all likelihood, fictional. It is much easier to record intercepts than to transcribe them. If one records, for example, between six and eight hours of radio intercepts over the course of a single day, it would take a transcriber one full day to transcribe

---

116    Statement of Emir Osmić, EDS file number 0084 8061.

60–90 minutes of recorded material. Even as early as the 1970s, no one was transcribing from ¼-inch reel-to-reel audio tape; audio cassettes were used instead. Cassette-tape transcription machines have a rewind feature on a foot pedal that allows the transcriber to rewind in one-, two-second, and longer increments as well as in fractions thereof. This is particularly helpful when the transcriber comes upon a passage which is difficult to understand or barely audible, which occurs rather frequently with documentary television work. In other words, it could take a transcriber an entire week to transcribe one day's worth of intercepts. How would Mr. Osmić know in advance how much reel-to-reel tape he needed to keep recording new intercepts without recording over old intercepts that had not yet been transcribed? Would he record over a reel-to-reel tape that he had not listened to? Was it acceptable practice at the ARBiH to wait a week before listening to an intercept? One would think not. Which leads to the next point. Audio cassette technology overtook reel-to-reel recording in the early 1970s, by which time the technology was ubiquitously available in the former Yugoslavia. No one would use reel-to-reel tape to record intercepts twenty years later in the 1990s, but even if one had, one would then have had the reel-to-reel tape transferred to audio cassette, which was cheap and readily available. If Mr. Osmić did run out of cassettes, it would have been easy to record the intercepts on erased music cassettes, which were available in abundance everywhere at that time. A radio used for intercepting messages could just as easily have been adapted to audio cassette as to reel-to-reel recording. An audio transfer from reel-to-reel to cassette was simple to do, if not routine. Besides, transcription machines were built for cassettes, not for reel-to-reel. Mr. Osmic makes it sound as though the ARBiH had only one 30 min. reel-to-reel tape. It is also worth noting that no professional transcription was ever done by hand. Professionals always typed while listening to a cassette on headphones because it's ten times faster. Lastly, even if we were to believe that the Bosnian Muslims had made handwritten "notes" of these purported intercepts, then we must insist that these "notes" not be called "transcriptions." A transcription is a word for word record. Otherwise, it's just the transcriber's selective interpretation. Mr. Osmić came to the ICTY with a my-dog-ate-my-homework excuse to explain the lack of original audio recordings, and the ICTY accepted it!

But there is another curious aspect to the intercept issue. In 1995, as part of his Srebrenica investigation in July of that year, ICTY chief investigator Jean-Rene Ruez forwarded a request to the Bosnian government to make available to the Prosecution relevant signal intercepts at their disposal. The Sarajevo authorities, however, took no action on that request during the following three years before finally complying in 1998. [117] That delay gave them plenty of time to doctor the evidence they were turning over, if they so wished. The fact that all but a handful of the alleged intercept transcripts they were disclosing was uncorroborated by any audio recordings would have greatly simplified their task. That raises the obvious question. It is established that the technologically sophisticated interested foreign intelligence entities surveilling the Bosnian battlefield had available to them satellites and spy planes capable of photographing action on the ground. Would it not be reasonable to expect that they would have had equipment of similar sophistication enabling them to listen to and record Bosnian Serb signal communications as well? Unlike the undersupplied Bosnian listening station in Srebrenica, they surely would have had access to more than just a single reel of recording tape. If so, they would not have been

---

117 *See* testimony of witness Stefanie Frease, *Tolimir* Trial Transcript, ICTY, 10 September 2010, p. 5172.

obliged to keep reusing the same tape continuously in order to make new recordings, nor would they have had to miss important enemy communications while laboriously transcribing each recording by hand. It is a mystery why Tribunal investigators did not seek Western countries' intercept records as a far more reliable source of the information they needed.

How consistent is the judicial branch of the ICTY in adhering to its stated principles? If they were consistent, would that not be reflected at key points where intercepts were used to buttress major elements of the Prosecution case? We saw some examples that indicate it was not. We may, for the moment, set aside the issue of purported audio intercepts made by foreign intelligence agencies during the Bosnian War. They were also used in proceedings at The Hague, but not to such a great extent (as in the case of "satellite photographs," where considerations of national security were advanced to prevent independent analysis of this form of signals intelligence[118]). Satellite photography didn't play a leading role in the courtroom as did locally produced intercepts, which purportedly originated from the monitoring resources of the ARBiH. Satellite photographs, to the extent that they had been used (*e.g.* at the *Popović et al.* trial), were subject to limitations which imposed a severe handicap on the Defense.

---

118  After leaving ICTY, Chief Prosecution Investigator Jean-René Ruez revealed in an interview that the renowned "satellite photographs" of the Srebrenica "killing fields" dramatically shown by Madeleine Albright at the UN had in fact been taken by obsolete U-2 planes, which obviated any grounds for keeping the images locked up for decades and preventing a thorough forensic examination of this evidence. [*Cultures & Conflicts*, 2007–1, no. 65; on the internet: http://conflits.revues.org/index2198.html]. More importantly, Ruez has testified that the much-touted satellite imagery notwithstanding, there is no photographic evidence of the actual executions but only "before and after" photographs. (*Prosecutor* v. *Karadžić*, Transcript, p. 24020, lines 20–22.)

It is important to bear the verification issue in mind because, just as with DNA evidence,[119] modern technology makes it easy to fabricate audio recordings. Whenever effective expert analysis of the evidence is thwarted — or is not insisted on — the purported evidence is practically as good as useless.

It is noteworthy that audio technology has advanced to hitherto unimagined levels, with a potentially direct impact on the trustworthiness of the relatively few — but in the context of some ICTY cases significant — recorded intercepts. (The famous "kill them all" audio intercept from the *Krstić* trial is a prime example.[120]) Although the Defense objected unsuccessfully on a variety of legal grounds to the admission of this recording in the *Krstić* case, its efforts stopped there. Neither in the *Krstić* case nor in any of the subsequent Srebrenica cases where similar evidence was tendered by the Prosecution did the Defense take the logical step of demanding that the audio material be subjected to a thorough and competent forensic analysis before any factual conclusions were drawn.

---

119   Insistence on verification is not mere hairsplitting. It is now known that not just DNA results, but even the DNA samples on which those results are based, can be plausibly faked. *See* "DNA evidence can be fabricated, scientists show," *The New York Times*, 18 August 2009; also, "Report: Israeli scientists discover way to counterfeit DNA," *Haaretz*, 18 August 2009. Dr. Dan Frumkin, a founder of Nucleix, a Tel Aviv company which has developed methods to distinguish genuine DNA from a counterfeit, has stated that "you can just engineer a crime scene" by planting authentic-looking counterfeit DNA and he adds that the task is so uncomplicated that "any biology undergraduate could perform this."

120   *Prosecutor* v. *Krstić*, "Decision on the defence motions to exclude exhibits in rebuttal and motion for continuance," 4 May 2001. The gist of the controversy was articulated by the Chamber in Par. 14 of its ruling: "...the Prosecution sought admission of the recorded intercept between Krstic and Obrenovic dated 2 August in which the accused is said to utter 'kill them all'. When confronted with this intercept, the accused denied that the conversation took place and called it a 'montage'."

Perhaps the Defense attorneys were inadequately informed of advances in audio technology and of their striking impact on the integrity of audio evidence. Just as it is now possible to create authentic-looking but completely false DNA readings, it is also possible to generate authentic-sounding voice recordings that convincingly imitate the voice of the purported speaker. The technology is known as "voice conversion" or "voice morphing." It is defined as "modifying the speech signal of one speaker (the source speaker) so that it sounds as if it had been spoken by a different speaker (the target speaker)."[121] A group of researchers describes it thus:

> Voice conversion ["VC"] is an area of speech pro-
> cessing that deals with the conversion of the per-
> ceived speaker identity. In other words, the speech
> signal uttered by a first speaker, the source speaker, is
> modified to sound as if it was spoken by a second
> speaker, referred to as the target speaker.[122]

The scientists also indicate some of the applications of voice conversion technology:

> The term voice conversion refers to the modification
> of speaker identity by modifying the speech signal ut-
> tered by a source speaker to sound as if it was spoken
> by a target speaker. In general, a voice conversion
> system is first trained using speech data from both the

---

121 Yannis Stylianou, Olivier Cappe, and Eric Moulines, "Continuous Prob-
abilistic Transform for Voice Conversion", IEEE TRANSACTIONS ON
SPEECH AND AUDIO PROCESSING, Vol. 6, No. 2 March 1998, p.
131.

122 Jani Nurminen et al., "Voice conversion", Speech Enhancement, Model-
ing and Recognition – Algorithms and Applications, Tampere University
of Technology, Finland
[http://www.cs.tut.fi/~moncef/publications/voice- conversionIntech-
2012.pdf].

source and the target speakers, and then the trained models can be used for performing the actual conversion. Potential applications for voice conversion include security related usage (hiding the identity of the speaker), entertainment applications, and text-to-speech (TTS) synthesis in which voice conversion techniques can be used for creating new and personalized voices in a cost- efficient way.[123]

As with many similar technologies, VC also is broadly dual-use. It clearly has benign applications (as in the dubbing of foreign films while preserving the original voice texture of the actors) but it also has nefarious potential. The falsification of evidence by recreating a defendant's voice and making him say self-incriminating things he may never have uttered is another such application that comes readily to mind. The possibility of the dishonest application of VC technology in the context of ICTY proceedings is an issue that remains unacknowledged as well as unaddressed. Until such a time as all audio intercept recordings that have been accepted into evidence and have influenced factual findings made by the various ICTY Srebrenica chambers are thoroughly examined by competent and independent forensic specialists, their integrity remains shadowed by doubt.

We are indebted to the BBC's zealous efforts to deceive the public for an example of irrefutable evidence that VC technology is not science fiction. In his *The Truth Seeker* broadcast, Russian RT channel host Daniel Bushell demonstrated how in 2013 these technological advances have actually been abused for political

---

123  Jani Nurminen et al., A parametric approach for voice conversion, TC-STAR Workshop on Speech-to-Speech Translation, June 19– 21, 2006, Barcelona, Spain, p. 225
[http://www.elda.org/tcstarworkshop_2006/pdfs/tts/tcstar06_nurminen.pdf].

purposes during the Syrian crisis.[124] On this particular occasion the fabrication attempted to discredit President Assad and buttress false accusations made against the Syrian government that it was "killing its own people."

In August 2013, the BBC broadcast a clip where an alleged doctor was claiming that Syrian forces had committed a "napalm" attack that killed a considerable number of innocent civilians. This dramatic statement, however, did not accomplish the desired goal, which was to mobilize Western public opinion to support military intervention in Syria. In September 2013, the very same video was rebroadcast, with the same actors and with an identical *mis-en-scène*, but with one key difference: The audio of the doctor's statement was digitally altered so that she was now being heard to say that the attack was committed using "chemical weapons" instead of "napalm," as in the earlier iteration. In both video clips, the speaker's voice sounds exactly the same.

Without a professional analysis of this audio recording, an ordinary layman could never detect the presence of a hoax, nor would he suspect that the words he was hearing were, in fact, digitally altered fakes.

The impression that VC is a new, cutting edge technology that burst onto the scene sometime around 2013 would also be incorrect. Even as long ago as February 1999, the *Washington*

---

124    The original YouTube clip of the fake
(//www.youtube.com/watch?v=blg9XVBUEZg) was removed for unexplained reasons; however, Craig Murray, former UK ambassador to Uzbekistan, who called the affair "Irrefutable evidence of a stunning bit of fakery by the BBC," posted an indignant comment about it on his blog at https://www.craigmurray.org.uk/archives/2013/10/fake-bbc-video/ and preserved both fake video clips there for posterity.

*Post* disclosed the existence of VC technology.[125] Even back then, which is precisely the time The Hague Tribunal was preparing its evidence for Srebrenica and other trials, VC technology had reached an enviably high level of development. So much so — as we learn from the *Washington Post* — that scientists at the Los Alamos National Laboratory in New Mexico, to whom credit for this invention is due, tried to impress their military and political sponsors by demonstrating VC's potential applications. They digitally altered the voice of a high-ranking U.S. general by making the general seditiously agitate for a *coup d'état* in a voice indistinguishable from his own.

This is proof positive that digital voice alteration, which is capable of generating the illusion that someone said something that he did not or never would have said, is a real possibility. The only way to verify this and remove any doubts is to perform a professional forensic analysis of the audio recordings. This has never taken place in any Srebrenica trial at the ICTY.

These are sufficient reasons to mistrust the intercept data used by the ICTY — and, by extension, its Sarajevo clone, the State War Crimes Court for Bosnia and Herzegovina, which follows identical procedures. It is right and just to sound the alarm. We need more than the disingenuous assurances of intercept operators of one of the warring parties or the "absolute certainty" of a Mrs. Frease. The trial records, particularly with respect to Srebrenica, where the greatest concentration of intercept evidence abuse by VC is likely to exist, should be subjected to thorough forensic scrutiny. At the ICTY — as well as the Sarajevo Court — intercepts that fail to meet fundamental standards of admissibility in ordinary criminal cases in national jurisdictions should

---

125   William M. Arkin, "When Seeing and Hearing Isn't Believing," *Washington Post*, 1 February, 1999.

have been excluded from consideration. Verdicts rendered by these courts must accordingly be modified as necessary to reflect the exclusion of such dubious evidence.

## 6. Genocide

The finding, which was heavily influenced for the duration of the conflict in Bosnia and Herzegovina by media-driven perception management, that the events that took place in Srebrenica in July 1995 constitute genocide under international law,[126] is central to the official ICTY Srebrenica narrative. A corollary assertion is that any resulting dilemmas regarding the narrative's veracity are now superfluous, based on judgments rendered by the International Criminal Tribunal for the Former Yugoslavia.

For all interested parties, the legal, political, and moral implications of genocide are so great that one must ask some hard questions. Is there evidence of genocidal intent in Srebrenica? If so, then how does The Hague Tribunal treat this issue?

This is the crux of the Srebrenica controversy regardless of what happened at any particular location and regardless of the total number of executed victims, at least in the legal and political sense, because genocidal intent, in legal terms *dolus specialis*, must be established; otherwise, the killing in Srebrenica cannot be raised to the level of genocide. Genocide is substantially more than simple killing, or killing on a particularly large scale, or a military operation conducted with uncommon brutality. The

---

126   This issue is particularly pertinent in light of the *Tolimir* Chamber's finding (2012) that the long-overlooked but practically simultaneous military operation in Žepa also constitutes "genocide," based on the assassination by Serbian forces of three indispensable community leaders (military commander, municipal president, and imam), without whom the community was left rudderless and unsustainable and therefore — even in the absence of Srebrenica-style mass executions — as good as "genocided." See *Tolimir* Trial Judgment, par. 780.

essence of the crime of genocide is *intent*, coupled with concrete acts designed to carry it out, to destroy one of the groups — be it ethnic, religious, or racial — protected by the Convention. All specialists in the legal field accept this. It is indisputable.

If we start from the assumption that logistical preparation for a genocidal undertaking requires a certain minimal time-frame to come to fruition, it is reasonable to pose the following question: At what moment can the existence of genocidal intent be established for Srebrenica, assuming there was one? and how long before the actual events did genocidal intent manifest itself?

In the *Krstić* Trial Judgment, the Chamber linked the inception of the Srebrenica plan to commit genocide to a meeting of Serbian military and political leaders at the Hotel Fontana in Bratunac on the morning of July 12, 1995, even though it admits that it lacks firm evidence for such a hypothesis.[127] Par. 573 of the *Krstić* Trial Judgment is a characteristic example of the Chamber drawing a pre-conceived conclusion, regardless of whether it is corroborated by factual evidence or not:

> The Trial Chamber is unable to determine the precise date on which the decision to kill all military age men was taken. Hence it cannot find that the killings committed in Potočari on 12 and 13 July 1995[128] formed part of the plan to kill all the military aged men. Nevertheless, the Trial Chamber is confident that the mass executions and other killings committed from July 13 onward were part of this plan.

---

127   See *Prosecutor v. Krstić*, Par. 126-134 and Par. 573 of the Trial Judgment and Par. 84, 85 and 91 of the Appellate Judgment for the way the Chambers treats the Hotel Fontana meetings on July 11 and 12, 1995.

128   If the Potočari killings on July 13 were not part of the "genocidal plan," then what unique circumstances make Kravica Warehouse killings — just a few kilometers away and committed on the same day — part of that plan?

How can "confidence" replace indisputable evidence, which admittedly is lacking?

The testimony of Jean-René Ruez, Chief Investigator for the Prosecution at the ICTY, given to the Srebrenica Commission established by the French Parliament in November of 2001, sheds light on the important chronological issue. Ruez, after having been asked by the Commission whether it was correct that prior to 9 July there was no Serbian plan to take over the enclave despite its enormous strategic significance, replied:

> In fact, the decision to take over the enclave was not taken before 9 July, when General Mladic understood that the enclave would not be defended. The original goal was for the enclave to be narrowed down to the territory of Srebrenica town, converting it into a huge open-air refugee camp, thus obliging the U.N. to commence evacuating the zone.[129]

The last part of Ruez's statement is pure speculation, but the first part about the non-existence of any Serbian plan to take over Srebrenica prior to 9 July is presumably based on documents to which Ruez had access in his official capacity as Chief Investigator. It is therefore credible and has the status of a provable fact.

Bearing in mind that the genocide in Srebrenica should have been committed between 13 and 17 July 1995, Ruez's revelation is of the utmost importance, precisely because it originates from a source so close to the Office of the Prosecutor of The Hague Tribunal. On Ruez's evidence, the intent to physically destroy the population of Srebrenica — or part of it — could not have

---

129   RAPPORT D'INFORMATION No. 3413, National Assembly of France, 22 November 2001, p. 43.

been formed before 9 July. Yet the genocide allegedly began only four days later.

Another significant clarification of the sequence of events was made by Richard Butler, the ICTY Prosecution's military expert. Like Ruez's statement, it also fits the definition of a "declaration against the superior's interest," which makes it all the more credible.

Butler testified before the Bosnia and Herzegovina War Crimes Court in Sarajevo as an expert witness at the *Pelemiš and Perić* trial in 2010. Butler's evidence sheds light not only on the sequence of events, but also on another key issue: *dolus specialis*, or genocidal intent. In his official capacity as Prosecution military expert, Butler also had access to the most sensitive and relevant documents.

Butler testified that he discovered no indication of a plan to exterminate Muslims at least up until 11 July, the date when Serbian forces took over Srebrenica. This advances Ruez's chronology by at least two additional days, which confirms that the intent on the part of the Serbs to commit genocide could not have been contemplated even forty-eight hours before the imputed crime began to unfold.[130]

Butler, while giving his testimony, disclosed additional details which — to put it charitably — cast reasonable doubt on the existence of genocidal intent.

First, Butler confirmed Ruez's report that the aim of the Serbian military operation, for which planning had begun on 30 June 1995, was confined to reducing the U.N. protected enclave to the city limits of the town of Srebrenica. Second, according to Butler, President Karadžić ordered Serbian forces to enter Sre-

---

130 State Court of Bosnia and Hercegovina, War Crimes Department, *Prosecutor v. Pelemiš et al*, X-KR-08/602, 22 March 2010.

brenica on 10 July, just one day before the takeover. This means that the takeover of the enclave was an improvised decision made in light of the operation's military success up to that moment, not a step taken as part of a pre-existing plan to capture and then exterminate a large portion of the male Muslim population. Third, Butler confirmed that, until the scope of the operation was unexpectedly broadened on July 10 to include taking full control of the enclave, the military campaign was being conducted exclusively by the Drina Corps[131] without the participation of the Bosnian Serb Army Main Staff or other superior command structures. Fourth, Butler said that he was "unaware" of any post-July 11 example, once takeover of the enclave had been completed and the operation was ended, of the VRS firing at civilians in Srebrenica. Fifth, as far as the deportation of civilians from the enclave is concerned, the documentary evidence according to Butler "does not show proof" of prior planning before the morning of 11 July, when the decision to enter Srebrenica was made. Finally, sixth, Butler accepted that among the ranks of the Army of the Republic of Srpska "at least until 12 or even 13 July" there was "no expectation that the prisoners might be executed."

How compatible is this sequence of events and its accompanying analysis, which was divulged by leading experts of ICTY Prosecution, with the Tribunal's conclusion that the political and military leadership of the Republic of Srpska intended the physical destruction of Muslim men, as an ethnic or religious community, in Srebrenica? The Convention on Genocide holds that the intent must be evident for a proper finding of genocide. So, if

---

131   The military unit of the Bosnian Serb Army in whose zone of responsibility Srebrenica was located.

genocide had occurred in Srebrenica, was it the calculated consequence of pre-existing intent — or an afterthought?

After the *Krstić* judgment, William Schabas, the Canadian legal scholar and expert in genocide studies, called attention to a dilemma which still remains eminently reasonable. After Schabas pointed out the Trial Chamber's apparent willingness in *Krstić* to "accept the Prosecutor's contention that the intent in killing the men and boys of military age was to eliminate the community as a whole,"[132] he observed that "this seems a rather enormous deduction to make on the basis that men and boys of military age were massacred." He then asks:

> Can there not be other plausible explanations for the destruction of 7,000 men and boys in Srebrenica? Could they not have been targeted precisely because they were of military age, and thus actual or potential combatants? Would someone truly bent upon the physical destruction of a group, and cold-blooded enough to murder more than 7,000 defenseless men and boys, go to the trouble of organizing transport so that women, children, and the elderly could be evacuated? It is certainly striking that another Trial Chamber, in Sikirica, dismissed the 'significant part' argument after noting that the common denominator of the victims was that they were men of military age and nothing more, as if this were insufficient.[133]

---

132  *Krstić* Trial Judgment, par. 594

133  William A. Schabas, "Was Genocide Committed in Bosnia and Herzegovina? First Judgments of the International Criminal Tribunal for the Former Yugoslavia," *Fordham Journal of International Law*, Vol. 25, No. 23, 2001-2002, p. 46.

Stephen Karganović

All professional observers of the ICTY agree that none of the six Srebrenica trials[134] ever produced a single item of evidence, originating at any command level, that demonstrated the existence of intent and ordered the necessary logistical preparations to destroy the Muslim community in Srebrenica. How did The Hague Tribunal then conclude that genocide did occur?

Par. 4 of the *Krstić* Trial Judgment provides a clue to answering this important question. The ICTY resorts to an inventive analytical technique as well as to a hitherto obscure legal doctrine:

> The Trial Chamber draws upon a mosaic of evidence that combines to paint a picture of what happened during those few days in July 1995.[135]

One possible implication is that the Court lacked firm and direct evidence upon which to base its judgment. The Chamber therefore decided to combine bits and pieces of potential evidence as tesserae in a mosaic, resulting in an image, an impression that could most accurately be compared to a Rorschach test. Each observer is free to interpret the abstract image placed before him in a unique and subjective way. This is the Chamber's "mosaic."

Deep-rooted assumptions about what constitutes a genocidal operation must be discarded in advance in order for the Chamber's interpretation to appear minimally plausible. One such common-sense assumption is that of the existence of a genocidal concept or plan. This is perhaps why, in Par. 225 of the *Krstić* Appellate Judgment, the Chamber expounds the amazing conten-

---

134  *Krstić, Blagojević and Jokić, Popović et al., Tolimir, Mladić,* and *Karadžić.*

135  ICTY, *Prosecutor v Krstić*, Trial Judgment, Par. 4.

tion that "'the existence of a plan or policy is not a legal ingredient of the crime' of genocide." The Appellate Chamber might welcome evidence of planning, if any could be found, but it maintains that its task can still be performed without it: "While the existence of such a plan may help to establish that the accused possessed the requisite genocidal intent, it remains only evidence supporting the inference of intent, and does not become a legal ingredient of the offence."[136]

The Chamber's verbal gymnastics fail. If there was no discernible plan or policy, then what were the specific causes of the alleged genocide in Srebrenica? If there was no coherent concept to commit the criminal act imputed to him, then why was General Krstić sentenced to lengthy imprisonment? The same may be asked of virtually every other Srebrenica defendant.

In Par. 26 of the *Krstić* Appellate Judgment, the Chamber drastically refashioned the very concept of intent: "The main evidence underlying the Trial Chamber's conclusion that the VRS forces intended to eliminate all the Bosnian Muslims of Srebrenica was the massacre by the VRS of all men of military age from that community." Whether all captured military-age men were massacred is doubtful.[137] But more to the point is the question whether the notion of "men of military age" is sufficiently broad to merit inclusion as one of the protected groups indicated in the Convention. Even if such genocidal intent did exist within the ranks of the military and political leadership of the Republic of Srpska, how does the fact that this leadership refrained from ordering the mass killing of Muslims approximately ten days later, during and immediately after the operation

---

136  ICTY, *Prosecutor v Krstić*, Appellate Judgment, Par. 225

137  *See* Annex V: Muslim Military Age Males Captured but not Executed by Serb Forces between 11 and 17 July 1995

that targeted the neighboring enclave of Žepa, fit in with the Appellate Chamber's scenario? [138]

In the *Krstić* case, the Chamber identified the inception of the Srebrenica genocide plan (the necessity of which it had just denied) in a meeting of members of Serbian political and military leadership at the Hotel Fontana in nearby Bratunac in the afternoon of 12 July 1995; however, the Chamber frankly admits that it lacks hard evidence even for that. [139]

When one is self-authorized to interpret one's own Rorschach test, problems are easily solved. One simply discards elements of the picture that do not conform to the concept, while at the same time claiming that what is seen — although others fail to notice it — is the most obvious part of the picture.

Finally, two important details frame this controversy.

The first has to do with the testimony of Dražen Erdemović, the ICTY Prosecution "crown witness," given at the trial of Radovan Karadžić. During his cross-examination, Karadžić asked Erdemović a direct question that touched the essence of the matter as far as Srebrenica is concerned, which is the *dolus specialis* or genocidal intent: [140]

---

138   For fairness' sake it should be noted that — by a curious act of omission — Žepa was not included in any of the Srebrenica indictments until the *Tolimir* trial, a decade after *Krstić*. Also, the *Tolimir* court had no need of mass slaughter to conclude that Žepa also constituted genocide. Prior to drawing this counter-intuitive conclusion, the court had prepared the theoretical groundwork by creatively redefining the concept of genocide so that three deaths were sufficient for its purposes. But the rhetorical question remains a valid one.

139   ICTY, *Prosecutor v. Krstić*, Trial Judgment, Par. 126-134 and Par. 573; Appellate Judgment, Par. 84-85 and Par. 91

140   ICTY, *Prosecutor v. Karadžić*, Transcript, 28 February 2012, p. 25410

"Did you fire at them with the intention of destroying the Muslims as an ethnic group in Bosnia, destroying them as a people?" to which Erdemović replied: "No, Mr. Karadžić." Karadžić's next question was whether anyone else in Erdemović's unit had the intention of exterminating Muslims. This was Erdemović's reply: "Mr. Karadzic, I cannot remember, but I do not believe that we discussed who had which intention on that day and whether anyone wanted to exterminate the Muslims. We did not have such discussions. I don't remember discussing that with anyone from my unit."[141]

So much about the frame of mind of the immediate perpetrators and about the intent that motivated them during the commission of the crime.

The other detail that needs to be highlighted is an astonishing reflection from the Separate Opinion of Judge Jean-Claude Antonetti written as part of the Appellate Judgment in the *Tolimir* case, in April of 2015. In the context of an incisive, Cartesian critique of the majority's view, Antonetti concludes with some poignant observations:

> [The Accused's] role, which was irreversibly determined by this Appeal Judgment, does not, however, provide an answer to the legitimate question of the victims' families as to who ordered the mass executions (...) In that respect, I must mention the expectation of the victims' families to learn the identity of the perpetrators of these tragic events that culminated in the executions of several thousand Muslims from Bosnia and Herzegovina (...) To this day, based on the evidence in the case file, I do not have an answer to this question.[142]

---

141   *Ibid.*, p. 25415

142   ICTY, *Prosecutor v. Tolimir*, Appellate Judgment, pp. 399 – 400.

Stephen Karganović

Everyone should ponder these devastating words of one of the most respected and fair-minded judges at The Hague Tribunal.[143] If, after more than twenty years of investigation, the Tribunal has failed to establish even the basic facts about Srebrenica, that strongly suggests that the ICTY was going about its job the wrong way and using a methodology that did not ensure professionally sustainable (or at least informative) conclusions, and that the ICTY was probably motivated by agendas that were, for the most part, without a juridical foundation.

If so, such an institution is manifestly unfit to make a finding of genocide.

## 7. Conclusions

This is a far from comprehensive essay, but it does test the coherence of some of the major building blocks of the ICTY's Srebrenica narrative. The underlying question was: How did the ICTY select, assemble, and evaluate evidence to support its conclusions? How the ICTY reached its conclusions is itself a pertinent question, but we can leave that aside for the moment because it would probably lead us out of the realm of jurisprudence. What matters is that in none of the four topics here examined (Branjevo/Pilica, the Kravica Warehouse, radio intercepts, and genocide) is there a clear nexus between the facts available to the Tribunal — as well as to its investigative organs — and the conclusions that were ultimately drawn.

It would take us too far afield to speculate about the reasons for this peculiar dissonance. It is enough for our purposes just to

---

143 Antonetti, driving the point home in the concluding remarks of his Dissenting Opinion, makes more disquieting comments about the Tribunal's performance: "The question is why did this military operation transform into a massacre of the prisoners of war? By failing to examine this avenue, the ICTY did not perform its duty to establish the truth," *ibid.*

establish the fact that it is so. We may never find out to our full satisfaction what occurred at those locations, but it is quite plain that the incidents at Branjevo/Pilica and Kravica Warehouse could not possibly have happened in real life as they are depicted in ICTY judgments. The so-called "intercept evidence," for the most part, turns out to be a spurious collection of unauthenticated notes by a party interested in the proceedings, while the few audio recordings that are available were never forensically scrutinized for fraud. Yet, based on this pseudo-evidence, ICTY chambers drew major conclusions, and it even determined the alleged number of captured prisoners. Information on the number of prisoners that were captured is a key point in this controversy because it is a prerequisite for raising the issue of how many prisoners could have been executed. As for the autopsy reports, which are the only link to the tangible evidence of the crime, if the expectation was that they would bolster the official version, then they manifestly failed to do their job. The ICTY's labored and convoluted interpretations of this forensic evidence (*see* Annex III) are a signal that this data is not what it is cracked up to be (for clarification, *see* Annex IV). More importantly, the DNA evidence — to which the Tribunal quietly switched around the time of the *Popović* trial after traditional autopsy-based forensic methodology proved incapable of delivering proof of 8,000 executed victims — is illusory. DNA evidence can only identify and re-associate mortal remains, but it cannot furnish any information about the time and manner of death, which are the only relevant data that would make DNA useful in the present case.[144] Finally, the ICTY's conclusion that genocide was

---

144  Under cross-examination by Radovan Karadžić, Thomas Parsons, Director of Science and Technology at the International Commission for Missing Persons (ICMP) in Tuzla, Bosnia and Herzegovina, the agency that performs DNA profiling for the Prosecution of The Hague Tribunal, ad-

(Footnote continued on next page)

Stephen Karganović

committed in Srebrenica is in complete factual and legal disarray. Significant problems have been identified in ICTY's fact-finding approach and its *ratio decidendi*. A comprehensive analysis of this important aspect of the ICTY's operation has yet to be written. This brief survey is but a prolegomenon for the pending task. Even so, this examination is sufficient to nullify the ICTY's pretensions to have created an authoritative historical account of events during the conflict in the Former Yugoslavia in the 1990s, supposedly based on a professionally impeccable contemplation of the best available evidence.

The ICTY's Srebrenica case is a house of cards.

---

(Footnote continued from previous page)

mitted the limited scientific scope of DNA technology: "**Karadžić**: So is it your claim that those people, whose DNA profiles you have established, were killed in an unlawful manner and did you separate that from those who were killed in action? **Parsons**: The ICMP does not concern itself with whether — with the legal question of how these people were killed or — particularly with whether their deaths were lawful or not. I'm reporting on the identifications that have been made with regard to mortal remains recovered from these graves." (*Prosecutor v. Karadžić*, Transcript, 22 March 2012, p. 26633.) At the *Popović* trial, Parsons was cross-examined by defense attorney Jelena Nikolić: "**Nikolić**: Does the ICMP issue death certificates? **Parsons**: No. **Nikolić**: Who is in charge of issuing those? **Parsons**: Court-appointed medical pathologists. **Nikolić**: It means that the ICMP establishes neither the year nor the manner and time of death? **Parsons**: That's correct." (*Prosecutor v. Popović*, Transcript, 1 February 2008, p. 20919) From the standpoint of a legal professional, Parsons' statement disposes of the matter.

# ANNEX I:
# DRAŽEN ERDEMOVIĆ'S
# ARMY OF REPUBLIKA SRPSKA CONTRACT
# WITH SIGNATURES OF GENERAL MLADIĆ (VERSION A)
# AND GENERAL DE GAULLE (VERSION B)

Stephen Karganović

ЈМБГ: 2511971... ...

**У Г О В О Р**
О ПРИЈЕМУ ЛИЦА У ВОЈСКУ РЕПУБЛИКЕ СРПСКЕ
ПО УГОВОРУ НА ОДРЕЂЕНО ВРЕМЕ

Закључен између:   Главног штаба Војске Републике Српске - ВП 7572 Сарајево

и ...Trišanović...Viktora...Dražen...
(презиме, очево име и име)

...Bijeljina ul. ...dojke....lukša 144...
(занимање и место боравка - адреса)

1. Главни штаб Војске Републике Српске - ВП 7572 Сарајево ...'...diverzantski mixa'...

1) прима ...Trišanović...Viktora...Dražen...
(презиме, очево име и име)

...Bijeljina ul. ...dojke....lukša 144...
(занимање и место боравка)

у војну службу по уговору на одређено време у својству ...padčicira-diverzant...

...na time...   , у чину ...vodnika...
(својство у коме се прима)

на време од ...2/dvije/godine... која ће трајати од ...01.04.1995.godine...
(трајање службе)                                             (дан, месец и година)

до ...31.01.1997.godine... ради обављања дужности ...komandira 1. M. vodа...
(дан, месец и година)                                           (назив дужности)

...у гарнизону ...Bijeljina...

2) Обавезује се да ...Trišanović Dražen,vodnik... обезбеди новчану
(презиме, име и чин који добија)

накнаду у складу са правилником.

3) Обавезује се да ...Trišanović Dražen,vodnik... постави на
(презиме, име и чин који добија)

дужност ...komandir 1. M. voda... у гарнизону ...Bijeljina...
(назив дужности)                                        (назив гарнизона)

и да му обезбеди права која према Закону о Војсци Републике Српске и другим прописима припа-
дају ...pravilnik o zakonima i izmoti pripadnika pripadnika V ...

4) Обавезује се да исплати посебну новчану награду ...Trišanović Dražen,vodnik...
(презиме, име и чин који добија)

за учешће у свакој појединачној диверзантској акцији у складу са нарадбом надлежног старешине;

5) Обавезује се да ...Dražen Trišavić,vodnik... обезбеди приоритет у додели
(име, презиме и чин)

стана на коришћење, преко надлежних органа власти, а на основу Наредбе Председника РС.

2. ...Trišanović Viktora, Dražen, stfvd...
(презиме, очево име и име, занимање)

...Bijeljina ul. čedojke lukša 144...
(место боравка-адреса)

обавезује се:

1) да ће ...01.04.1995.god... ступити на дужност ...komandire 1. M. voda...
(дан, месец и година)                                          (назив дужности)

у гарнизону ...Bijeljina... а према постављењу надлежног старешине;
(назив гарнизона)

00399985

130

# VERSION A:

2) да ће у војној служби по уговору, уколико на провери оспособљености за дужност покаже задовољавајуће резултате, остати ~~~~~~~~ односно до __31.01.1997.__ године;
(дан, месец и година)

3) да ће дужност вршити савесно и у складу са прописима;

4) да ће се за време службе по уговору придржавати свих прописа који се односе на службу у
овој јединици.

3. ~~~~~~~~~~~~ за време ратног стања и непосредне ратне опасности има
(име, презиме и чин)
обезбеђену бесплатну исхрану и смештај;

4. У случају рањавања ~~~~~~~~~~~~~~~~~~ задржава право на пла-
(чин, презиме и чин)
ту у износу одређеном у тачки 1. под 2) овог уговора, и распоређује се на лакшу дужност у оквиру
своје или друге јединице, уколико га надлежна војно-лекарска комисија огласи неспособним за
извршавање диверзантских задатака.

5. Од дана ступања на дужност ~~~~~~~~~~~~~~~~~~ почиње да тече војна служба по
(име, презиме и чин)
овом уговору и од тог дана стиче права и обавезе по основу уговора и својство
~~~~~~~~~~~~~~~~~~~~~~~~

6. Ако ~~~~~~~~~~~~~~~ без оправданог разлога не ступи на дужност на дан
(име, презиме и чин)
утврђен у тачки 2. под 1) овог уговора, сматраће се да овај уговор није закључен.

7. Војна служба по овом уговору престаје под условима прописаним одредбама члана 216. Закона
~о Војсци Републике Српске.

8. Овај уговор сачињен је у пет примерака за војника по уговору, односно у шест примерака за
подофицира по уговору и официра по уговору. По један примерак доставља се:
лицу које је ступило у војну службу по уговору; војној јединици односно војној установи у којој је
на служби; за сваки примерак досијеа персоналних података и војном рачуноводственом центру.

~~~~~~~~~~, 23. februar 1995. godine
(место, дан, месец и година закључења уговора)

_(потпис лица које се прима)_

_(потпис старешине надлежног за закључивање уговора)_
Komandant Glavnog štaba
Vojske Republike Srpske
general-pukovnik
Ratko Mladić
_(дужност, чин, презиме и име
старешине надлежног за закључивање уговора)_

(откуцати машином: презиме, очево име и име,
~~~~~~~~~~~~~~~~~)

Датум ступања на дужност:
01. februar 1995. godine
(дан, месец и година)

ОВЕРАВА

_(потпис старешине)_
Komandant 10 diverzantskog odreda
potporučnik, Milorad Pelemiš

_(потпис примљеног лица)_
(дужност, чин, презиме и име старешине
који оверава датум ступања на дужност)

131

Stephen Karganović

## VERSION B:

2) да ће у војној служби по уговору, уколико на провери оспособљености за дужност покаже задовољавајуће резултате, остати 2/ивије/године односно до 31.01.1997. године;
(дан, месец и година)

3) да ће дужност вршити савесно и у складу са прописима;

4) да ће се за време службе по уговору придржавати свих прописа који се односе на службу у овој јединици.

3. _____ за време ратног стања и непосредне ратне опасности има
(име, презиме и чин)
обезбеђену бесплатну исхрану и смештај;

4. У случају рањавања _____ задржава право на плату у износу одређеном у тачки 1. под 2) овог уговора, и распоређује се на лакшу дужност у оквиру своје или друге јединице, уколико га надлежна војно-лекарска комисија огласи неспособним за извршавање диверзантских задатака.

5. Од дана ступања на дужност _____ почиње да тече војна служба по овом уговору и од тог дана стиче права и обавезе по основу уговора и својство _____

6. Ако _____ без оправданог разлога не ступи на дужност на дан
(име, презиме и чин)
утврђен у тачки 1. под 1) овог уговора, сматраће се да овај уговор није закључен.

7. Војна служба по овом уговору престаје под условима прописаним одредбама члана 216. Закона о Војсци Републике Српске.

8. Овај уговор сачињен је у пет примерака за војника по уговору, односно у шест примерака за подофицира по уговору и официра по уговору. По један примерак доставља се: лицу које је ступило у војну службу по уговору; војној јединици односно војној установи у којој је на служби; за сваки примерак досијеа персоналних података и војном рачуноводственом центру.

Билјина, 23.фебруар 1995.године
(место, дан, месец и година закључења уговора)

_____
(потпис лица које се прима)

Станковић Виктор, Младен,бравар

Билјина, Недојке Белића 144
(откуцати машином: презиме, очево име и име,

Датум ступања на дужност:

01.фебруар 1995. године
(дан, месец и година)

_____
(потпис примљеног лица)

(потпис старешине надлежног за закључивање уговора)
Командант Главног штаба
војске Републике Српске
генерал-пуковник
Charles de Gaulle

(укуцати чин, презиме и име
старешине надлежног за закључивање уговора)

ОВЕРАВА

_____
(потпис старешине)
Командант 10 диверзантског одреда
потпоручник,Милорад Пелемиш

(дужност, чин, презиме и име старешине
који оверава датум ступања на дужност)

00399986

132

# ANNEX II:
## MODEL WITH HANDS TIED IN THE BACK
## AND LYING FACE DOWN
## AS DESCRIBED BY WITNESS "Q"

ANNEX III:
INTERPRETATION OF FORENSIC EVIDENCE
RELATED TO THE KRAVICA WAREHOUSE
IN ICTY JUDGMENTS

## POPOVIĆ ET AL., TRIAL JUDGMENT

439. Primary graves at two different locations were found to have forensic links to the events at Kravica Warehouse: two graves at Ravnice — Ravnice 1 and Ravnice 2 — were found to have building materials including foam, concrete and plaster linking them to Kravica Warehouse, and two graves at Glogova — Glogova 1 and Glogova 2 — were found to have broken masonry and door frames indistinguishable from those located at Kravica Warehouse.

440. In addition, forensic evidence links secondary graves at three different locations to the events at Kravica Warehouse. At Zeleni Jadar, seven gravesites can be linked to Kravica Warehouse: in Zeleni Jadar 5 and 6, concrete, plaster and other building materials located in the grave established a link; in Zeleni Jadar 2, body parts located in the grave were matched with a tooth found at Kravica Warehouse. Furthermore, in all of the Zeleni Jadar graves — Zeleni Jadar 1A, 1B, 2, 3, 4, 5, and 6 — links with the Glogova 1 primary grave were established through the identification of body parts belonging to the same individuals in both the Glogova 1 grave and the relevant secondary grave.

443. Prosecution investigator Dusan Janc prepared an expert report in which he concluded that the remains of 1,319 individuals have been found in primary and secondary graves associated with the Kravica Warehouse killings. Janc subsequently filed a

corrigendum to his report in which he stated that some of these 1,319 persons may have died in circumstances unrelated to the Kravica Warehouse events. Janc does not explicitly state by how many the number should be reduced, however he indicates that the following bodies were buried in graves related to Kravica Warehouse, but cannot be linked to the Kravica Warehouse killings: (a) 12 individuals who were returned to the VRS from Serbia; 1604 (b) up to 80 bodies from the area around the Vuk Karadžić School; (c) 6–7 bodies from Potočari; (d) 10–15 bodies from Konjević Polje; and (e) one truck load of bodies from the area along the Bratunac-Konjević Polje Road. Further, the Trial Chamber notes that there is evidence before it regarding three persons buried in the Glogova grave, which indicates that they were not victims of the Kravica Warehouse killings. In addition, one individual from the Blječeva secondary grave was last seen on 18 July and therefore cannot be linked to the Kravica Warehouse execution. As stated below, the Trial Chamber accepts the evidence presented by Janc regarding the DNA and forensic links established between the primary and secondary graves. Taking the evidence outlined above into account, the Trial Chamber concludes that at least 1,000 people were killed in Kravica Warehouse.

## KARADŽIĆ TRIAL JUDGMENT

5257. The Accused argues in his final brief that the Glogova gravesite was a "mixed grave" which contained not only victims from the Kravica Warehouse incident but from other killing incidents related to the fall of Srebrenica, as well as victims who had died years earlier. The Prosecution acknowledges that a number of bodies found in the Glogova gravesites were brought from places other than the Kravica Warehouse. The Prosecution explains that this number includes at least 80 victims executed in Bratunac, including at the Vuk Karadžić School, plus approximately 100 individuals who cannot be determined beyond reasonable doubt to have been executed.

5258. As of 13 January 2012, DNA analysis led to the identification of 226 bodies from Glogova 1 and 171 from Glogova 2, as persons listed as missing following the take-over of Srebrenica. However, Dušan Janc clarified that not all of these 397 individuals can be linked to the killings at the Kravica Warehouse, since bodies which cannot be linked to this execution site were brought to Glogova, namely at least 80 victims executed in Bratunac, plus approximately 100 bodies brought from other locations. This is consistent with other evidence received by the Chamber that bodies collected from various places, including the Konjević Polje intersection, the Konjević Polje-Bratunac Road, Potočari, the areas of Rađno Buljek, Kamenica, and Pobuđe, and around the Vuk Karadžić School in Bratunac, were brought to Glogova to be buried.

5282. While the Chamber considers that some of these 235 individuals who were reported to have been seen alive on or after 14 July 1995 likely overlap with the approximately 180 individuals who were brought to Glogova from sites or incidents other than the Kravica Warehouse, the degree to which the two groups overlap cannot be determined beyond reasonable doubt. Therefore, in order to reach the minimum number of Kravica Warehouse victims found in Glogova and the related secondary gravesites, the Chamber has deducted both groups from the total of 1,168 bodies, leading to a minimum of 753 victims. Further, the maximum number of possible Kravica Warehouse victims found in Glogova and the related secondary gravesites can be reached by deducting those 235 individuals who were reported to have been seen last on or after 14 July 1995, as well as the approximately 80 individuals killed at the Vuk Karadžić School, from the total of 1,168 bodies, leading to a maximum total of 853 victims. Therefore, the Chamber finds that a minimum of 753 individuals and a maximum of 853 individuals found in Glogova and the related secondary gravesites were executed at the Kravica Warehouse incident.

## ANNEX IV:
## FORENSIC SITUATION AT MASS BURIAL SITES
## LINKED TO THE KRAVICA WAREHOUSE

RAVNICE

Exhumations at this location were carried out twice, first in September of 2000, then in August and September of 2001. What characterizes this mass grave is the high number of cases where only body fragments were located. Out of a total of 495 autopsy reports, 275 refer to cases involving only a fragment. These proportions can easily be seen in the graph but for the data to be even clearer, this means that in 55% of the cases only a body part, often just one or more bones, was found. Perhaps even more significantly, out of 275 reports which involve only a few bones, in 259, or 94.2%, the cause of death was not determined. As far as incomplete bodies are concerned, the cause of death could not be determined in 17 out of 65 cases. In one hundred cases, injuries were either caused by a bullet or the bullet itself was found. The cause of death was left undetermined in 13 complete or almost complete bodies. In 44 cases, various metal fragments with or without bullets were found, which is indicative of different kinds of weapons that were used there. One ligature was also found in this grave.

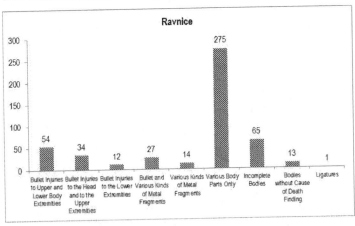

## GLOGOVA

At this location, several mass graves were found, some of which contained the remains of two to three bodies, while others contained a much greater number. Almost all mass graves at this location were exhumed between September and October 1999, except for the mass grave denoted as Glogova 1, which was exhumed in May 2001. As the graph shows, the column representing body parts plays the dominant role. In a significant number of cases, five or fewer bones are involved. Given that the human body is composed of over 200 bones, it is clear that such a small sample is insufficient for drawing any forensically significant conclusions unless it involves cranial or other bones that shield vital organs, and unless the bones themselves exhibit injuries caused by bullets or other weapons. It is important to note that out of 295 cases at this location where only a small body fragment was found, Prosecution experts were themselves unable to determine the cause of death in 280 of these cases. Thirty-five bodies exhibited traces of shrapnel, which unambiguously indicates that these persons died from the impact of a grenade, mortar, or another heavy weapon. Blast wounds were the cause of death in 32 cases. It is also relevant that 53.3% of the Glogova material does consists of incomplete bodies, *i.e.*, only of body parts and/or fragments. Of that percentage, in 95% of the cases the cause of death could not be determined by the ICTY's forensic experts. With reference to incomplete bodies, in 33 cases the cause of death could not be determined; in eight cases the cause of death was injury to the upper body region, and in one case injuries to the lower body region were cited as the cause of death. A total of 14 bodies had blindfolds and/or ligatures, which may be interpreted as suggesting execution.

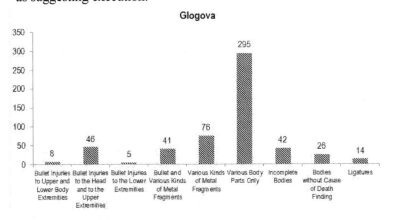

Glogova

Stephen Karganović

## ZELENI JADAR

Zeleni Jadar mass graves, exhumed in October of 1998, also contain a significant number of reports with very few bones. The percentage of cases where only a body part was found, e.g. a thigh or a foot, is 31,5%. Out of a total of 64 reports where only a body part was located, in 54 cases, or 84,3%, the cause of death was not determined. Where incomplete bodies are concerned, of 58 such cases the cause of death was not determined in 28 cases. In two cases ligatures were found, and in 12 cases complete or almost complete bodies were found, but the cause of death *was undetermined. In 44 cases there were found bullet injuries in different parts of body.* The rest of 23 bodies contain injuries made by different kinds of weapons which includes mines and artillery.

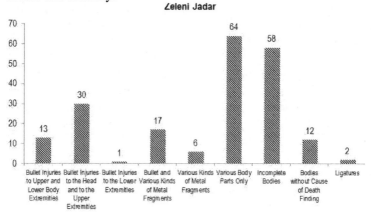

Zeleni Jadar

**Source**: Dr. Ljubiša Simić, General Presentation and Interpretation of Srebrenica Forensic Data (Pattern of Injury Breakdown), in S. Karganović and Lj. Simić, *Rethinking Srebrenica*: New York, 2013, pp. 108–129.

140

ANNEX V:
MUSLIM MILITARY AGE MALES CAPTURED
BUT NOT EXECUTED BY SERB FORCES
BETWEEN 11 AND 17 JULY 1995

*Here follow brief summaries of debriefing statements made by Bosnian Muslim prisoners after their release. These statements were recorded by Bosnian Muslim authorities. Reference is made to EDS document reference numbers in ICTY Prosecution database.*

1. **Ademović, Bekir** (1975), 01185273. Soldier, captured July 13 with seventeen wounded individuals. He mentions the names of five other individuals who were captured with him. During the column's withdrawal, he witnessed combat activity around Konjević Polje and he gave an estimate of Muslim casualties. After having been captured, he was taken to the Bratunac Health Clinic, where he spent two days waiting for treatment. He was then placed in the care of a Dutch doctor. During the night of July 17–18, he was transferred to the Batković Prisoner of War Camp. He witnessed prisoners being beaten but he himself was not mistreated.

2. **Memišević, Nurudim**. Civilian, captured on July 14 near Baljkovica. For further details, see the statement given by father, **Memišević, Nurif** 00396028. He was transferred to Batković on July 14, where he was beaten.

3. **Ahmetović, Nedžad** (1953) 01189539. Soldier, captured on July 13. He was taken to Karakaj (near Zvornik) where he was held for two-to-three days. While retreating with the column, he witnessed combat activity and subsequently gave an assessment

of casualties. He was transferred to the Batković POW camp where he was exchanged on December 24, 1995.

4. **Mustafić, Zazim** (1964), 01185284. Soldier who was wounded and later captured by the Drina Corps military police on July 12. He names ten other individuals who were captured with him. He was transferred to Batković on July 18 and was exchanged on September 29, 1995.

5. **Hašemović, Aziz** (1960), 01185332. Soldier, captured on July 16 with nine other wounded persons, of whom he names four. He received medical assistance at the Bratunac Health Clinic, following which he was transferred to the Batković POW camp on July 17. He was exempted from labor obligations because of his medical condition. He was exchanged on September 29, 1995.

6. **Vilić, Sadik** (1960), 00401652. Civilian, captured on July 13. After the withdrawal of the Dutch Battalion, he was captured by the VRS with a large group of wounded Muslims in Potočari. He confirms that the entire group received proper medical treatment at the health clinic in Bratunac. He was not mistreated. He was interrogated by VRS intelligence personnel, registered with the ICRC on July 18, and evacuated to the Batković POW camp on July 19 with twenty-two other wounded prisoners. He was exchanged on September 29, 1995. In Batković, he was interrogated by a VRS officer on military matters, but he was not mistreated, although he was later abused by a war crimes investigator during interrogation.

7. **Tabaković, Reuf** (1960), 01185288. Soldier, wounded, captured July 12. He was held in Bratunac for five days. On July 17, he was transferred to Batković where he was exchanged on December 24, 1995.

8. **Tabaković, Šukrija** (1973), 00371755. Soldier, wounded, then captured on July 11–12, according to the best of his recollection. He spent six days at the UN camp in Potočari, then was taken to the hospital in Bratunac for treatment with six other wounded Muslims (July 17–18). He provided the names of other wounded prisoners who had been captured and treated with him. He was transferred to Batković on July 18, where he was treated in accordance with the Geneva Convention. He was exchanged on September 30, 1995.

9. **Kaljević, Rifet** (1945), 01185280. Soldier, wounded, then captured on July 14. He took part in the withdrawal, during which time he attempted to commit suicide. He was later captured and then taken by Serbian forces to the Bratunac Hospital for treatment after his suicide attempt. He mentions a "gravely ill" prisoner, also from Srebrenica, who was being treated but who expired at the Bratunac hospital. He was transferred to Batković and then exchanged on December 24, 1995.

10. **Smajlović, Idriz** (1956), 12122824. Soldier, wounded, then captured on July 11. He spent several days at the clinic in Potočari, where he was registered with the Red Cross. He was transferred to Bratunac on July 15, where he was interrogated and mistreated. He was transferred to Batković on July 16 and then exchanged on September 29, 1995. The witness expressed bitterness toward the Serbs because he had been wounded after stepping on a landmine, but he states that as a prisoner he was treated properly. He confirmed that the 28th Division of the B-H Army from Srebrenica was conducting attacks on surrounding Serbian villages.

11. **Selimović, Sadik** (1962), 03052246 (statement number in the files of the Muslim intelligence service, AID); 02131234. Soldier, wounded, captured in Potočari on July 12. He was taken to the Bratunac Hospital with other wounded soldiers where

some of the staff treated them properly, but others did not. Eight days after his capture, he was transferred to Batković where he was registered with the Red Cross. He gave statements to both the Muslim authorities (AID) and to the ICTY Prosecution (OTP).

12. **Hasić, Sakib** (1968), 00588878 (statement number in the database of ICTY Office of the Prosecutor). Status unclear: wounded, then captured by the VRS at the UN clinic in Potočari. Serbian soldiers separated gravely wounded Muslim prisoners who were to be freed. In Bratunac, he saw wounded Muslims with Red Cross registration cards. He was given a medical exam on July 13. He was interrogated on July 15 and he was then registered with the Red Cross a day or two later. He was transferred to Batković and exchanged on December 24, 1995.

13. **Gračanlić, Džemo** (1974), 00371741. Status unclear: wounded, then captured by the VRS at the UN clinic in Potočari with twenty-three other wounded Muslims. He was transferred to the Bratunac hospital on July 14, then on July 19 transferred to Bijeljina, and finally transferred to the Batković POW camp. He was registered with the Red Cross and exchanged on September 29, 1995.

# PERCEPTIONS OF INJUSTICE: THE ICTY HAS PLANTED THE SEEDS OF FUTURE BALKAN WARS[1]

by

Višeslav Simić

*"Not only must Justice be done; it must also be seen to be done."*

R v Sussex Justices,
*Ex parte* McCarthy ([1924] 1 KB 256, [1923] All ER Rep 233)
is a leading English case
on the impartiality and recusal of judges.

The founders and current directors of the International Criminal Tribunal for the Former Yugoslavia (hereinafter either the "ICTY" or "the Tribunal") in The Hague have declared it a success for its efforts to punish criminals and render justice to victims. The ICTY's sponsors in the international community have written its annals in stone. Nevertheless, the Balkan peoples have viewed the ICTY's questionable — even suspicious — methods and results as unjust and prejudiced. In the Balkans, its decisions have entered national, religious, and political discourse and the leaders of these peoples are mobilizing confrontations with other national and religious communities. This essay presents a sampling of their perceptions.

---

1    "Injustice is the seed of future wars." Carla Del Ponte, ICTY Prosecutor; Politika; Belgrade, Serbia; May 1–2, 2008; p. 33.

Višeslav Simić

**Introduction**

*No one is happy and no one is satisfied,*
*no one is at peace, and no one is serene.*[2]

These verses written by the great nineteenth-century Serbian poet, His Grace the Bishop and Sovereign Prince of the Ecclesiastical State of Montenegro Petar Petrović Njegoš, concisely describe the outcome of the ICTY's prosecutions as perceived by the peoples of former Yugoslavia, especially by the Serbs and Croats. These verses also shed additional light on the Tribunal's prosecutorial praxis, because ICTY Prosecutor Katrina Gustafson even prosecuted the late poet posthumously.[3] Prosecutor Gustafson calumniated Njegoš' *magnum opus* "The Mountain Wreath," which was written almost 150 years before the outbreak of the civil war that devastated the Socialist Federative Republic of Yugoslavia.[4]

Such outbursts of prosecutorial zeal often provide much needed comic relief to the tragic circumstances surrounding the proceedings, and this has convinced many Southern Slavs and

---

2  Njegoš, Petar Petrović; The Mountain Wreath; Izdavačko preduzeće "Rad"; Belgrade, Serbia; 1997; page 165.

3  The Tribunal has a curious sense of chronology. A poet who has been dead for 150 years may be prosecuted, but contemporary crimes against Serbs are frequently not. There was plenty of evidence of crimes committed against Serbs and their property in Croatia, as well as of genocidal crimes against Serbs by administrative organs of the government of Macedonia. For example, this author's father had his surname "Macedonized" on his birth certificate, which most Serbs in Macedonia experienced because the Skoplje government officially denied the existence of Serbs. Not one of these crimes was taken into consideration as contributing to the rise of inter-ethnic tensions in Yugoslavia; however, a literary work written almost two centuries ago was.

4  InSerbia Today; *ICTY: Njegos celebrated ethnic cleansing of Muslims*; Feb 13, 2014, https://inserbia.info/today/2014/02/icty-njegos-celebrated-ethnic-cleansing-of-muslims/

ex-Yugoslavs alike of the ICTY's dilettantism and buffoonery. The ICTY staged another circus act when its prosecutors called an eyewitness to the stand who was going to testify about alleged crimes committed by Slobodan Milošević, President of Serbia. Since the trial was being broadcast live in the Balkans, viewers were able to see a legally blind man take the witness stand, who then admitted under oath that he hadn't seen anything but had only heard some third- and fourth-hand village gossip. The ICTY Rules of Procedure and Evidence, Rule 89(c), states: "A witness who has heard the testimony of another witness shall not for that reason alone be disqualified from testifying."[5] Angela Stavrianou correctly pointed out in her article *Admissibility of Hearsay Evidence in the Special Court for Sierra Leone* that: "The Trial Chamber in the ICTY has held that the admission of hearsay does not compromise the rights of the accused."[6]

These procedural high jinx call Hannah Arendt[7] to mind and invert her conclusion about the banality of evil and the ordinariness of Nazi war criminals by attributing these stupefying qualities to the bureaucrats who have gathered at the ICTY in The Hague. Helle Porsdam[8] points out that "the world's only remaining superpower" established the ICTY in order to fulfill its teleology.

---

5  ITCY Rules of Procedure and Evidence; Rule 89(c), http://www.icty.org/en/documents/rules-procedure-evidence

6  Stavrianou, Angela; *Admissibility of Hearsay Evidence in the Special Court for Sierra Leone*; Centre for Accountability and the Rule of Law website; Freetown, Sierra Leone; Aug. 11, 2016, http://www.carl-sl.org/pres/admissibility-of-hearsay-evidence-in-the-special-court-for-sierra-leone/#_ftn6

7  Arendt, Hannah; *Eichmann in Jerusalem: A Report on the Banality of Evil*; Penguin Books; New York; 2006.

8  Porsdam, Helle; *From Civil to Human Rights: Dialogues on Law and Humanities in the United States and Europe*; Edward Elgar Publishing; Cheltenham, UK; 2009; page 5.

The Nuremberg trials established the principle that:

> Individuals have international duties which transcend the national obligations of obedience imposed by the individual State. He who violates the laws of war cannot obtain immunity while acting in pursuance of the authority of the State if the State in authorizing action moves outside its competence under international law.[9]

Yet, the individuals who were recruited by the ICTY to break new ground in international law chose either to abandon or abolish international legal standards. In the Western Balkans, skeptics have recalled the infamous agreement between Stalin and Churchill on the fate of the Nazis after WWII. According to Michael Bess,[10] Churchill wanted them executed but Stalin reprimanded him by saying: "[I]n the Soviet Union, we never execute anyone without a trial." Churchill reportedly snapped: "Of course, of course. We should give them a trial first." Many jokes made the rounds in the former Yugoslavia about Andrei Kozyrev similarly reprimanding Madeleine Albright, who was obsessed with overcoming "the Munich Syndrome"; and there were jokes involving François Mitterrand rebuking Bill Clinton, who was also desperate to show off his competence in foreign relations. Ex-Yugoslavs often wondered who could reprimand ICTY judges for applying "The Führer Principle," i.e., the basis for political authority in government organs in Germany during the Third Reich, which meant that the Führer's word superseded written

---

9   Judgment of the International Military Tribunal, Nuremberg, October 1946; Yale Law School; Lillian Goldman Law Library; The Avalon Project.

10  Bess, Michael; *Choices Under Fire: Moral Dimensions of World War II*; Chapter: Justice for the unspeakable? The Enduring Legacy of the War Crimes Trials at Nuremberg and Tokyo; Random House; New York; 2006; page 263.

laws. In the case of ICTY judges, the Führer is understood to be the collective Washington-Brussels-London elites whose uncompromising[11] words have likewise superseded written laws. The Führer Principle, one may note, was ruled to be inadmissible as a defense during the Judges' Trial at Nuremberg, where sixteen Nazi jurists and lawyers were tried for implementing Nazi racial purity laws.

Prince-Bishop Njegoš was accused by the ICTY of instigating a civil war in the Balkans, although he was removed by a century and a half from the disintegration of Yugoslavia in the 1990s, and had written his epic poem about events that transpired a century before his own time. Be that as it may, another religious leader, the Bishop of Rome, John Paul II, who was alive and directly involved in armed conflict in Yugoslavia, was never called to testify at the ICTY, much less was he either accused for his personal participation in the crimes against peace or was the state he represented (*i.e.*, the Vatican) ever accused of preparing the destruction of a sovereign state, a founding member of the UN, one of whose organs, incidentally, is the ICTY. To wit, the last president of Yugoslavia, Stipe Mesić, testified to John Paul II's complicity publicly:

> I wanted to convey the idea of the break-up of Yugoslavia to those who had the greatest influence on its fate, to Genscher and the Pope. In fact, I had three meetings with Genscher. He enabled a contact with

---

11 Madeleine Albright infamously declared the that the UN Food and Agriculture Organization's preliminary estimate of 567,000 deaths of Iraqi children was an acceptable sacrifice in order to enforce sanctions on the Iraqi regime: "I think this is a very hard choice, but the price — we think the price is worth it." *60 Minutes* (TV program hosted by Lesley Stahl); CBS News; May 12, 1996; FAIR website: https://fair.org/extra/we-think-the-price-is-worth-it/

the Holy See. The Pope and Genscher agreed with
the total break-up of SFRY.[12]

Milan Kučan, the first President of Slovenia, also testified to that
effect:

JUDGE MAY: [...] That is what Mr. Mesic said,
something along those lines; is that right?

THE WITNESS: (Interpretation) Yes.[13]

These perceived derelictions of duty on the part of the ICTY are
not going to be forgotten — at least not by the Serbs — because
the 1946 Nuremberg Judgment of the International Military Tribunal ruled that "the [Nuremberg] Charter makes the planning or
waging of a war of aggression or a war in violation of international treaties a crime." And "Article 7 of its Charter expressly
declares: "The official position of defendants, whether as Heads
of State, or responsible officials in government departments,
shall not be considered as freeing them from responsibility, or
mitigating punishment."

## Unexpected Agreement
## on the Need for a War Crimes Tribunal

A surprising development took place in the former Yugoslavia: overwhelming majorities of each national group, ethnic minorities, and religious communities that theretofore seemed unable to agree on anything at all, did agree on the need for a war
crimes tribunal. Every non-Serbian group acted as if it expected
such a war crimes tribunal would try only the "others" (*i.e.*,

---

12 Mesić, Stipe, NTV broadcast, November 8, 1995.
http://yugoslavtruth.blogspot.mx/2005/04/john-paul-ii-and-break-up-
of.html

13 Kučan, Milan; *Cross-examination of Prosecution witness by President Slobodan Milošević on May 21, 2003, at ICTY,*
http://www.icty.org/en/content/milan-ku%C4%8Dan

Serbs for the most part). These non-Serbian groups were alleging that "our people" committed no war crimes; instead, they alleged: "we defended ourselves from Serb aggression." Most Serbs also appeared to want a war crimes tribunal established largely because they hoped that crimes against Serbs in this war — unlike others — would be punished, but also because most Serbian intellectuals wanted a war crimes tribunal to prosecute Serbian suspects as individuals in order to avoid collective Serbian responsibility that would result in even greater demonization, as strongly advocated by many Western media, some Western politicians, as well as by other former Yugoslavs.

After the ICTY was established and began trying suspects, Croats, Bosnia-Herzegovinians, and Serbia's Muslims (both Slavic and Albanian) supported its efforts enthusiastically because Serbs preponderated among the accused. As soon as non-Serbs started getting indicted and arrested by the ICTY, Catholic Croats and Bosnia-Herzegovinian Muslims began withdrawing their support for the Tribunal. Prominent politicians and intellectuals in these former Yugoslav regions came out against the ICTY and they published critical appraisals of it and as well as of the West in general.[14] The same pattern appeared when Albanians from Serbia were indicted and taken to the ICTY.[15]

As time passed, another trend began uniting former Yugoslav national groups in mistrust and condemnation of the Tribunal: the ICTY's complete blindness to crimes committed by anyone from the West, especially the U.S. It revived the old proverb da-

14 Pečarić, Josip; *Sramotni sud u Haagu* (The Shameful Tribunal in the Hague); Stih; Zagreb; 2001.

15 RTS; *Лимај ухапшен, па пуштен* (Limaj arrested, then released); March 16, 2011 –
http://www.rts.rs/page/stories/ci/story/134/hronika/859646/ljimaj-uhapsen-pa-pusten.html

ting from the Ottoman occupation, which attested to the impotence of the conquered: "The kadi[16] accuses you, then the kadi judges you."[17] The ICTY dismissed such criticism. It emphasized that its jurisdiction was limited to crimes committed on the territory of the former Yugoslavia. Even so, one of the individuals understood to be most responsible for the civil war in Bosnia-Herzegovina was Warren Zimmerman, the U.S. Ambassador to Yugoslavia, who was physically present in the country during the period under the ICTY's purview, yet he was never indicted for the greatest of all crimes — the crime against peace. He was first and foremost responsible for sabotaging an agreement by Yugoslav authorities to end the armed conflict, as Jean Bricmont states:

> [...] of the Lisbon agreements of February 1992, the Canadian Ambassador to Yugoslavia at the time, James Bissett, has written, "The entire diplomatic corps was very happy that the civil war had been avoided — except the Americans. The American Ambassador, Warren Zimmerman, immediately took off for Sarajevo to convince [the Bosnian Muslim leader] Izetbegovic not to sign the agreement." Zimmerman later admitted this, although he claimed, implausibly, just to be helping Izetbegovic out of an agreement with which the latter was uncomfortable. However, according to "a high-ranking State Department official who asked not to be identified," quoted in *The New York Times*, "The policy was to

16 kadi, a Muslim magistrate who, of course, bases his decisions on Sharia law. He has the power to charge, try, and sentence the accused.

17 Ranke, Leopold; *Serbian Revolution* (Die Serbische Revolution; Aus serbischen Papieren und Mitteilungen; Hamburg; Perthes; 1829); Serbian Literary Association; Belgrade, 1965; page 59.

encourage Izetbegovic to break the partition plan. It was not committed to paper." That was Bush, Sr.[18]

James Bissett, the former Canadian Ambassador to Yugoslavia, also testified that Zimmerman was crucial in causing Bosnia-Herzegovina's Muslims to renege on the Lisbon Agreement brokered by Cutilheiro in February 1992. This paved the way for war. According to Andy Wilcoxson:

> The former Canadian ambassador testified that American interference caused war to erupt in Bosnia and Kosovo. He testified that in March 1992 (one month before the outbreak of war in Bosnia) Portuguese diplomat Jose Cutilheiro brokered a peace agreement in Lisbon between Bosnia's Serbs, Croats, and Muslims. Bissett said that the agreement had been signed by Karadzic for the Serbs, Boban for the Croats, and Izetbegovic for the Muslims. The witness, a career diplomat, believed that the Cutilheiro plan was a good plan that would have avoided war in Bosnia if it had been implemented. Unfortunately, the Cutilheiro plan was never implemented. Bissett testified that the then American ambassador to Yugoslavia, Warren Zimmerman, flew to Sarajevo and met with Izetbegovic. He testified that Zimmerman sabotaged the peace plan by encouraging Izetbegovic to remove his signature from the agreement. Soon after his meeting with Zimmerman, Izetbegovic reneged on the agreement and civil war broke out in Bosnia. Far from being the peace seeking humanitarians they claimed to be, Bissett testified that the Clinton Administration prolonged the Bosnian war by sabotag-

---

18 Bricmont, Jean, *Humanitarian Imperialism: Using Human Rights to Sell War*, translated by Diana Johnstone, NYU Press; New York; 2006; page 50.

ing the Vance-Owen plan and the Owen-Stoltenberg plan.[19]

The Recommendations in ICTY's *Final Report to the Prosecutor* by the Committee Established to Review the NATO Bombing Campaign against the Federal Republic of Yugoslavia are still remembered in the Balkans as just one of many egregious examples of Western hypocrisy:

> 90. [...] NATO has admitted that mistakes did occur during the bombing campaign; errors of judgment may also have occurred. Selection of certain objectives for attack may be subject to legal debate. On the basis of the information reviewed, however, the committee is of the opinion that neither an in-depth investigation related to the bombing campaign as a whole nor investigations related to specific incidents are justified. In all cases, either the law is not sufficiently clear or investigations are unlikely to result in the acquisition of sufficient evidence to substantiate charges against high level accused or against lower accused for particularly heinous offences.

> 91. On the basis of information available, the committee recommends that no investigation be commenced by the OTP in relation to the NATO bombing campaign or incidents occurring during the campaign.[20]

---

19 Wilcoxson, Andy; *Lipstick on a Pig: Corrupt "Justice" at the ICTY*; Slobodan-milosevic.org; Oct. 20, 2013 – http://www.slobodan-milosevic.org/news/awrch102013.htm

20 *Final Report to the Prosecutor* by the Committee Established to Review the NATO Bombing Campaign Against the Federal Republic of Yugoslavia, http://www.icty.org/en/press/final-report-prosecutor-committee-established-review-nato-bombing-campaign-against-federal

Jared Israel pointed out in his article "The Boss Pushes for Civil War in Yugoslavia" that Peter Galbraith, another U.S. citizen,

> was ambassador to Croatia during the planning and execution of Operation Storm. In that massive military assault, during which he was shown on Croatian TV riding a tank, 250,000 Serbs, mostly farming families, were driven from their ancestral lands by the Croatian Army.[21]

Yet Galbraith, like Pope John Paul II and Warren Zimmerman, was never charged by the ICTY; instead, he advanced his diplomatic career.

Pointing out such examples is not a case of *tu quoque,* in other words, an attempt to evade responsibility. That defense strategy was also declared invalid at Nuremberg.[22] This is a grave and legitimate charge against the ICTY; it is an accusation of a breach of legal and professional duty through the application of the very "measure" (this term will be revisited later) that was purportedly created in order to provide a global mechanism for achieving legal and legitimate long-term — if not permanent — security, justice, and peace in international affairs.

## Many Former Yugoslavs, Particularly Serbs, Believe the ICTY Is an Illegitimate Institution

On the one hand, Lee Atwater coined the phrase "perception is reality";[23] on the other hand, the former Yugoslav peoples

---

21 Israel, Jared; *The Boss Pushes for Civil War in Yugoslavia*; 9/16/99, http://emperors-clothes.com/misc/civil.htm

22 Heise, Nicole A., *Deciding Not to Decide: Nuremberg and the Ambiguous History of the Tu Quoque Defense*; January 1, 2009; Available at SSRN: https://ssrn.com/abstract=1354048      or http://dx.doi.org/10.2139/ssrn.1354048

23 Kelner, Simon; *Perception is reality: The facts won't matter in next year's general election*; The Independent; October 30, 2014,

(Footnote continued on next page)

have indeed constructed their own reality, based on their perceptions, of the ICTY. It is a reality opposed to the one created by
the ICTY, which believes its mission is to create and manage
global public opinion.

A range of objections, starting with the legal basis for the
creation of the Tribunal and ending with its declaration of success in fulfilling its self-proclaimed mission, challenge the IC-
TY's seamless narrative, the foundation upon which the New
World Order's edifice of peaceful coexistence is built. Each hole
in this narrative is fertile soil for doubt and suspicion; these are
the seeds of future discord, hatred, and desire for revenge which
may germinate and then ripen into a new Balkan war.

Even groups that have benefitted the most from the ICTY's
decisions recognize that they could have been on the losing side
under a different set of geopolitical caprices. They may grumble
behind the back of the Western strongmen and warlords[24] who
supported them, but they know that their imaginary victory has
been erected on shifting sands. This is because the Tribunal is
generally understood to have been created illegally, so each of its
rulings may potentially be regarded as null and void, which re-
duces the ICTY to another vain exercise in the projection of
power based on the principle that might makes right.

Most legal scholars, even if they are reluctant to admit it publicly for fear of ostracism, are acutely aware of the UN Security
Council's legal inability to create by *fiat* a subsidiary body dedi-

---

(Footnote continued from previous page)

https://www.independent.co.uk/voices/comment/perception-is-reality-the-
facts-wont-matter-in-next-years-general-election-9829132.html

24 Technically this patriarchal figure of speech is politically and factually
incorrect. Many of the most fervent and ruthlessly militant Western leaders
who were calling for the bombardment of Serbia were women.

cated to criminal justice. The West's belief in the *fiat* is supported by a famous exchange reported by James Rubin, the U.S. Assistant Secretary of State for Public Affairs in the Clinton Administration.[25] According to Rubin, British Foreign Secretary Robin Cook advised U.S. Secretary of State Madeleine Albright that the British government "had problems with their lawyers [who believed] it was illegal [to attack Serbia]." Albright's infamous reply was: "Get more lawyers" to provide the political — if not legal — arguments she sought and eventually obtained.

At the time of the ICTY's creation, the Secretary General of the UN Boutros Boutros-Ghali warned that the UN's own procedures were being violated because there was no universal legislative organ that could create the Tribunal:

> The approach which in the normal course of events would be followed in establishing an international tribunal would be the conclusion of a treaty by which the member states would establish a tribunal and approve its statute. This treaty would be drawn up and adopted by an appropriate international body [*e.g.* the General Assembly or a specially convened conference], following which it would be opened for signing and ratification. Such an approach would have the advantage of allowing for a detailed examination and elaboration of all issues pertaining to the establishment of the international tribunal. It would also allow the states participating in the negotiation and conclusion of the treaty to fully exercise their sovereign will

---

25 Thakur, Ramesh; *Responsibility to Protect and Sovereignty*; Charles Sampford's Chapter 8: Legality and Legitimacy: A Dozen Years after Goldstone; Routledge; London; 2013; p. 146.

in particular whether they wish to become parties to the treaty or not.[26]

The UNSC resolution that was used to create the Tribunal made it clear that semantics did not play a significant role in the minds of its authors, who turned the ICTY into a "measure" instead of an "institution." They interpreted the clause in Chapter VII of the UN Charter as one that grants the Security Council the right to take *measures* to maintain or restore international peace and security. Even this was conveniently ignored when NATO attacked Yugoslavia in 1999, since no international war was taking place until NATO violated the peace and started bombing.

Boutros-Ghali also made it clear that "this approach would have the advantage of being expeditious and immediately effective,"[27] and it would thus substitute political expediency in advancing U.S. policy at the expense of legality and proper form.

Another important aspect of international law and custom was abolished by the illegal creation the ICTY. The Convention on the Prevention and Punishment of the Crime of Genocide of 1948 and the Geneva Conventions of 1949 entrusted prosecution of those crimes to national courts of the signatory states. This provision was suspended, which thus annulled the competence of national courts. This decision by the UNSC also allowed the ICTY, by operation of Article 15 of its Statute, to create its own rules of procedure and write its own laws.

This *ultra vires* action by the UNSC, which came at a time when Russia and China were politically incapacitated, was a self-abrogating act because Chapter VII of the UN Charter,

---

26 Boutros-Ghali, Boutros; *UN Secretary General's Report no. S/25704*; 3 May 1993, http://www.securitycouncilreport.org/un-documents/document/icty-s-25704-statute-re808-1993-en.php

27 *Ibid.*, Sect. 23.

which was used to endow the ICTY with putative legality, did not grant it such authority at all but limited it to the sphere of international security. Judicial matters were to be handled only by the International Court of Justice; however, the U.S., which pushed for the creation of ICTY, had withdrawn from the ICJ in 1986 after the Court ruled against U.S. interests by declaring that the U.S. mining of the Bay of Managua, Nicaragua, was a war crime. The U.S. later decided to accept the ICJ's jurisdiction only on a case-by-case basis. The U.S. also regularly used its veto power to prevent enforcement of the court's rulings through resolutions of the UN Security Council.

In addition to this, legal scholars — as well as cognoscenti in the Balkans — know that the U.S. never submitted to the jurisdiction of the International Criminal Court, in spite of the Clinton administration having toyed with the idea when in 2000 it signed the Rome Statute, but which it never submitted to the U.S. Senate for ratification. The U.S. Congress elevated its hypocrisy to new heights when it passed a law — *The American Service-Members' Protection Act* — in 2002 whose Title 2 authorized the U.S. President to "use all means necessary and appropriate to bring about the release of any U.S. or allied personnel being detained by, on behalf of, or at the request of the International Criminal Court."[28]

The West ensured its complete moral bankruptcy in the eyes of former Yugoslavs when the U.S. developed a legal loophole by citing the Rome Statute's Article 98 as a basis for bilateral immunity agreements with foreign governments, which prohibit the transfer of U.S. citizens to the custody of the ICC, even if a

---

28 ASPA, Title 2 of Pub.L. 107–206, H.R. 4775, 116 Stat. 820, enacted August 2, 2002, https://www.congress.gov/bill/107th-congress/house-bill/4775

state has signed and ratified the Rome Statute. The European Union struck a pose to uphold international law and justice in 2002 by issuing a common EU position that "candidate states" may enter "into U.S. agreements . . . tak[ing] into account that some persons enjoy State or diplomatic immunity" and are "present on the territory of a requested State because they have been sent by a sending State."[29] A running joke in the Balkans has it that "powerful and sovereign" states such as Albania, Bosnia-Herzegovina, Macedonia, and Montenegro have concluded infamous Article 98 agreements with the U.S.[30] The "sovereign" state of Kosovo incorporated into Article 153 of its Constitution the provision that the "final authority in theatre" is "the Head of the international military presence," which in reality means it is the U.S.[31] In 2006, Serbia's new pro-US/NATO government also signed a special agreement[32] with NATO — of which the U.S. is the undisputed leader — which was reconfirmed in 2016 by Serbia's — not Kosovo's — new and even more pro-US/NATO government. This agreement, the NATO Partnership for Peace Program, grants unimpeded access and immunity to NATO troops on the supposedly sovereign territory of Serbia and it guarantees that the "authorities" in Serbia shall not detain NATO

---

29  General Affairs and External Relations Council of the European Commission; 2450th Council session; 12134/02 (Presse 279); Sept. 20, 2002; Brussels; p.10.

30  Georgetown Law Library; *International Criminal Court – Article 98 Agreements Research Guide,*
http://guides.ll.georgetown.edu/c.php?g=363527&p=2456099

31  Constitution of the Republic of Kosovo; Republic of Kosovo Assembly – http://www.kuvendikosoves.org/?cid=2,1058

32  Srbija Danas; *NATO dobio diplomatski imunitet: Ovo je Sporazum koji je Srbija potpisala sa NATO!*; Feb. 19, 2016,
https://www.srbijadanas.com/clanak/nato-dobio-diplomatski-imunitet-ovo-je-sporazum-koji-je-srbija-potpisala-sa-nato-19-02-2016

personnel. In 2003, Croatia and Slovenia "suffered" the loss of U.S. military aid by not signing this agreement. They were attempting to please their EU overlords in Brussels. Croatia and Slovenia, being NATO members, fall under the direct control of the U.S. through NATO's command structure and political architecture. But NATO troops have obtained immunity from prosecution, at least in Serbia. Thus, not a single right-thinking person in the former Yugoslavia will be fooled into believing the posturing by the U.S., the UK, France, *etc.* (countries that are the principal powers behind the ICTY) about taking the moral high ground.

## The ICTY as a Western Political Tool

U.S. Ambassador Richard Holbrooke in his 2003 BBC radio interview "United Nations or Not?" proclaimed with a magnificent lack of concern that the "[ICTY is a] huge valuable tool."[33] With Karadžić and Mladić having being indicted by the ICTY, Holbrooke added: "[t]hey cannot participate in an international peace conference of any sort." Charles Ingrao, a U.S. Professor of History and a Balkans expert, stated in a 2008 *Deutsche Welle* interview that "Holbrooke promised Karadžić that he wouldn't be arrested."[34] The U.S. State Department also revealed that Ambassador Holbrooke used the ICTY as a political bargaining chip. Ambassador Holbrooke absolutely disregarded a principle of justice by "promising Karadžić freedom from arrest if he stepped down from office and disappeared," because his resigna-

---

33  Holbrooke, Richard; Radio Interview; *United Nations or Not? The Final Judgment: Searching for International Justice*; BBC Radio; Sept. 9, 2003.

34  Ingrao, Charles; *Holbrooke promised Karadžić that he wouldn't be arrested*; Deutsche Welle (in Serbian); August 7, 2008, http://www.dw.com/sr/%C4%8Darls-ingrao-holbruk-obe%C4%87ao-karad%C5%BEi%C4%87u-da-ne%C4%87e-biti-uhap%C5%A1en/a-3543935

tion would then allow Serbia's President Milošević, who was malleable, to be the official legal representative of the Bosnia-Herzegovinian Serbs at the Dayton Peace Conference. Since then, many Balkan commentators have tartly noted that Serbia's citizens had suffered for years under UN sanctions simply because the U.S. claimed that Milošević did not have the right to interfere in the affairs of Bosnia-Herzegovina, an independent and sovereign state. The U.S. eventually became the sole representative of only one of Bosnia-Herzegovina's ethnic groups at a major international peace conference. Peace, as always, is a life-and-death matter.

One of the most problematic aspects of the ICTY was its "sealed indictments,"[35] which had been introduced by Louise Arbour, the Canadian jurist. This provoked uncertainty and fear among political leaders in the Balkans, especially Serbs, because no politician was able to know whether he would be walking into a meeting either to negotiate with former Yugoslav adversaries and their Western representatives — or into a trap. This uncertainty put Serbian leaders in a vulnerable psychological state, because they were targets of witch hunts and potential arrests, which could result in the loss of personal freedom, dignity, office and property. The West applied a behavior modification schedule, with rewards or punishments as possible outcomes each step of the way — so Serbian politicians developed the behavioral patterns of a gambler. They never knew whether they would end up being indicted by the ICTY or end up being praised as peacemakers and reliable partners. As experiments with laboratory rats have shown, an organism subjected to a random reinforcement schedule keeps repeating the behavior for which it

---

35 Stover, Eric; *The Witnesses: War Crimes and the Promise of Justice in The Hague*; University of Pennsylvania Press; 2011; pp. 36–37.

was rewarded over long periods of time, even after punishment had been replaced by a reward. This in turn caused Serbian officials to respond to each and every stimulus administered by the West. It perpetuated confusion by programming the Serbs to respond in their hope of eventually guessing correctly and being rewarded instead of punished.

Another ICTY Prosecutor, Carla del Ponte, made it clear that the Tribunal was a political tool of the West. She stated that "the primary focus of the Office of the Prosecutor must be on the investigation and prosecution of the five leaders of the FRY and Serbia who have already been indicted,"[36] but she uttered not a word on the ICTY's possible plans to indict any of the Western leaders who were responsible for numerous crimes committed during NATO's illegal bombardment of Serbia in 1999. They were, after all, guilty of the supreme offense, the crime against peace. The *Interim Agreement for Peace and Self-Government in Kosovo*, the peace treaty that was the putative objective of the failed Rambouillet conference in February 1999, clearly established a pretext for the bombardment. It later served as a basis for UN Security Council Resolution 1244, which expanded the scope of immunity from prosecution that NATO had demanded as well as privileges accorded to U.N. personnel in occupied Kosovo. In 1999, U.S. President Clinton spoke before the Legislative Convention of the American Federation of State, County, and Municipal Employees, and he claimed that: "Milosevic, on the other hand, [...] refused even to discuss key elements of the agreement."[37] President Clinton failed to say that the so-called

---

36 Stover, 2011, pp. 36–37.

37 Clinton, William J.; *Remarks at the Legislative Convention of the American Federation of State, County, and Municipal Employees*; March 23, 1999, http://www.presidency.ucsb.edu/ws/?pid=57294#axzz2iFJfcG7P

negotiations were conducted in the most hostile manner toward the Serbs, and that the so-called peace agreement contained secret clauses that not only completely negated the sovereignty and freedom of Serbia if President Milošević were to sign it, but it also set the stage for fundamentally changing the country's social system, management of its natural resources, and its economy. It was an ultimatum[38] designed to be rejected in order to trigger a war against Serbia.

U.S. Congressman Tom Lantos (D-CA), Chairman of the Foreign Affairs Committee of the U.S. House of Representatives, provided further proof that the ICTY was part of a well-planned U.S. political ambush. He spoke at a Hearing before the Committee on Foreign Affairs of the U.S. House of Representatives, where he said:

> Just a reminder to the predominantly Muslim-led government[s] in this world that here is yet another example that the United States leads the way for the creation of a predominantly Muslim country in the very heart of Europe. This should be noted by both responsible leaders of Islamic governments, such as Indonesia, and also by jihadists of all color and hue. The United States' principles are universal, and in this instance, the United States stands foursquare for the creation of an overwhelmingly Muslim country in the very heart of Europe.[39]

---

38 Not even a year later, U.S. Ambassador Richard Holbrooke's assistant Jonathan Levitsky proudly stated to the author of this text (at the U.S. Mission to the UN) that he was "the author of the Rambouillet Accord," and that he "used the 1914 Austro-Hungarian ultimatum to Serbia as a blueprint," so that the Serbs would not sign it and thus provide an opening for the NATO bombardment.

39 *The Outlook for the Independence of Kosova*, Hearing before the Committee on Foreign Affairs; House of Representatives; 110th Congress, First Session; April 17, 2007; Serial No. 110-44; page 16.

(Footnote continued on next page)

NATO Spokesman Jamie Shea also made it clear at a May 1999 press conference that the ICTY was a political tool of the U.S. and NATO:

> As you know, without NATO countries there would be no International Court of Justice, nor would there be any International Criminal Tribunal for the former Yugoslavia because NATO countries are in the forefront of those who have established these two tribunals, who fund these tribunals and who support on a daily basis their activities. We are the upholders, not the violators, of international law. We obviously recognise the jurisdiction of these tribunals, but I can assure you, when these tribunals look at Yugoslavia I think they will find themselves fully occupied with the far more obvious breaches of international law that have been committed by Belgrade than any hypothetical breaches that may have occurred by the NATO countries, and I expect that to apply to both. So that is our position on that, we recognise international law, in fact we recognise international law so much that when we see a massive violation of it, [...], we don't just shout about it, we do something to stop it because we uphold international law. The charge by Yugoslavia was brought under the genocide convention. That does not apply to NATO countries. As to whom it does apply, I think we know the answer there.[40]

---

(Footnote continued from previous page)

http://www.gpo.gov/fdsys/pkg/CHRG-110hhrg34713/pdf/CHRG-110hhrg34713.pdf

40  Shea, Jamie; Press Conference; May 16, 1999,
https://www.nato.int/kosovo/press/p990516b.htm

Justice Louise Arbour refined this conclusion during a joint press conference with the U.S. Secretary of State Madeleine Albright in Washington, D.C., on April 30, 1999, when she said:

> We have long-standing relationships with [NATO] information providers. We are now looking at trying to accelerate the flow of that kind of information and the quality of the product. [...] It's a dialogue and a partnership that we have to maintain. [...] [W]e have partners who have the political will and the operational skills to execute arrest warrants even in hostile environments. [...][W]e've now put in place mechanisms that allow us, in partnership with many others who are in the field in Albania and in Macedonia, to try to process refugee accounts and, from our point of view, select those who will provide the best base for a court case.[41]

## Problems with the
## Rules of Procedure and Evidence at the ICTY

In the interest of brevity, only the ICTY rules of procedure and evidence most damaging to the dispensation of justice will be commented upon.

The Tribunal adapted practices from different judicial traditions, but only to the extent that they suited the realization of Western political goals; at the same time, the Tribunal disregarded all the safeguards that had been developed over the centuries to guarantee the impartiality and trustworthiness of courts as well as the legal profession. The Tribunal will long be remembered for its unprecedented and destructive mishmash of rules, of

---

41 Arbour, Louise; *Press Conference with Madeleine Albright*; Washington, DC; April 30, 1999. The original link: http://secretary.state.gov/www/statements/1999/990430a.html, has since been replaced by: https://1997-2001.state.gov/statements/1999/990430a.html

which neither the Spanish Inquisition nor Stalinist courts could ever have been accused. These include:

amending the rules with disregard for their prejudice to the rights of the accused;

rule amendments that have the effect of *ex post facto* law;

rules that may be amended by the chamber with no further discussion if the judges accept them unanimously;

the Prosecution may create rules by *fiat* but the Defense is accorded no similar right;

the Prosecution was declared an organ of the Tribunal, so it also has the right to amend the rules;

the Prosecution may deny the Defense access to evidence and it may present its reasons for such refusal to the judges without the Defense either being present or having a right to challenge it subsequently;

the Tribunal may prohibit the disclosure of not only the indictment, but also of any documents or information to the Defense;

hearsay evidence may be admitted;

witnesses are allowed to testify anonymously;

witnesses are allowed to refuse to appear in court and they may have their identities permanently concealed;

names and identifying information may be expunged from the public record;

closed hearings (*i.e.*, secret trials) are permitted;

trial by jury (which might have introduced some common sense into the courtroom proceedings) is not allowed;

sealed indictments[42] may be issued;

facts, documents, and information may be concealed from the general public, especially if it is contrary to the interests of any state (*i.e.*, the U.S. and its vassals);

detention of non-indicted suspects for up to ninety days is permitted, and no evidence is required;

a suspect who had already been acquitted may be re-arrested and may be held in detention for ninety days for no stated reason;

forced self-incrimination is permitted;

confessions are presumed to be "free and voluntary," even after a long period of detention without either indictments or evidence, while the prisoner must bear the burden of proof to prove the contrary;

the conditions of detention may be modified;[43]

the Registrar has the almost arbitrary right to disqualify any counsel, if said counsel is regarded as "unfriendly" to the Tribunal;

the ICTY may limit the number of attorneys a defendant may have if it determines too many attorneys already represent the aforementioned defendant;

---

42 A survey of Bosnian judges revealed that the Muslim judges "generally found the sealed indictments acceptable." They reasoned that since "Bosnia was 'totally undemocratic'" this practice was absolutely permissible. *International Law and Society: Empirical Approaches to Human Rights*; edited by Laura A. Dickinson; Chapter 7; Justice, Accountability and Social Reconstruction: An Interview Study of Bosnian Judges and Prosecutors, by The Human Rights Center and the International Human Rights Law Clinic, University of California, Berkeley, and the Centre for Human Rights, University of Sarajevo; Routledge; 2017.

43 Serbs were generally denied modification of detention even for life-threatening medical reasons; however, a Croatian general Tihomir Blaškić was allowed to await trial in a private villa.

the Tribunal allowed itself to be funded, staffed, and assisted by private citizens, NGOs, corporations, military alliances, and governments (all of the aforementioned enjoy practical immunity from prosecution at the Tribunal) that had a direct stake in the results of the trials.

Gabrielle Kirk McDonald, a U.S. citizen and an ITCY President, pointed out during her 1999 statement before the U.S. Supreme Court:

We benefited from the strong support of concerned governments and dedicated individuals such as Secretary Albright. As the permanent representative to the United Nations, she had worked with unceasing resolve to establish the Tribunal. Indeed, we often refer to her as the 'mother of the Tribunal'.[44]

## The Problem of Biased and Selective Indictments

Today, human rights groups as well as legal scholars in the U.S. are expressing grave concerns about the disproportionate number of minorities who have been incarcerated in U.S. prisons. *National Geographic* magazine recently published an article entitled "The Stop."[45] It begins: "Black motorists are pulled over by police at rates exceeding those for whites. It's a flash point in the national debate over race, as many minorities see a troubling message: You don't belong here." These words are powerful. Yet, the UN's own ICTY published in November 2017 *Key Figures of the Cases*,[46] which showed little regard for the stunning disproportionality in the number of Serbs who have been indict-

---

44 Ali, Tariq: *Masters of the Universe? NATO's Balkan Crusade.* London: Verso, 2000, pp. 164-165.

45 *The Stop*, National Geographic — Special Issue; (unattributed authorship); Vol. 233; No. 4; April 2018; p. 100.

46 ITCY, *Key Figures of the Cases*, Nov. 2017, http://www.icty.org/sid/24

ed, detained, and sentenced, and who even died during the process, when compared to the number of prisoners of other ethnic backgrounds. Even though conscientious observers had voiced these concerns, they were dismissed by the facile explanation that Serbs committed more crimes than all the other ethnic groups in the former Yugoslavia. Imagine the resulting outrage if this simplistic justification had been given as an official explanation for the disproportionately large number of arrests, detentions, prosecutions, and incarcerations of minorities in the U.S.

In the aftermath of the ICTY's closing, some Serbs are left wondering whether their nation even has a right to exist; others believe that the West used demonization techniques in its discourse on the Balkans, especially with respect to Serbs. Generally, Serbs have come to believe that the West applied nineteenth century quasi-scientific concepts, disguised by PR buzzwords and spin, to portray Serbs, in up-to-date and seemingly reasonable terms, as a pathological and deviant people. The purpose was to divide individuals and societies deemed progressive, well-adjusted, stable, and advanced[47] from those deemed backward, historically unstable, pathologically self-destructive — even retarded. In the case of the Serbs, among others, Western discourse relied on selective and decontextualized quotations from the theories of Darwin and Smith as well as from latter-day proponents of their ideas. The West gussied up its discourse on Ser-

---

47 The author's personal experience testifies to this search for atavist Serbian pathology. An American journalist interviewed the author together with a visiting Croatian journalist in 1992. She could not conceal her surprise when she realized that the fair-skinned, blue-eyed, English speaker before her, who was cleanly shaven and who wore a suit and a tie, was actually a Serb; the dark-skinned, black-eyed, bearded, non-English-speaker was the Croat. Her sub-conscious racial impressions pervaded the published text of the interview. *See* Purdy, Penelope; *Tales of Anguish Revealed in Soft Voices*; *The Denver Post*; June 28, 1992.

bian pathology with pseudo-scientific language, but there was an underlying aspect of mediaeval demonization to it: the "others" were hurting "us," so the "others" had to be eliminated. It was a smug moralistic creation of superior and inferior categories of human beings. The discourse appeared anchored in biological determinism. It presented alleged evidence of the Serbs pathology and their dysgenic[48] heritage: they were reduced to the status disease bearers.[49] Inferior peoples are incapable of understanding the benefits of a superior civilization. Thus, the West had to make an example of them, punish them, and if not eliminate, at least contain, control, and reduce their numbers and confine them to a minimal territory where they would never again interfere with glorious progress and irreversible advancement of the human species. These opinions have come from the top down since the 1990s, when the U.S. Senator at the time, Joseph Biden (later U.S. Vice President) declared that the Serbs were just "a bunch of illiterate degenerates, baby killers, butchers, and rapists."[50]

It wasn't simply this racist approach that outraged even Serbs who were supportive of the ICTY. Some suspects were apprehended as political payback to cooperative local officials for their promotion of Western interests. The most blatant example is the case of Dr. Vojislav Šešelj, who, according to the ITCY's Prosecutor Carla Del Ponte, was indicted at the request of the Prime Minister of Serbia at the time, Zoran Djindjić. As reported

---

48 Lynn, Richard; *Dysgenics — Genetic Deterioration in Modern Populations*; Human Evolution, Behavior, and Intelligence; Praeger; 1996; pp. 206–7.

49 Savich, Carl K.; *War, Journalism, and Propaganda – An Analysis of Media Coverage of the Bosnian and Kosovo Conflicts*; Project Rastko; 2000, http://www.rastko.rs/kosovo/istorija/ccsavich-propaganda.html

50 "Biden does the Balkans," by N. Malić. https://original.antiwar.com/malic/2009/05/19/biden-does-the-balkans/

by the Belgrade daily *Politika* in 2008, she recorded in her memoir *Madame Prosecutor: Confrontations with Humanity's Worst Criminals and the Culture of Impunity*, that Djindjić had told her: "Take Šešelj away and don't send him back to us again."[51] Dr. Šešelj actually surrendered to the Tribunal voluntarily and spent eleven and one half years in The Hague as a prisoner before he was acquitted on all counts and released in 2014. He returned to Serbia where he has since been actively participating in political life. Even so, news just came from The Hague as of this writing that the ITCY has partially overturned Šešelj's acquittal and that it sentenced him to ten years in prison. The ICTY overstepped the traditional appellate court's writ. It is not supposed to pass a final sentence but only to rule on points of law in the lower court's verdict. With the ICTY, anything is possible.

How many other Serbian political leaders might have cut a deal with either the Tribunal or the U.S. government in order to avoid being arrested because they feared the existence of a "sealed indictment" against them?

One such political leader might be Vuk Drašković, the controversial novelist and "master of Serbia's public squares" during the 1990s. Although he used more inflammatory language in his nationalistic and anti-Muslim speeches than Dr. Šešelj ever did, Drašković was never arrested, despite rumors of the existence of a "sealed indictment" against him. He even became Foreign Minister of Serbia in 2004 after the regime change that overthrew President Milošević. This writer remembers a Bosnian Muslim interpreter openly boasting during a February 2004 Prayer Breakfast at the Washington, D.C., Hilton as she informed her audience that Mr. Drašković had been "worked over"

---

51 *Politika*, 14 April 2008, http://www.politika.rs/sr/clanak/39448/Dindic-Vodi-Seselja-i-nemoj-vise-da-nam-ga-vracas

by a representative of the U.S. Institute for Peace in order to prepare him to undertake his responsibilities as Foreign Minister the following month. During Drašković's term of office, Serbia signed on to the infamous NATO Partnership for Peace Program. Many suspect Drašković committed his signature to this document simply because he was being blackmailed by a secret ICTY indictment. Drašković shocked many in Serbia by his about-face. He transformed himself from a chauvinist into the greatest proponent of Western superiority; from inciting violence to abjectly confessing the Serbian people's genetic deficiencies and perpetual guilt for crimes committed during the Yugoslav civil wars.

Ante Gotovina, a French citizen and Foreign Legion *caporal-chef*, and later Croatian General, who was indicted by the ICTY in 2001, presents another interesting case. He promptly disappeared. Gotovina was eventually apprehended in 2005 in the Canary Islands. Many Croats, especially those who had fought for what they believed was the liberation of Croatia from Serbian occupation, were angered by the indictment of a man whom they considered a national hero. They were further enraged by allegations that the Croatian government collaborated with the Tribunal in his apprehension. They believed that the Croatian government had exchanged Gotovina for future membership in the EU and NATO. During his absence, it was supposed that General Gotovina was hiding in one of the many Roman Catholic monasteries in Croatia. He was not. This writer had a surreal encounter during a trip to San Francisco in the spring of 2006. A young Mexican man stopped me on the street and called to my attention my personal resemblance to the fugitive Croatian general. He shed tears as he claimed that I looked like his "lover, the greatest hero of his people." During a long and emotionally charged conversation, this young man claimed that General Gotovina had lived with him (with the blessing of U.S. authorities) in a hotel in San Francisco until Mr. Gotovina decided to go to the Canary

Islands despite his lover's pleadings not to do so. If we accept the aforementioned ICTY ruling that the admission of hearsay evidence does not compromise the rights of the accused, then this "lover's testimony" would carry even more weight than ordinary hearsay evidence because it would have come from an allegedly first-hand source.

To illustrate The Hague's bias in selecting individuals for indictment one need only quote the principal Western leaders who held office the time of the Kosovo "war." One may start with Madeleine Albright, U.S. Secretary of State and the principal initiator of the attack on Serbia, who admitted during a 2013 NPR interview that: "what we did there was not legal." Walter Isaacson pointed out in *Time Magazine*[52] that in March 2014, Gerhard Schröder, German Chancellor at the time of the NATO bombardment of Serbia in 1999, said[53] during a conference organized by the weekly *Die Zeit* in Hamburg: "We sent our planes there . . . against Serbia, and together with NATO forces bombed a sovereign state, and at the same time there was no decision of the UN Security Council."[54]

Even NATO officially admitted in its Fact Sheet *Russia's Accusations — Setting the Record Straight*, dated April 13, 2014,

---

52  "Madeleine's War," *Time Magazine*, May 10, 1999,
     http://edition.cnn.com/ALLPOLITICS/time/1999/05/10/albright.html

53  TANJUG; March 10, 2014:
     http://www.b92.net/eng/news/comments.php?nav_id=89568

54  Reported by *Telegraf.rs*, 9 March 2014,
     http://www.telegraf.rs/vesti/981087-gerhard-sreder-priznao-da-je-nato-
     nelegalno-bombardovao-srbiju; see also *B92*, 10 March 2014: "International-
     al law was broken when Serbia was attacked: Gerhard Schroeder has admit-
     ted that "like the situation in Crimea," the NATO attack on Serbia in 1999
     was also "a violation of international law,"
     https://www.b92.net/eng/news/world.php?yyyy=2014&mm=03&dd=10&n
     av_id=89568

that its "Operation Allied Force was launched despite the lack of Security Council authorization."[55]

Western leaders, who were acutely aware that they were committing serious violations of both international[56] and domestic laws and principles,[57] and who were especially concerned about being accused of a crime against peace,[58] made certain from the onset of the "war" that no official declaration of war was to be made by any of the states involved in the aggression against Serbia. George Robertson, the UK Defense Secretary, when he was questioned in Parliament about the possibility of British casualties during the "war" against Yugoslavia, replied: "[The military experts] rightly warn that we cannot have a casualty-free war. This is not a war." Robinson's entire testimony was reported in the 1999 UK Select Committee on Defence Minutes of Evidence.[59] Robertson testified with an air of ritual

---

55 NATO website (no longer available)
http://www.nato.int/nato_static/assets/pdf/pdf_2014/20140411_140411-factsheet_russia_en.pdf &
http://www.nato.int/cps/en/natolive/topics_109141.htm – accessed: April 13, 2014

56 Montevideo Convention on the Rights and Duties of States; Article 11; Montevideo, Uruguay; December 26, 1933.
http://www.jus.uio.no/english/services/library/treaties/01/1-02/rights-duties-states.xml and http://www.cfr.org/sovereignty/montevideo-convention-rights-duties-states/p15897

57 The U.N. General Assembly Resolution 2131 (XX); Declaration on the Inadmissibility of Intervention in the Domestic Affairs of States and the Protection of Their Independence and Sovereignty. http://www.un-documents.net/a20r2131.htm

58 The Nuremberg Final Declaration; 1946: "To initiate a war of aggression is not only an international crime; it is the supreme international crime, differing only from other war crimes in that it contains within itself the accumulated evil of the whole." http://www.economist.com/node/14205505

59 Robertson, George Rt. Hon. MP; U.K. Select Committee on Defence; Minutes of Evidence; Examination of Witnesses (Questions 380-399);

(Footnote continued on next page)

farce. The Chairman then asked: "Having clarified their legal status, I presume there will be no formal declaration of war." To which Robertson replied: "It is not a war." The Chairman then asked: "If a NATO pilot is shot down [...] what under the Geneva Convention [...] can [he] demand under international law?" Mr. Robertson answered as follows:

> The full protection of the Geneva Conventions. [...]
> All parties to any conflict must be bound by the GC.
> [...] This is not a war. We are not declaring war on
> Serbia. We are not bombing Serbia. We are damag-
> ing the military capability to destroy civilians in that
> part of the world.[60]

The Tribunal indicted not one Western leader for any of the crimes the ICTY had been established to prosecute and punish in the pursuit of transnational justice. The peoples of the former Yugoslavia are not likely to forget this.

## The Deaths of Accused Persons *en Route* to The Hague as well as of Those in Its Custody

Hitler's close associate, Hermann Göring, committed suicide in his jail cell in Nuremberg after he had been sentenced to death. General Praljak of the Croatian Republic of Herzeg-Bosnia flamboyantly committed suicide by swallowing poison in the ICTY courtroom — right in front of the judges — when he rejected the final guilty verdict they handed to him in 2017. This grotesquerie takes absurd dimensions when one notes that the

---

(Footnote continued from previous page)

March 24, 1999, http://www.parliament.the-stationery-office.co.uk/pa/cm199899/cmselect/cmdfence/39/9032403.htm

60 Young, Hugo; *The Lord Robertson of Port Ellen? Oh, good grief*; The Guardian; Sept. 2, 1999, https://www.theguardian.com/politics/1999/sep/02/labour.labour1997to991

ICTY withheld legitimate medications from another prisoner, President Slobodan Milošević.[61] A deadly poison somehow passed, despite "strict" security measures in the ICTY, into the hands of a convicted war criminal so that he could commit suicide theatrically before video cameras in the courtroom and thus gain eternal glory among his sympathizers. Yet President Milošević was not allowed to receive necessary medications because of these same "strict" security measures.

The ICTY officially attributed President Milošević's death in 2006 to "a heart attack" — but not to murder, as it was widely thought to be. Others (mostly Serbs) died either *en route* to the ICTY or in its custody or during temporary release from the ICTY (the ICTY, as it may be surmised, did not want these suspects to die in its custody): Slavko Dokmanović, in detention (1998); Simo Drljača, before his transfer to The Hague; Dušan Dunjić, a forensic pathologist, in a hotel in The Hague on the eve of his important testimony in the trial of General Ratko Mladić; Dr. Milan Kovačević (1998); Milan Babić (2006); General Zdravko Tolimir (2016); Miroslav Deronjić (2007); General Mile Mrkšić in prison in Portugal (2017); Goran Hadžić, while on temporary release (2016); as well as Generals Djordje Djukić (1996), Momir Tarlać (2002), and Milan Gvero (2013).

Any other organ of justice that had such an alarmingly high death rate among prisoners in its custody would have come under intense scrutiny — but not the ICTY. This added dimension leads one to believe that the ICTY spectacularly miscarried justice, especially with respect to Serbs. This perception will not die

---

61 Wilcoxson, Andy; *Tribunal denies Milosevic medical treatment as Canadian ambassador concludes his testimony*; February 24, 2006, http://www.slobodan-milosevic.org/news/smorg022406.htm

as easily as the Tribunal's detainees did, nor as fast the "international community" might wish it to.

## The Disparity in Acquittals and Length of Sentencing with Respect to the Nationality and Religion of Those Who Have Been Detained, Accused, and Convicted

This writer once worked as a researcher who gathered evidence on the Čelebići Camp Case, which was a prisoner-of-war camp jointly operated by Croats and Muslims. I was shocked that Zejnil Delalić, who was the Coordinator of the Bosnian Muslim and Bosnian Croat forces in the Konjic area in 1992, and who was Commander of the First Tactical Group of the Bosnian Army, was acquitted. *The Hague Justice Portal* reported that the ICTY's

> Trial Chamber II found that he did not have command and control over the prison-camp and over the guards who worked there and, accordingly, determined that he could not be held criminally responsible for their actions."[62]

Yet nearly the entire Serbian leadership was held responsible for command and control for each subordinate who was accused of committing even the slightest infraction of the rules of war.[63]

Blatant bias is also evident in the case of former Republika Srpska President Biljana Plavšić, whose indictment for genocide was based on statements she made regarding the genetic shortcomings of Muslims in Bosnia-Herzegovina,[64] but not a single

---

62  http://www.haguejusticeportal.net/index.php?id=6112

63  For details of Delalić acquittal, *see* ICTY Trial Judgment, 16 November 1998, http://www.icty.org/x/file/Legal%20Library/jud_supplement/suppl-e/celebici.htm

64  Black, Ian; *The Iron Lady of the Balkans*; The Guardian; Gender; Special report: war crimes in the former Yugoslavia; Sept. 10, 2001; https://www.theguardian.com/world/2001/sep/10/gender.uk1

Western official was ever indicted for racist and warmongering invectives directed against Serbs.[65]

The ITCY's own website provides shocking statistics of its impressive inability to find evidence of the guilt of non-Serbs, while it displays near magical capabilities to do so in cases involving Serbian suspects: 72 Serbs have been sentenced to a total 1,138 years of prison; Croats, Albanians, and Bosnian Muslims together have been sentenced to a total of 361 years. Of the latter, only 20 Croats, 5 Bosnian Muslims, and 1 Albanian were found guilty.[66] One must be reminded that many of the witnesses, who could have provided evidence of criminal acts committed by Albanian leaders, have mysteriously committed suicide, died in accidents, or simply disappeared, which allowed the ICTY to release the suspects and leave them free to return to politics and high office. Today, many of these former suspects (*e.g.* Ramush Haradinaj) are addressed as "your excellency."

### Racism as a Perceived Basis for the Establishment of the Tribunal

The UN created *ad hoc* tribunals solely for Eastern Europeans (*i.e.*, Slavs), Albanians, and Africans, which provides ample evidence that Western leaders were acting on their well-concealed racism. The permanent Russophobia that afflicts Western leaders was projected for the most part on Serbs, who are treated as substitute Russians simply because Western leaders have no jurisdiction over Russians. The Balkan crisis provided these Western leaders with an opportunity to vent their frustrations, which they could not otherwise express in today's politically correct world.

---

65 *Biden's Racist Slurs and Searing Insults Documented*, Free Republic, May 15, 2009, http://www.freerepublic.com/focus/news/2253148/posts

66 https://en.wikipedia.org/wiki/List_of_people_indicted_in_the_International _Criminal_Tribunal_for_the_former_Yugoslavia

The Balkan peoples hold this perception strongly, and they will not change their minds anytime soon.

## Conclusions

The nineteenth century German historian Leopold von Ranke held that the discipline of history must find out "how things actually were." Generations of conscientious investigators of the past have obeyed his dictum. The ICTY, however, departs from this principle of historical honesty in its fanatical pursuit of a politically correct narrative for the events that have taken place in Yugoslavia since 1991.

The ICTY's approach to the evidence and its historical context caused even the Muslims of Bosnia and Kosovo — the sides which benefitted the most from U.S. intervention in the Yugoslav conflict — to be dissatisfied, disappointed, and distressed as soon as their own war heroes were indicted, arrested, and in rare and isolated instances found guilty and sentenced by the Tribunal. The Croats, the second most guilty ethnic group according to the number of war criminals who have been convicted and sentenced, eventually turned against the ICTY after the death of their *pater patriae*, Dr. Franjo Tudjman, when it became known that he had been under investigation for genocide which Croatian forces had allegedly committed against Bosnian Muslims, to be sure, but not against Serbs. With the passage of time, the world has become much more aware of the countless horrific crimes committed by the U.S. and its vassals who have left a smoldering trail of destruction from Libya to Pakistan. Not one of the nationalities, ethnic groups, minorities, or religious communities of Yugoslavia either felt guilt or regret for any *actus reus* committed in their name, because they had learned that the death and destruction inflicted on their enemy would be declared by the West to be collateral damage, a byproduct of the fog of war, which would then free the perpetrators of responsibility and even turn them into national heroes and champions of freedom and democracy. Instead of remorse, the Americans have engineered an alleviation of guilt, a clearing of the conscience of the peoples of the former Yugoslavia. Some collateral damage!

If one considers the likely possibility that the ICTY is not a true global judicial mechanism but is simply the West's military/political/diplomatic apparatus for projecting force, then one may call to mind Article 16 of President Abraham Lincoln's General Order No. 100, otherwise known as the 1863 "Lieber Code." Article 16, defines the rules of engagement in war as well as the conduct of soldiers. It states that:

> Military necessity does not admit of cruelty — that is, the infliction of suffering for the sake of suffering or for revenge [...]. It admits of deception, but disclaims acts of perfidy; and, in general, military necessity does not include any act of hostility which makes the return to peace unnecessarily difficult.[67]

In this context, the ICTY clearly failed to fulfill this noble yet politically motivated directive — especially with respect to the last sentence. The ICTY has actually made the return to true and lasting peace in former Yugoslavia unnecessarily difficult.

In conclusion, it is helpful to recall the noble aspiration of Lord Acton: someday a history of Europe will be written in such a fashion that it would be impossible to detect the nationality of its contributors. A desire might be expressed that the ICTY should pass judgments in a similar fashion, so that the citizenship and political loyalty of its judges would not prejudice them or much less even be perceived. Yet U.S. historian Anthony

---

67 Lieber, Francis; Instructions for the Government of Armies of the United States in the Field; LL.D.; (Originally Issued as General Orders No. 100, Adjutant General's Office, 1863); Government Printing Office; Washington, DC; 1898: http://avalon.law.yale.edu/19th_century/lieber.asp

Grafton concluded that Lord Acton's aspiration was utterly unfeasible. He believed that such a history would be written when the seas turn to lemonade — in other words, never.

The gullible may wish to believe the ICTY has brought lasting peace to the Balkans; the skeptics understand that the ICTY has instead planted the seeds of future Balkan wars.

## General References

Balkan Insight; *Kosovars Stage Protest Against Limaj Trial*; Jan. 31, 2012 – http://www.balkaninsight.com/en/article/protest-in-support-of-commander-steel/1458/196

Becker, Richard; *Chapter 22: The Rambouillet Accord-Pretext for a War of Aggression*; Selected Research Findings; Independent Commission of Inquiry to Investigate U.S./NATO War Crimes Against the People of Yugoslavia –
http://www.iacenter.org/warcrime/22_rambo.htm

Collon, Michel; *Liar's Poker: The Great Powers, Yugoslavia and the wars of the future*; Translated from French by Milo Yelesiyevich and Terence McGee; International Action Center; NY; 1998; page 25.

Durant, Will; *Our Oriental Heritage; The Story of Civilization*; Part 1; Simon and Schuster; New York; 1954; Chapter 10, Assyria, 1 Chronicles; page 265.

Gould, Stephen Jay; *In response to Mindless Societies*; New York Review of Books; Vol. 22; No. 18; Nov. 13, 1975.

Holbrooke, Richard; *To End a War*; Modern Library; 1999; p. 107.

Jennings, Peter; *Land of The Demons*; Special News Broadcast recorded from ABC Evening News; March 18, 1993 –
http://tvnews.vanderbilt.edu/siteindex/1993-Specials/special-1993-03-18-ABC-1.html

Judgment of the International Military Tribunal, Nuremberg, October 1946; Yale Law School; Lillian Goldman Law Library; The Avalon Project – http://avalon.law.yale.edu/imt/judlawch.asp

Libal, Michael; *Limits of Persuasion: Germany and the Yugoslav Crisis, 1991–1992*; Praeger Publishers; Westport, CT; 1997.

Longinović, Tomislav; *Vampire Nation: Violence as Cultural Imaginary*; Duke University Press; Durham, NC; 2011.

Memorandum of Understanding between the Office of the Prosecutor and Supreme Headquarters Allied Powers Europe (SHAPE) was signed – In The Trial Chambers; Prosecutor v. B. Simic, M. Simic, M. Tadic, S. Zivkovic, S. Todorovic and S. Zaric; 2. Cooperation between SFOR and the International Tribunal; May 9, 1999; paragraph 4. - http://www.icty.org/x/cases/simic/tdec/en/01018EV513778.htm

NPR; *Albright: U.N. Needs To Show Its Relevance On Syrian Issue*; Sept. 26, 2013 – http://www.npr.org/2013/09/26/226375391/albright-u-n-needs-to-show-its-relevance-on-syrian-issue

Pfaff, William; *Hague Tribunal Indictment Clarifies New NATO Strategy*; Chicago Tribune; June 1, 1999 – http://articles.chicagotribune.com/1999-06-01/news/9906010161_1_indictment-of-slobodan-milosevic-war-crimes-international-criminal-tribunal

The Hague Justice Portal; Delalić, Zejnil; no date available – http://www.haguejusticeportal.net/index.php?id=6112

# WHEN JUSTICE FAILS

by

Jovan Milojevich

The International Criminal Tribunal for the Former Yugoslavia (the "ICTY" or the "Tribunal") in The Hague, Netherlands, was founded in 1993 to prosecute alleged war criminals involved in conflicts on the territory of the former Yugoslavia. From 1993 until its closure in 2017, the ICTY indicted 161 individuals from all the ethnic groups involved in the various conflicts. Nevertheless, the Tribunal has been embroiled in controversy ever since its inception, with accusations of ethnic bias, the destruction of evidence, the violation of defendants due process, and censorship to name a few. The controversy culminated with the last verdict handed down by the Tribunal on December 4, 2017, when the accused, Slobodan Praljak, drank poison as the judge read out a guilty verdict, and thus committed suicide in the courtroom for the entire world to see. He died at a local hospital shortly afterwards. The shocking video footage created a media frenzy. The Western press generally characterized the incident as merely the desperate act of an insane war criminal, which was undoubtedly an oversimplification. Considering the context of the incident, the former Bosnian Croat general's belief that the court had wronged him seemed genuine, and it was clearly important to him to share his feelings about the court with the world. Ultimately, he chose death over a life under what he believed to be the Tribunal's false authority.

Praljak's protest by suicide certainly did not prove his innocence. It did, however, shed light on the workings of the Tribunal — especially on its many contentious verdicts — which may have been one of Praljak's intentions. The acquittal of the former

Bosnian military commander Naser Orić, who had publicly boasted of his crimes, is a prime example of the court's controversial verdicts. His victims included women and children who "had been tortured and mutilated and others were burned alive when their houses were torched [by Orić and his men]" (Szamuely 2013: 278). Prosecution witness General Morillon, Commander of the United Nations Forces in Bosnia from 1992–93, stated during his testimony at the Milošević Trial that "Orić engaged in attacks during Orthodox holidays and destroyed villages, massacring all the inhabitants... [He] was a warlord who reigned by terror in his area and over the population itself.... he could not allow himself to take prisoners."[1]

Schindler (2007: 229) says that Orić's "tenure as Srebrenica's commander was marked by horrifying atrocities against those he took a disliking to. Orić's crimes against Serb civilians were among the worst perpetrated by anyone in the Bosnian civil war, including much wanton butchery against innocent victims." He also notes that in February 1994 Orić "entertained a *Washington Post* reporter by showing him a videotape of his soldiers decapitating Serbs" (229). Similarly, Johnstone (2002) concludes that Orić had a propensity to attack Serbs on Serbian holidays as well as to brag to Western reporters of his exploits. She states:

> Orić's raiders chose the Orthodox Christmas day, 7 January 1993, to attack the village of Kravica, slaughtering villagers and burning homes. Forty-six Serbs were killed outright, some as they left church after Christmas service. [Between 1992–94] some 192 Serb villages were pillaged and burnt, and over 1,300 villagers were killed, while many more fled.... Orić actually invited foreign reporters to his comfort-

---

1   Trial transcript, 12 February 2004, 31965, 31966, www.icty.org.

able apartment to show off his "war trophies": vide-
ocassette tapes of his exploits displaying severed
heads and dead bodies of Serbs, burning houses, and
heaps of corpses (111).

Serbs expressed outrage over Orić's acquittal and, as one
study conducted in Bosnia shows, Serbs tend to cite this case as
evidence of the Tribunal's bias against their ethnic group (Clark
2011: 67). Accusations of bias are not limited to Serbs because
Croats have also accused the Tribunal of bias against them
(Clark 2011, Saxon 2005). Nevertheless, the Tribunal denies
these allegations and argues that its "judgements demonstrate
that all parties in the conflicts committed crimes," and that it
"regards its fairness and impartiality to be of paramount importance."[2] Furthermore, the Tribunal stresses that it has "contributed to an indisputable historical record, combating denial
and helping communities come to terms with their recent history.
Crimes across the region can no longer be denied."[3] In light of its
acquittal of one of the worst war-criminals of the Yugoslav wars,
these self-aggrandizing claims are highly suspect.

In addition, the Tribunal's unwillingness to indict well-
known war criminals further contradicts its claims. For example,
the former commander of the 5th Corps of the Bosnian Army
during the Bosnian war, Atif Dudaković, is an alleged war criminal the Tribunal failed to indict. Over a decade ago various vid-
eos surfaced of Dudaković and his troops committing war crimes
in multiple locations (B92 2007). One video shows him ordering
the execution of two Bosnian Muslim prisoners of war and then

---

2    http://www.icty.org/en/about

3    *Ibid.*

congratulating the two soldiers who carried out the order.[4] It is disconcerting that the ICTY did not indict any of the individuals involved, nor did it launch an investigation. Today, Dudaković is considered a hero in Bosnia and he has been heralded as such by the country's main politicians, which certainly does not support the Tribunal's claim that its workings have combated denial and helped communities come to terms with their recent history. On the contrary, as Akrivoulis (2017: 372) notes: "Given the public mistrust to the Tribunal in the region, its workings seem to aggravate the already existing tensions between the conflicting communities, rather than facilitate their reconciliation."

It seems as though the Tribunal had difficulties reaching any of its stated goals. According to the Tribunal's founding 1993 UNSC Resolution, its fundamental goals were to bring peace and justice to all the peoples of the former Yugoslavia (Akrivoulis 2017: 372). Yet, as far back as 1995, when the ICTY was in its infancy, Woodward (1995) offered an insightful and prescient analysis that exposed the flaws in the court's supposed intentions. She described how the threat of prosecution from the court backed the fighters into a corner and increased their incentives to find sanctuary within their own sovereign states, which made them less likely to stop the fighting — and when one considers that perhaps the worst atrocities came *after* 1993, Woodward made a compelling case. Furthermore, she found that by "ignoring this counterproductive result — encouraging the conditions that led to violations — supporters of the War Crimes Tribunal appeared to give priority to defending the norms rather than to

---

4    The video can be viewed at
     https://www.youtube.com/watch?v=5hLgUH_60Fk. The two men fought
     with Fikret Abdic's Bosnian Muslim forces, which opposed the Bosnian
     government.

preventing conditions that would result in more victims" (324). Lastly, she pointed out that because "the procedure was pushed largely by the United States, the accusations became a servant of American policy toward the conflict itself, which required a conspiracy of silence about the atrocities committed by parties who were not considered aggressors" (324). The cases of Orić and Dudaković attest to the soundness of her conclusion.

## Critics Versus Supporters of the ICTY

Woodward is not alone in pointing out the (alleged) connection between the ICTY and the United States. Thomas (2003: 171), for instance, states that:

> selective manipulation of the international justice system and process has become one of the means of conducting U.S. foreign policy. The U.S.-sponsored and -supported creation of the International Criminal Tribunal for the Former Yugoslavia (ICTY) is an illustration of such a system of biased justice where the main goal is to indict Serbs while preventing any indictment of NATO leaders and minimizing those against Croats and Muslims.

Black (2000: 29–30) argues that "it was necessary to discredit the existing leadership" of Yugoslavia in order to break it up "into quasi-independent colonies, principally of Germany and the United States," and that an "effective propaganda weapon in such an exercise is, of course, a tribunal with an international character, which the public will accept as a neutral instrument of justice but which is controlled for political ends." Dickson and Jokic (2006: 355) assert that the Tribunal has violated the procedural rights of defendants by "gagging" them. The Tribunal has gone as far as to remove defendants from the courtroom altogether so they don't "see and hear the evil" that NATO leaders carried out against Serbs.

Correspondingly, Bardos (2013: 15) argues that former ICTY justice Frederik Harhoff's allegation of political interference in the decision-making process by the former (American) President of the Tribunal,[5] as well as the subsequent accusations of political interference triggered by Harhoff's allegation, have reinforced the view that "the tribunal's work is determined not by impartial standards of justice, but by the great powers' political interests." Furthermore, Hayden (1999) argues that the ICTY delivers "biased justice" because prosecutorial decisions are based on the national characteristics (ethnic background) of the accused rather than on solid evidence. He maintains that the Tribunal's dereliction of duty to prosecute NATO leaders for *prima facie* war crimes, as well as for crimes comparable to those who have been indicted, is evidence of its bias.

Scharf (2002), on the other hand, legitimizes the creation of the Tribunal and minimizes its association with the United States. He argues that the founding of the Tribunal by the United Nations, and not by the victors or those who were involved in the conflict, legitimizes it because there was a general consensus within the 'international community' that an *ad hoc* tribunal was necessary in order to bring peace and stability to the region (2002: 394). This view, however, overlooks the integral role of the United States in creating the Tribunal — especially the role of former Secretary of State Madeleine Albright, who is referred to as the "mother of the Tribunal" (Johnstone 2002). More accurately, it was the five-member United Nations Security Council ("UNSC") that created the Tribunal, even though the UN Charter

5    Harhoff alleged that former President of the ICTY and Presiding Judge of the Appeals Chambers, American Theodor Meron, pressured his colleagues to overturn decisions related to cases involving war crimes in Croatia and Serbia (Bardos 2013: 15).

does not grant it the power to do so; nor does the Tribunal have the legal jurisdiction to try anyone for war crimes in the former Yugoslavia (Laughland 2007). As Johnstone (2000: 164) emphasizes: "The Security Council's ICTY went over the heads of the states concerned and simply imposed its authority on them, without their consent." According to Laughland (2007), there are only two possible ways to legally create an international criminal court: 1) by amending the UN Charter; or 2) through a multinational treaty, neither of which occurred during the process of the creation of the ICTY.

In addition, the Tribunal seemingly acted on a direct order from the U.S. government to indict Slobodan Milošević. As the U.S. was beginning to lose public support for its war (NATO's 1999 bombing campaign against Yugoslavia), the Tribunal indicted Milošević. It was a peculiar time to charge him with war crimes because there was a war raging throughout Kosovo as Yugoslav armed forces battled the so-called Kosovo Liberation Army (KLA) and because bombs were raining down from unrelenting U.S./NATO bombers, which made it impossible to conduct any type of investigation into alleged war crimes. Without an investigation having been conducted, there would be no way to collect the evidence necessary for an indictment. Yet, to the ICTY and the United States, evidence was just a minor technicality. The lack of evidence did not preclude an indictment against Milošević.

The lack of evidence against Milošević became increasingly more apparent during the trial as the Prosecution found it difficult to prove that Milošević had committed the alleged crimes in Kosovo. Fortunately for the Tribunal, however, it had amended the original indictment just before the trial had begun by adding two more indictments: one for Croatia and the other for Bosnia. Evidently, the Prosecution did this hoping the new indictments would make it easier to build a case against Milošević. As Laughland (2007: 110) illustrates:

> The extravagant claims made by NATO during the bombing of Yugoslavia were obviously incapable of standing up in court.... In the absence of evidence for ethnic persecution in Kosovo, the Prosecution evidently decided to cast the net as widely as possible in the hope that it might 'get' Milošević for Bosnia and Croatia instead.

Furthermore, if certain information not approved by the Tribunal or the U.S. government surfaced during a trial, then the Tribunal either redacted the testimony or silenced the defendant, and it sometimes even blacked out entire witness testimonies.

For instance, when Slobodan Milošević cross-examined former NATO Commander General Wesley Clark, the presiding judge, Richard May, forbade Milošević to ask any questions about the NATO bombardment. According to Mandel (2004: 174), Milošević was not allowed to cross-examine Clark on the "more likely US reasons for the war or its legitimacy or legality, or Clark's own status as a war criminal, no matter how *relevant* such questions might be." Moreover, before releasing the transcript to the public, the Tribunal gave the United States government permission to censor the entire transcript of General Clark's testimony as it saw fit (Dickson and Jokic 2006, Laughland 2007). Indicting individuals without evidence, redacting testimony, censoring defendants, and violating their due process are just some of the controversial issues pointed out by critics of the Tribunal. Other notable issues include trying defendants *in absentia*, allowing hearsay evidence, allowing and admitting evidence obtained through torture, accepting testimony from perjured witnesses, not allowing defendants to confront their accusers, violating defendants' right to a public hearing, and giving accused war criminals immunity from prosecution in exchange for their testimony.[6] In addition, the Tribunal was caught destroying physical evidence of crimes committed against Serbs, a revelation brought to light by one of its former lead prosecutors, Carla Del Ponte (Ching 2014, Del Ponte, Sudetic, and Amato 2008). Nevertheless, there are many scholars who support the workings as well as the legacy of the Tribunal.

Scharf (2002: 394), for example, claims that the "message of the International Tribunal's indictments, prosecutions, and convictions to date of Muslims and Croats, as well as of Serbs, has been that a war crime is a war crime, whoever it is committed by. The Tribunal has taken no sides." Smith (2012: 166) makes an analogous claim when he asserts: "The effective prosecution of those accused of war crimes regardless of the side of the conflict the defendant was on is a critical progression here that cannot be understated." Both Scharf and Smith argue that the workings of the Tribunal attest to its fairness and impartiality, however the validity of this claim is dubious. For instance, convictions of some non-Serbs do not necessarily lead to the conclusion that "the Tribunal has taken no sides," which may be either true or false. Therefore, this argument is a *non sequitur*, a logical fallacy.

*A propos* the rights of the accused, Smith claims that the "ICTY proceedings at the Hague seem to deliver justice to the accused because both the procedural due process and substantive due process dimensions of the institutional arrangement are soundly constructed. Specifically, there can be no serious argument that the accused are not entitled to a full and fair defense" (2000: 163-164). By sagaciously choosing his words, Smith creates an impression of making a profound statement, yet there are

---

6    *See* Black (2000), Brock (1996), Dickson and Jokic (2006), Laughland (2007), Mandel (2004) and Thomas (2000).

two fundamental problems with this claim: 1) it is a logical red herring; and 2) it is inaccurate. First, the concern is not whether the accused *deserve* a fair defense, but whether they actually *receive* one. By framing the argument as "there can be no serious argument that the accused are not **entitled** to a full and fair defense" as opposed to "are not **receiving** a full and fair defense" is disingenuous. Any defendant on trial, in any court, anywhere in the world, is *entitled* to a full and fair defense, whether the defendant actually *receives* one is another matter. Secondly, the ICTY has forcibly appointed defense council for a defendant against his will, which was a clear violation of a defendant's due process and is evidence that contradicts Smith's claim that due process at the ICTY was soundly constructed (Dickson and Jokic 2006, Laughland 2007).

Scharf (1997) also maintains that due process was soundly implemented at the Tribunal. He states that during the Tadić Trial facts were established "one witness at a time in the face of vigilant cross-examination by distinguished defense counsel," which, he argues, is evidence that the accused was accorded full due process and, as a result, the trial produced a "definitive account that can endure the test of time and resist the forces of revision" (215–216). Nonetheless, Scharf contradicts himself. Only seven pages earlier, he claimed that the Defense strategy was to accept the full account of the atrocities as presented by the Prosecution and it was not to challenge the Prosecution's version of events in any way, so the Defense focused instead on making a case that the evidence given by Prosecution witnesses was "unreliable because in many cases it was prejudiced testimony of Muslim victims who saw all Serbs as their oppressors" (208–209). As Mandel (2004: 240) astutely notes, the "defense strategy was not at all to challenge the historical claims by 'vigilant cross-examination by distinguished defense counsel', but rather to concede the prosecution version of history and try instead to cast doubt on the individual guilt of the accused."[7] The position that due process at the ICTY was soundly constructed and implemented does not seem well-founded.

Finally, a recent empirical study — conducted by this author (Milojevich 2018) — found that the only two predictors of outcome of verdicts at the Tribunal were 'defendant ethnicity' and 'victim ethnicity', which indicates an anti-Serb bias. However, the study was conducted before the Appeals Chamber pronounced its judgement in *Prosecutor v. Jadranko Prlić et al.*, which affirmed almost all of the Trial Chamber's convictions of Jadranko Prlić, Bruno Stojić, Slobodan Praljak, Milivoj Petković, Valentin Ćorić, and Berislav Pušić.[8] Therefore, these outcomes were not included in the data analyses of the 2018 study. However, with the completion of this case, as well as a few others, the number of defendants in the data set increased, which allowed for additional quantitative analyses to be conducted. The present study, like the previous one, examined case facts and outcomes for possible bias. However, this study included the final total ($N = 109$) defendants who went through the entire trial proceedings at the ICTY, including those who received a final verdict. This increase (in the population size)[9] also increases the power to detect significant effects.

In light of the findings of the previous study (Milojevich 2018), it was predicted that there would be an association between verdict and defendant ethnicity (Hypothesis 1 (H1)) as

---

7    For a full analysis, *see* Mandel (2004: 239-240).

8    *See*    http://www.icty.org/en/press/the-icty-renders-its-final-judgement-in-the-prli%C4%87-et-al-appeal-case

9    'Population' size is used instead of 'sample' size as both the previous and present studies included all of the completed cases at the time they were conducted. Since the ICTY has operationally shutdown, the population size will no longer increase.

well as an association between sentencing and defendant ethnicity (Hypothesis 2 (H2)) at the ICTY. Furthermore, it was predicted that there would be an association between verdict and victim ethnicity (Hypothesis 3 (H3)). With the increase in population size, this study also focused on analyzing differences between the conviction rates as well as the sentencing of defendants from only non-Serb groups. This distinction is important because the increase in cases involving non-Serb defendants now allows for analyses to be conducted without including cases involving Serb defendants.

## Method

### Sample

The ICTY indicted 161 individuals, however only those who went through the Tribunal's entire process were used for this study. One hundred and nine defendants were either 'sentenced' or 'acquitted' ($N = 109$) — all of whom were included in this study.[10] The remaining individuals: 1) had their indictments withdrawn ($N = 20$); 2) died either before or during trial ($N = 17$); 3) were transferred to a national jurisdiction ($N = 13$); or 4) had retrials ordered ($N = 2$). The data were collected from the Tribunal website's *Cases* section.[11]

### Coding

A thorough review was conducted on all of the completed cases at the ICTY in order to obtain the exact number of convictions, acquittals, and the number of years to which those who were convicted had been sentenced. Other important data were

---

10   See http://www.icty.org/en/cases/key-figures-cases

11   See http://www.icty.org/en/action/cases/4

also collected: the ethnicity of each defendant as well as the ethnicity/ethnicities of their (alleged) victims; the age of each defendant at the start of his or her trial; the category — Military, Political, or Paramilitary — to which each defendant belonged when the alleged crimes occurred; the type of charges being pressed (which takes into account the number of victims, the type of involvement in as well as the overall scope of the crimes); and lastly, in which of the three conflicts — Croatian, Bosnian, and/or Serbian (Kosovo) — the defendant was involved.

In addition, a categorical variable was created for 'victim ethnicity'. Thus, victims were divided into two categories: 'Serbs' and 'non-Serbs'. Two categorical variables were created for 'defendant ethnicity'. In one, the defendant was either categorized as 'non-Serb' ("0") or 'Serb' ("1"), and in the other as 'Bosnian Croat' ("0"), 'Serb' ("1"), and 'remaining non-Serb groups' ("2"). Each defendant was further categorized as either 'acquitted' ("0") or 'convicted' ("1"). 'Years sentenced' was coded as a scale variable from 1–50 years. Those who were given life sentences received a score of 50 years.

Two categorical variables were also created for the type of charges that were pressed (which take into account the numbers of victims, the type of involvement in the crimes, and the overall scope of the crimes). It was not possible to create a continuous variable for the number of victims because roughly half of the defendants were charged for 'indirect' involvement in crimes that were committed as part of a Joint Criminal Enterprise ("JCE") — a legal doctrine the ICTY uses to assign liability. The ICTY used JCE mainly for cases involving mass crimes such as the 'ethnic cleansing' of villages, and it may essentially be understood as a concept of 'collective liability'.

Jovan Milojevich

**Results**

## Preliminary Analyses

Preliminary analyses were conducted by examining potential confounding variables and covariates, including the age and gender of the defendants, group membership of the defendants (Military, Political, or Paramilitary), which theatre/s of the civil war the defendants were involved in, and the type of charges that were pressed (which take into account the number of victims, the type of involvement in the crimes, and the overall scope of the crimes). Results indicated that age differed significantly between Serbian and non-Serbian defendants, $t(107) = -4.277; p < .001$. Specifically, non-Serbs ($M = 43.571; SD = 9.0612$) were significantly younger than Serbs ($M = 51.970; SD = 10.5054$). Significant effects also emerged for group membership, $F(2, 106) = 3.410, p < .05$, as 67.2 % of Serbian defendants were members of the military, 23.9% were members of the political establishment and 9.0% were members of a paramilitary formation. In comparison, non-Serb defendants had a higher percentage in the military at 88.1 %, while 11.9% were members of the political establishment and 0.0% were members of a paramilitary unit. Neither gender nor location of conflict differed by defendant ethnicity (gender: $t(107) = .790$, *n.s.*; location of conflict: $\chi^2(2) = .668$, *n.s.*), therefore, neither variable was further considered.

Lastly, Chi-squares were run to examine the association between the type of charges that were pressed (which takes into account the number of victims, the type of involvement in the crimes, and the overall scope of the crimes), and verdict. In the first analysis, the variable used for the former placed the defendants into either of two categories: 1) indirect involvement (high-level officials/mass war crimes); or 2) direct involvement (low-level officials/active role in perpetrating atrocities). Eight cases were excluded from the analysis as these individuals were tried for both direct and indirect involvement. Most of these accused were commanders who were neither high-level nor low-level military figures but somewhere in between, who were accused of actively having taken part in war crimes as well as of 'creating an environment that encouraged and permitted war crimes to be committed' — mainly against prisoners of various camps. The result of the Chi-square showed there was not a significant difference in the verdict based on indirect or direct involvement; $\chi^2(1) = .619, p = n.s.$

In order to test this association by using the entire population size ($N = 109$) a variable was created that placed defendants in one of two categories: those who were tried under the Joint Criminal Enterprise ('JCE') doctrine and those who were not ('non-JCE'). This was done in anticipation of a significant association between the two variables: the 'JCE' category would be associated with the 'indirect involvement' (high-level officials/mass war crimes) category; and the 'non-JCE' category would be associated with the 'direct involvement' (low-level officials/active role in perpetrating atrocities) category. The former may also be classified as 'collective responsibility'; and the latter as 'individual responsibility'. As expected, the association between the two variables was significant; $\chi^2(1) = 38.378, p < .001$; therefore, another Chi-square was run to examine the association between the type of charges that were pressed and verdict but with the 'JCE/non-JCE' variable in place of the 'indirect/direct involvement' variable. The result showed that there was no significant difference in verdict based on those who were tried as part of a JCE and those who were not; $\chi^2(1) = .016, p = n.s.$ Overall, the Chi-squares indicate that there was no association between the type of charges that were pressed (which take into account the number of victims, the type of involvement in the crimes, and the overall scope of the crimes), and verdict. Therefore, neither variable was considered further.

Jovan Milojevich

## Sample Characterization

Descriptive statistics were conducted to characterize the length of sentencing based on (victim and defendant) ethnicity.

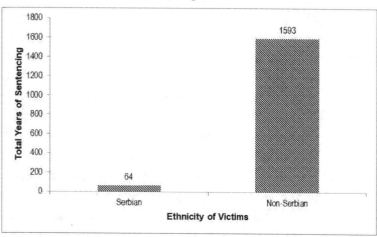

*Figure 1.* Sentencing at the ICTY based on the ethnicity of the victims. This figure illustrates the lack of representation of Serb victims compared to non-Serb victims in the total number of years of sentencing handed down by the ICTY.

As shown in Figure 1, 64 out of 1,657 total years of sentencing at the ICTY were for crimes committed against Serbs (3.86%), while 1,593 years were given for crimes against non-Serbs (96.14%) — this is a difference of almost 2,400%. These statistics are alarming when one considers the number of Serbian victims resulting from the conflicts in Croatia, Bosnia, and Kosovo.

## Sentencing at the ICTY — II

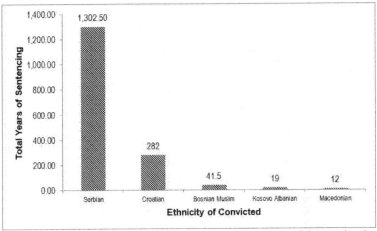

*Figure 2.* Sentencing at the ICTY based on the ethnicity of the convicted. This figure illustrates the disparity between the total number of years of sentencing handed down for each ethnic group.

Next, Figure 2 shows that defendants of Serbian ethnicity were sentenced to 1,302.5 out of 1,657 total years of sentencing (78.6%), leaving only 354.5 years (21.4%) for all of the other ethnic groups combined. Furthermore, since only 64 years of sentencing were handed down for crimes committed by non-Serbs against Serbs, the remaining 290.5 years were for crimes committed by non-Serbs against other non-Serbs, which is 354% more years sentenced than for crimes committed by non-Serbs against Serbs. This statistic is also alarming when one considers fighting between non-Serb groups made up only a tiny fraction of the civil war. Finally, Croatians made up 80% (282 years) of the remaining 354.5 years. Figure 3 shows the difference in years of sentencing between Bosnian Croatians and Croatians.

## Sentencing at the ICTY — III

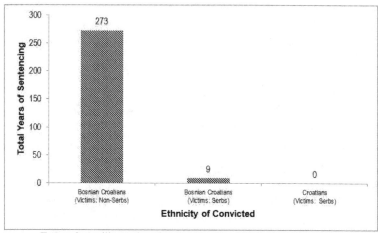

*Figure 3.* An illustration showing the disparity in the number of years of sentencing given to Croatians whose victims were non-Serbs and to those Croatians whose victims were Serbs.

As shown in Figure 3, Bosnian Croats were sentenced to serve 273 years in prison for crimes committed against non-Serbs — compared to only 9 years for crimes committed against Serbs — while no Croatians (involved in the Croatian conflict and whose victims were Serbs) were convicted of war crimes. Bosnian Croatians whose victims were non-Serbs were sentenced to almost 3,000% more years in prison than Croatians (from Bosnia and Croatia) whose victims were Serbs. Overall, Bosnian Croats received 100% of the 282 years of sentencing that were handed down to defendants of Croatian ethnicity.

### Ethnicity of Victims

Analyses were run to examine whether or not there was an association between victim ethnicity and verdict within the non-Serb groups (Hypothesis 3 (H3)). It was expected that those who committed crimes against non-Serbs would be more likely to be convicted than those who had committed crimes against Serbs. First, a Fisher's exact test was run to examine the association between victim ethnicity and verdict by using the entire population.

**Table 1**
**Verdict Totals Based on the Ethnicity of the Victims**

| | | Verdict | | | | Total | |
|---|---|---|---|---|---|---|---|
| | | Acquitted | | Convicted | | | |
| Victim Ethnicity | Non-Serbian | 9 | 9.6% | 85 | 90.4% | 94 | 100% |
| | | 50.0% | | 93.4% | | 86.2% | |
| | Serbian | 9 | 60.0% | 6 | 40.0% | 15 | 100% |
| | | 50.0% | | 6.6% | | 13.8% | |
| | Total | 18 | 16.5% | 91 | 83.5% | 109 | 100% |
| | | 100% | | 100% | | 100% | |

*Note*: 90.4% versus 40.0% respectively, p < .001, Fisher's exact test.

A significant difference in verdict emerged based on victim ethnicity: 90.4% versus 40.0% respectively, $p < .001$, according to Fisher's exact test. As seen in Table 1, 9 out of 94 defendants whose purported victims were non-Serbs were acquitted by the ICTY, which is a rate of 9.6% and a conviction rate of 90.4%, while 9 out of 15 defendants whose purported victims were Serbs were acquitted, for a 60.0% acquittal rate and a 40.0% conviction rate. Furthermore, 6 out of 91 total convictions (6.6%) were for crimes committed against Serbs, leaving 85 out of 91 convictions (93.4%) for crimes committed against non-Serbs. Next, a Chi-square was run to examine the association between conviction and acquittal rates of non-Serbs ($N = 42$) and the ethnicity of their victims.

## Table 2
## Verdict Totals of Non-Serbs
## Based on the Ethnicity of the Victims

| | | Verdict | | | | Total | |
| | | Acquitted | | Convicted | | | |
|---|---|---|---|---|---|---|---|
| **Victim Ethnicity** | Non-Serbian | 6 | 22.2% | 21 | 77.8% | **27** | 100% |
| | | 40.0% | | 77.8% | | 64.3% | |
| | Serbian | 9 | 60.0% | 6 | 40.0% | **15** | 100% |
| | | 60.0% | | 22.2% | | 35.7% | |
| | **Total** | **15** | 37.5% | **27** | 64.3% | **42** | 100% |
| | | 100% | | 100% | | 100% | |

*Note:* $\chi^2(1) = 5.994, p < .05$

Results from the Chi-square indicate a significant association between verdict and victim ethnicity for non-Serb defendants: $\chi^2(1) = 5.994$, $p = .014$. As seen in Table 2, 6 out of 27 total convictions (22.2%) were for crimes committed against Serbs, compared to 21 out of 27 convictions (77.8%) for crimes committed against non-Serbs. Furthermore, 6 out of 27 of the non-Serb defendants whose purported victims were non-Serbs were acquitted by the ICTY, which is an acquittal rate of 22.2% and a conviction rate of 77.8%. In comparison, 9 out of 15 non-Serb defendants whose purported victims were Serbs were acquitted, for a 60.0% acquittal rate and a 40.0% conviction rate — Conviction Rates: 77.8% compared to 40.0%; Acquittal Rates: 22.2% compared to 60.0%.

### Ethnicity of Defendants

To test Hypothesis 1 (H1), a Chi-square was run to examine the association between verdict and defendant ethnicity. To be more precise, it was conducted to test for differences between the verdicts of Bosnian Croats and the verdicts of the remaining non-Serbs.

### Table 3
### Verdict Totals Based on Ethnicity of the Defendants

| | | Verdict | | | | Total | |
| | | Acquitted | | Convicted | | | |
|---|---|---|---|---|---|---|---|
| **Defendant Ethnicity** | Remaining Non-Serb Groups | 11 | 57.9% | 8 | 42.1% | **19** | 100% |
| | | 73.3% | | 29.6% | | 45.2% | |
| | Bosnian Croat | 4 | 17.4% | 19 | 82.6% | **23** | 100% |
| | | 26.7% | | 70.4% | | 54.8% | |
| | **Total** | **15** | 37.5% | **27** | 64.3% | **42** | 100% |
| | | 100% | | 100% | | 100% | |

*Note:* $\chi^2(1) = 7.435, p < .01$

Results from the Chi-square indicate a significant association between verdict and defendant ethnicity for non-Serb defendants: $\chi^2(1) = 7.435, p = .006$. As seen in Table 4, 8 out of the 27 total convictions (29.6%) were against the 'remaining non-Serb groups', compared to 19 out of 27 (70.4%) for Bosnian Croats. Furthermore, 11 out of 19 of the 'remaining non-Serb' defendants were acquitted by the ICTY, which is an acquittal rate of 57.9% and a conviction rate of 42.1%. In comparison, 4 out of 23 Bosnian Croat defendants were acquitted, for a 17.4% acquittal rate and an 82.6% conviction rate — Conviction Rates: 42.1% compared to 82.6%; Acquittal Rates: 57.9% compared to 17.4%.

To note, 64 out of 67 Serbian defendants have been convicted at the ICTY, which is a 95.5% conviction rate and 4.5% acquittal rate. Further analyses indicated that there was not a significant difference between the conviction rates of Serbians and Bosnian Croats — although it was trending in that direction — (95.5% versus 82.6% respectively, $p = .068$, Fisher's exact test) — yet there was a significant difference between the conviction rates of Serbians and non-Serbians, $\chi^2(1) = 18.271$, $p < .001$. Next, a Chi-square was run to test for differences between the victims of Bosnian Croats and the victims of the remaining non-Serb groups.

### Table 4
### Victim Ethnicity of Bosnian Croats
### and the Remaining Non-Serb Groups

|  |  | Victim Ethnicity | | | | Total | |
|---|---|---|---|---|---|---|---|
|  |  | Non-Serbian | | Serbian | | | |
| Defendant Ethnicity | Remaining Non-Serb Groups | 5 | 26.3% | 14 | 73.7% | 19 | 100% |
|  |  | 18.5% |  | 93.3% |  | 42.5% |  |
|  | Bosnian Croat | 22 | 95.7% | 1 | 4.3% | 23 | 100% |
|  |  | 81.5% |  | 6.7% |  | 54.8% |  |
|  | Total | 27 | 64.3% | 15 | 35.7% | 42 | 100% |
|  |  | 100% |  | 100% |  | 100% |  |

Note: $\chi^2(1) = 21.787, p < .001$

As seen in Table 4, the results show a significant association between victim ethnicity and defendant ethnicity. Only 1 (4.3%) Bosnian Croat defendant was tried for committing crimes against Serbs while 22 (95.7%) were tried for crimes committed against non-Serbs, whereas 14 defendants from the remaining non-Serb groups were tried for committing crimes against Serbs (73.7%) and 5 (26.3%) were tried for committing crimes against non-Serbs. Another important statistic to note from Table 4 is that the ICTY tried more Bosnian Croats, 23 (54.8%), than the rest of the non-Serb groups combined, 19 (45.2%), which includes Bosnian Muslims, Kosovo Albanians, Croatians, and Macedonians. In addition, when examining the entire population, the association between defendant ethnicity and victim ethnicity becomes even more apparent.

### Table 5
### Association between
### Defendant Ethnicity and Victim Ethnicity

| | | Victim Ethnicity | | | | | |
| | | Non-Serbian | | Serbian | | Total | |
| --- | --- | --- | --- | --- | --- | --- | --- |
| | Remaining Non-Serb Groups | 5 | 26.3% | 14 | 73.7% | **19** | *100%* |
| | | *5.3%* | | *93.3%* | | *17.4%* | |
| | Bosnian Croat | 22 | *95.7%* | 1 | *4.3%* | **23** | *100%* |
| | | *23.4%* | | *6.7%* | | *21.1%* | |
| | Serbian | 67 | 100% | 0 | *0%* | 67 | *100%* |
| | | *71.3%* | | *0%* | | *61.5%* | |
| **Total** | | **94** | *86.2%* | **15** | *13.8%* | **109** | *100%* |
| | | *100%* | | *100%* | | *100%* | |

*(row label, left margin, rotated: Defendant Ethnicity)*

As indicated in Table 5, the victims of all but one of the Bosnian Croat and Serbian defendants (98.9%) were non-Serbian. Only 1 out of the 15 non-Serb defendants (6.7%) whose victims were Serbian was a Bosnian Croat, leaving the remaining 14 defendants (93.3%) coming from one of the 'remaining non-Serb groups'. Finally, 89 out of the 94 defendants (94.7%) whose victims were non-Serbs were Serbian or Bosnian Croat. Due to the significant association between defendant ethnicity and victim ethnicity, these variables were analyzed separately in the following logistic regression analyses. This was done to avoid multicollinearity, which occurs when there are high correlations among predictor variables which can lead to unreliable and unstable estimates of regression coefficients.[12]

Next, to further test H1 and H3, binary logistic regressions were conducted to test for effects of defendant ethnicity, victim ethnicity, age of defendants, and membership group (political/military) of defendants on the verdicts of the ICTY.

---

12   Taken from www.statisticalhorizons.com/multicollinearity

| | Model 1 | | | Model 2 | | | Model 3 | | | Model 4 | | |
| | DV: Verdict | | | DV: Verdict | | | DV: Verdict | | | DV: Verdict | | |
| | B | SE B | $e^B$ | B | SE B | $e^B$ | B | SE B | $e^B$ | B | SE B | $e^B$ |
|---|---|---|---|---|---|---|---|---|---|---|---|---|
| Age | -.025 | .031 | .975 | -.002 | .029 | .998 | -.023 | .032 | .977 | .002 | .028 | 1.002 |
| Membership Group | .303 | .862 | 1.354 | .407 | .887 | 1.502 | .248 | .906 | 1.282 | -.066 | .846 | .936 |
| Defendant Ethnicity 1 | 2.681 | .749 | 14.593** | — | — | — | — | — | — | — | — | — |
| Defendant Ethnicity 2 | — | — | — | 2.777 | .632 | 16.075** | — | — | — | — | — | — |
| Defendant Ethnicity: Remaining non-Serbian Groups (Reference Group) | — | — | — | — | — | — | — | — | — | — | — | — |
| Defendant Ethnicity: Remaining non-Serbian | — | — | — | — | — | — | — | — | — | — | — | — |
| Defendant Ethnicity: Serbian | — | — | — | — | — | — | 3.560 | .830 | 35.161** | — | — | — |
| Defendant Ethnicity: Bosnian-Croat | — | — | — | — | — | — | 1.861 | .724 | 6.431* | — | — | — |
| Victim Ethnicity | — | — | — | — | — | — | — | — | — | 2.652 | .675 | 14.177** |
| Constant | 1.644 | | | -.257 | | | 2.468 | | | -.511 | | |
| $\chi^2$ | 19.267** | | | 22.853** | | | 26.669** | | | 18.168** | | |
| df | 3 | | | 3 | | | 4 | | | 3 | | |

*$p < .01$, **$p < .001$

*Note:* (N = 109); Verdict: Acquitted = 0, Convicted = 1; Membership Group: Non-Political = 0, Political = 1; Defendant Ethnicity 1: Non-Serbian = 0, Serbian = 1; Defendant Ethnicity 2: Remaining Non-Serbian Groups = 0, Serbian/Bosnian-Croatian = 1; Victim Ethnicity: Serbian = 0; Non-Serbian = 1.

Overall, the models were statistically significant, Model 1: $\chi^2(3) = 19.267$, $p < .001$; Model 2: $\chi^2(3) = 22.853$, $p < .001$; Model 3: $\chi^2(4) = 26.669$, $p < .001$; and Model 4: $\chi^2(3) = 18.168$, $p < .001$. Model 1 explained 27.4% (Nagelkerke $R2$) of the variance in conviction rate and correctly classified 83.5% of cases. Model 2 explained 32.0% (Nagelkerke $R2$) of the variance in conviction rate and correctly classified 86.2% of cases. Model 3 explained 36.7% (Nagelkerke $R2$) of the variance in conviction rate and correctly classified 88.1% of cases. Model 4 explained 25.9% (Nagelkerke $R2$) of the variance in conviction rate and correctly classified 86.2% of cases.

As Table 6 shows, defendants of Serbian ethnicity were significantly more likely to be convicted than non-Serbs ($OR = 14.59$), after controlling for age and membership group. When Serbians and Bosnian Croats were combined into one group, they were also significantly more likely to be convicted than the 'remaining non-Serb groups' ($OR = 16.08$). Furthermore, Bosnian Croat ($OR = 6.43$) and Serbian ($OR = 35.16$) defendants were significantly more likely to be convicted than defendants from the 'remaining non-Serb groups' after controlling for age and membership group. Lastly, defendants whose victims were non-Serb were 14 times more likely to be convicted than defendants whose victims were Serbian ($OR = 14.177$). The results support H1 and H3.

Finally, a one-way analysis of variance (ANOVA) and a t-test were performed to test the hypothesis (H2) that Bosnian Croats were more likely to receive longer sentences for similar crimes than those who were convicted from the 'remaining non-Serb groups', as well as the more general claim that there was an association between defendant ethnicity and sentencing at the IC-TY. The result of the ANOVA was significant, $F(2, 88) = 4.330$, $p = .016$, $\eta2 = .09$. However, due to the small population size of convictions from the 'remaining non-Serb groups' ($N = 7$), the test had low statistical power which, therefore, considerably reduced the chance of detecting a true effect. Nonetheless, the result showed that convicted defendants of Serbian ethnicity ($M$ = 20.35, $SD$ = 13.20) were more likely to be given longer sentences than convicted defendants from the 'remaining non-Serb groups' ($M$ = 9.50, $SD$ = 6.53). The differences in sentencing between Bosnian Croats ($M$ = 14.84, $SD$ = 6.36) and the 'remaining non-Serbian' group and between Bosnian Croats and Serbs were not significant, yet they were trending in that direction. Next, a t-test was performed to test the difference in sentencing between Serbs and non-Serbs. The analysis indicated that there was a significant association between sentencing and defendant ethnicity, $t(89)$ = -2.692; $p < .01$. In sum, Serbians ($M$ = 20.35, $SD$ = 13.20) were more likely to receive longer sentences than non-Serbians ($M$ = 13.13, $SD$ = 6.74), which supports the general claim of H2 that there was an association between defendant ethnicity and sentencing at the ICTY.

## Discussion

This study examined whether ethnicity was associated with case outcomes (verdict and sentencing) in order to obtain new insights on the issue of bias. The results strongly suggest that defendant ethnicity *and* victim ethnicity shaped case outcomes (verdict and sentencing) at the ICTY. The results support the claim of bias by the Tribunal — against both Serbs and, to a lesser (yet still significant) extent, Bosnian Croats. In general, Bosnian Croats have been left out of the discussion of possible bias by the Tribunal, however Slobodan Praljak's suicide has again raised the question of bias by the Tribunal and forced the Bosnian Croats into the discussion.

## Ethnicity Versus Other Factors

Although the results of this study reveal that ethnicity influenced case outcomes, other important factors were also taken into account such as: the type of charges that were pressed; the crimes committed; the overall scope of the crimes; the level of involvement in crimes (direct or indirect); the number of victims; the defendant's gender and age; the locations of crimes and/or conflicts that the accused was involved in; the defendant's group membership (Political, Military, or Paramilitary); and the defendant's position of power within the group. Overall, none of these factors were associated with verdict or sentencing. In fact, the *only* factors that predicted verdict and sentencing were defendant ethnicity and victim ethnicity.

For instance, when comparing convictions at the ICTY by ethnicity, the results showed that defendants of Serbian ethnicity were almost fifteen (15) times more likely to be convicted than defendants of non-Serbian ethnicity, and that the defendants — regardless of ethnicity — whose victims were non-Serb were 14 times more likely to be convicted than defendants whose victims were Serbian. Furthermore, Bosnian Croats were over six (6) times more likely to be convicted than defendants from one of the 'remaining non-Serb groups', while Serbian defendants were inordinately thirty-five (35) times more likely to be convicted than defendants from one of the 'remaining non-Serb groups'. Also, only sixty-four (64) out of 1,657 years of sentencing (3.86%) were handed down for crimes committed against Serbs. Furthermore, the conviction rate of Serbs at the ICTY was 95.5%, compared to 82.6% for Bosnian Croats and 42.1% for the remaining non-Serbs groups.

To put the ICTY cases into a domestic perspective, a recent study shows that African-Americans are incarcerated at 5.1 times the rate of whites in state prisons.[13] In addition, a recent report

---

13    http://www.sentencingproject.org/wp-content/uploads/2016/06/The-Color-of-Justice-Racial-and-Ethnic-Disparity-in-State-Prisons.pdf

found that African-American males received sentences that averaged 19.1% longer than white males for similar offences.[142] In comparison, Serbs received sentences that averaged 55% longer than non-Serbs for similar offences. When comparing Serbs and Bosnian Croats to defendants from the 'remaining non-Serb groups', the disparity becomes even more apparent. Bosnian Croats received sentences (on average) 56% longer than those convicted from the 'remaining non-Serb groups', while Serbs received sentences that averaged 114% longer than the convicted from the 'remaining non-Serb groups'.

## Bosnian Croatians Versus "Croatian Croatians"

Bosnian Croats were sentenced to 366% more years in prison than Bosnian Muslims, Kosovo Albanians, and (Croatian) Croatians *combined*. Furthermore, twenty-three (23) Bosnian Croatians were prosecuted at the ICTY compared to only three (3) (Croatian) Croatians, or 667% more. This is significantly disproportionate to the actual conflicts in Yugoslavia as the conflict between the Croatian government and the Serbs (from the Krajina region) lasted around 4.5 years (March 1991–November 1995) with tens of thousands of victims on all sides. In comparison, the Croat-Muslim conflict in Bosnia and Herzegovina lasted less than a year and a half (October 1992–February 1994) with significantly fewer victims. Furthermore, Bosnian Croats and Bosnian Muslims were allies and fought together against Bosnian Serbs before and after their aforementioned conflict — in some areas of Bosnia even during it (Woodward 2000: 244). The time frame, combat zone, and crimes committed were much greater in scope in the Croat-Serb (Croatian) conflict than in the

---

14   https://www.ussc.gov/sites/default/files/pdf/research-and-publications/research-publications/2017/20171114_Demographics.pdf

Croat-Muslim (Bosnian) conflict, which includes the gravest of crimes — such as 'ethnic cleansing'.

Parenti (2000: 156) notes that

> what is still not widely understood in the West is that most of the ethnic cleansing throughout the former Yugoslavia was perpetrated not *by* the Serbs but *against* them. More than one million Serbs were driven from their ancestral homes in the breakaway republics.

Furthermore, Herman and Peterson (2010: 82) state that "Operation Storm drove some 250,000 ethnic Serbs out of the Krajina.... killing several thousand, including several hundred women and children." They further add that this "ethnic cleansing of 250,000 Serbs was the single largest event of its kind in the Balkan wars." Unfortunately, no one was convicted by the ICTY for this war crime — nor for similar crimes that were committed much earlier in the conflict, including those of Miro Bajramović.

Bajramović, a former Croatian policeman, claimed that in September 1991 his unit carried out orders to "perform ethnic cleansing" in Gospić. He estimated that in less than a month he and his unit had "liquidated some 90–100 people" and that he was personally responsible for the death of 86 people (Johnstone 2002: 29–30). He implicated Tomislav Merčep, a paramilitary leader turned politician, as well as his "gang of killers" known as the "Croatian Knights," during his confession and disclosed their killing operations in Gospić, Lika, and the Pakrac Valley (Johnstone 2002: 29-30).

Six months after Bajramović's revelations, three former Croatian soldiers risked their lives by taking evidence of these massacres, including videotapes of the killings, to the ICTY. The soldiers confessed to witnessing:

> scores of abductions and killings in and around the town of Gospic... [and claimed that hundreds of eth-

nic Serbs] were executed and buried in mass graves around Gospic by the Croatian Army, paramilitary groups and the police. They also contend that documents they have turned over to The Hague implicate senior Croatian officials, including Defense Minister Gojko Susak, in the killings (Hedges 1998).

These revelations sparked virtually no reaction by the ICTY, which did not indict any of the individuals implicated in the killings nor did it conduct a serious investigation into the matter (Johnstone 2002: 31).

These incongruities are highlighted not to dispute the verdicts of the ICTY but to shine a light on the lack of justice for certain victims. Clearly, the Tribunal needed at least some convictions of *non-Serbs* to at least appear to be fair, yet it could not go after the U.S. government's main allies in the conflicts: Bosnian Muslims, Kosovo Albanians, and (Croatian) Croatians, whose victims were primarily Serbs. Unfortunately for the Bosnian Croats, this meant they had to be 'thrown under the bus'. There is no disputing that every side was victimized and each group had its own perpetrators, as even the verdicts at the ICTY — however disproportionate — demonstrate. What should be of concern, however, is the manner in which the Tribunal carried out justice and the possible repercussions of such a policy.

**Limitations and Future Directions**

There were some limitations to conducting a quantitative study on this subject, mainly due to the complexities and uniqueness of the institution. For instance, the Tribunal often made changes to its rules of procedure, sometimes even after the trials had already begun. Furthermore, the defense was often not allowed to cross-examine witnesses; large portions of trial proceedings were held either in private or in closed session; and the Tribunal frequently redacted testimonies and censored defendants. Finally, the Prosecution "made widespread use of the IC-

TY's Rule 92*bis*, which allows witnesses to submit written statements, and for these statements to be presented as evidence to the court. The consequence is that statements can be admitted as evidence without the witness appearing for cross-examination" (Laughland 2004: 153). In some cases, this resulted in hundreds of thousands of pages of evidence. Therefore, there were many factors that either could not be tested or were unfeasible for inclusion in the analyses.

The literature on the ICTY is vast; however, research that focuses on bias is still lacking. The present study should help fill this void; nevertheless, more research needs to be conducted on this issue. Directions for future analysis could include comparative studies of cases, specifically ones that compare Serb cases with similar non-Serb cases. Finally, more research needs to be conducted on the Tribunal's impact on peace-building and reconciliation in the region.

**Conclusion**

The possible consequences of a biased international court could be serious, but perhaps nowhere greater than the region in question here. For instance, a biased court could lead to a contrived historical record of the war, which could in turn contribute to a denial of responsibility by certain groups; encourage revisionist narratives that will disavow victims and marginalize groups; and adversely affect reconciliation and peace-building efforts in the region. A prime example of the animosity that exists in the region occurred during a recent FIFA World Cup qualifying match between Kosovo and Croatia (October 6, 2016), when fans of both teams chanted 'Kill the Serbs' and other fascist slogans (Mejdini and Milekic 2016).

It has been decades since the conflicts ended, yet after all the time that has passed "the bitter resentment, grief, hatred and distrust — emotions that block reconciliation" (Johnstone 2015: 86)

— have changed little for the better, if at all. Of course, there are many contributing factors for the lack of reconciliation in the Balkans; however, the absence of justice being served in a fair and balanced manner certainly will not alleviate this problem. On the contrary, it will most likely exacerbate it.

Jovan Milojevich

## References

Akrivoulis, Dimitrios E. 2017. "Memory, Forgiveness and Unfinished Justice in the Former Yugoslavia." *Journal of Balkan and Near Eastern Studies* 19, no. 4: 366-387

Bandow, Doug. 2017, Jan. 24. "Bungled Intervention in Kosovo Risks Unraveling: A new deal needed for peace," *Forbes.* Retrieved from https://www.forbes.com/sites/dougbandow/2017/01/24/bungled-intervention-in-kosovo-risks-unraveling-a-new-deal-needed-for-peace/#572b2aac1b16.

Bardos, Gordon N. 2013. "Trials and Tribulations: Politics as Justice at the ICTY. *World Affairs*, 176, no. 3: 15-24.

Black, Christopher. 2000. "The International Criminal Tribunal for the Former Yugoslavia: Impartial?", *Mediterranean Quarterly*, 11, no. 2: 29–40.

Boyd-Barrett, Oliver. 2016. *Western mainstream media and the Ukraine crisis: A study in conflict propaganda.* Taylor & Francis, United Kingdom.

Brock, Peter. 1996. "The Hague: Experiment in Orwellian justice." *Mediterranean Quarterly*, 7: 55-74.

Brock, Peter. 2005. *Media Cleansing: Dirty Reporting — Journalism and Tragedy in Yugoslavia*, GM Books, Los Angeles.

Ching, Carrie. 2014. *Strange border kidnappings in Kosovo: Correspondent confidential.* Documentary. Directed by Carrie Ching. Los Angeles: VICE Media LLC, 2014. Retrieved from https://www.youtube.com/watch?v=nUzdXoRH2H8

Clark, Janine Natalya. 2011. The impact question: the ICTY and the restoration and maintenance of peace. In B. Swart, A. H. J. Swart, A. Zahar, and G. Sluiter (Eds.), *The legacy of the International Criminal Tribunal for the former Yugoslavia:* 55-80. Oxford University Press, Oxford.

Del Ponte, Carla, Chuck Sudetic, and Bruno Amato. 2008. *La caccia: Io ei criminali di guerra.* Feltrinelli Traveller, Italy.

Dickson, Tiphaine and Alexandar Jokic. 2006. "Hear no evil, see no evil, speak no evil: The unsightly Milosevic case", *International Journal for the Semiotics of Law*, 19, no. 4: 355-387

"Evidence of Bosnian army crimes emerges in video," *B92,* February 10, 2007. Retrieved from https://www.b92.net/eng/news/region.php?yyyy=2007&mm=02&dd=10&nav_id=39542

Hayden, Robert M. 1999. "Biased justice: Humanrightsism and the International Criminal Tribunal for the Former Yugoslavia", *Cleveland State Law Review*, 47: 549

Hedges, Chris. 1998, Feb. 15. "Threats Worry 3 Who Tied Croatian Army to Atrocities," *The New York Times,* Retrieved from https://www.nytimes.com/1998/02/15/world/threats-worry-3-who-tied-croatian-army-to-atrocities.html

Herman, Edward S., and David Peterson. 2010. *The Politics of Genocide*, NYU Press, New York.

Johnstone, Diana. 2000. "Humanitarian war: Making the crime fit the punishment." In Tariq Ali (ed), *Masters of the Universe? Nato's Balkan Crusade,* Verso, London: 147-170.

Johnstone, Diana. 2002. *Fool's Crusade: Yugoslavia, NATO and Western Delusions*, Monthly Review Press, New York.

Johnstone, Diana. 2015. *Queen of Chaos: The Misadventures of Hillary Clinton.* CounterPunch, Petrolia.

Laughland, John. 2007. *Travesty: The Trial of Slobodan Milosevic and the Corruption of International Justice,* Pluto Press, London.

Mandel, Michael. 2004. *How America Gets Away with Murder: Illegal Wars, Collateral Damage and Crimes against Humanity,* Pluto Press, London and Ann Arbor, MI.

Mejdini Fatjona, and Sven Milekic. 2016, Oct. 7. "Kosovo-Croatia match marred by anti-Serbian chants," *Balkan Insight.* Retrieved from http://www.balkaninsight.com/en/article/kovoso-croatia-football-match-emerge-racial-slurs-10-07-2016

Milojevich, Jovan. 2018. "Justified Grievances? A Quantitative Examination of Case Outcomes at the International Tribunal for the For-

Jovan Milojevich

mer Yugoslavia (ICTY)." *Journal of Balkan and Near Eastern Studies* (2018): 1-24.

Saxon, Dan. 2005. "Exporting Justice: Perceptions of the ICTY among the Serbian, Croatian, and Muslim Communities in the Former Yugoslavia." *Journal of Human Rights* 4, no.4: 559-572.

Scharf, Michael P. 1997. *Balkan Justice: The Story behind the First International War Crimes Trial since Nuremberg.* Carolina Academic Press, Durham, N.C.

Scharf, Michael P. 2002. "The International Trial of Slobodan Milosevic: Real Justice or Realpolitik." *ILSA Journal of International and Comparative Law* Vol. 8: 389.

Schindler, John R. 2007. *Unholy Terror: Bosnia, Al-Qa'ida, and the Rise of Global Jihad*, Zenith Press, St. Paul, MN.

Smith, Charles A. 2012. *The Rise and Fall of War Crimes Trials: From Charles I to Bush II*, Cambridge University Press, Cambridge.

Szamuely, George. 2013. *Bombs for Peace: NATO's Humanitarian War on Yugoslavia*, Amsterdam University Press, Amsterdam.

Thomas, Raju G. C. 2000. "The US, Nato and the UN: Lessons from Yugoslavia." *Global Dialogue, 2*, no. 2: 52.

Thomas, Raju G. C. 2003. "Wars, Humanitarian Intervention, and International Law: Perceptions and Reality", In Raju G. C. Thomas (ed), *Yugoslavia Unraveled: Sovereignty, Self-determination, Intervention*, Lexington Books, United States.

Woodward, Susan L. 1995. *Balkan Tragedy: Chaos and Dissolution after the Cold War*, Brookings Institution Press, Washington D. C.

# AFTERWORD:

## CARICATURE

by

Peter Brock

*Hang 'em first. Try 'em later.*
— Judge Roy Bean

*Summum ius summa iniuria.*
*(Extreme justice is extreme injustice.)*
— Cicero

This book extinguishes a quarter-century of caricature after five civil wars in the "bloody, bloody Balkans"[1] — and it proclaims moral victors as well as damnable villains.

Certainly the authors of *The Hague Tribunal, Srebrenica, and the Miscarriage of Justice* will be branded "genocide deniers" by Orwellian practitioners at The Hague courts who succeeded in using tribunal voodoo and selective prosecution to seed future wars from a region where a few short centuries ago Dutch pirates stashed booty and evaded justice!

The unpronounceable "ICTY" acronym[2] designates the 87 supposed arbiters — 68 men and 19 women — who concocted

---

1    *Media Cleansing: Dirty Reporting* by the author, GMBooks, Los Angeles (2005-06), p. ix.

2    The less tedious acronym "ICTY" (for International Criminal Tribunal [for the former] Yugoslavia is used instead of the official and cumbersome 12-word title with 31 vowels and 44 consonants: "The International Tribunal To Adjudicate War Crimes Committed In The Former Yugoslavia."

duplicities and hoaxes against the late "former" (politically-corrected) ... Yugoslavia.[3]

Piously attired in appropriate blood-red robes — contrasting the insipid, pale-blue helmets of UN mercenaries — the presiding "excellencies" conjured the demons of Versailles and Nuremburg to provoke Euro-*ethnocracies* to obligingly burn these judges in effigy.[4]

The Hague Tribunal, presiding over this the grim burlesque of "impunity and transitional justice," mesmerized itself into going on a *jihad* against the South Slavs — and the West.

Ninety men and one woman got lengthy prison sentences.[5] They were judged on little more than their nationalities. Most of the condemned were portrayed as reincarnations of Gavrilo Princip. It was a scandalously cruel joke.

The Hague Tribunal staged marathon trials for higher-ups (Milošević, Karadžić, Mladić), but the flamboyant Serbian radical Vojislav Šešelj left the ICTY judges and inept prosecutors tongue-tied and spluttering. A law professor himself, Šešelj had surrendered voluntarily to The Hague Tribunal in 2003. He awaited a trial that was delayed for more than four years. He had to go on a month-long hunger-strike to win the right to defend himself. He was unpredictable and freely resorted to full-throated obscenities. He shredded Carla Del Ponte's 99 prosecu-

---

3    http://www.icty.org/en/about/chambers/judges; An abundance of American participation guided the formation of the ICTY from the beginning, although U.S. constitutional law is not fundamentally prescribed in lieu of official tribunal law. Even so, American lawyers participated on defense teams and served in numerous roles in The Hague and ICTY machinery.

4    https://wonkawbih.wordpress.com/2018/02/15/b03/. The term is deservedly dredged in the aftermath of Yugoslavia's uncivil dismemberment.

5    Former Bosnian Serb Vice President Biljana Plavšić (now 89) plea-bargained for an 11-year term and was released after six years from a Swedish prison.

tion witnesses and 1,400 trial exhibits in connection to multiple "war crimes" throughout 175 trial days.

Over the course of thirteen years, the prosecutors became obsessed with Šešelj's repeated use of "Greater Serbia," which Del Ponte alleged constituted incitement and abetted crimes against humanity. Co-prosecutor Christine Dahl, during the recitation of the itemized charges in 2007, lamely called Šešelj a "scandalmaster and skillful politician."[6]

But he had already won before the opening shot was fired.

Šešelj, who stands over 6' 5" tall, hijacked the courtroom with persistent controversy; he harangued judges and lawyers alike throughout the volatile proceedings; and he even identified "protected" witnesses. The court declared him repeatedly in contempt — and Šešelj finally topped off his mockery of the court by not calling *any* defense witnesses!

Šešelj kept provoking Danish Judge Frederik Harhoff until he displayed his bias in favor of Šešelj's conviction. That got Harhoff to disqualify himself, so he was removed from the case.

Chief Judge Jean-Claude Lionetti (France), Mandiaye Niang (Senegal), and Flavia Lattanzi (Italy) could not wait to eject him from The Hague and send him back to Belgrade after Šešelj said he had cancer and that oncological examinations performed on him at The Hague had been bungled!

Šešelj, now 64, returned to Serbia in time to lead his party's electoral campaign to win 23 seats in Parliament. Ultimately, he was acquitted in 2016. He rebuffs prosecution attempts to renew appeals.

---

6    "The Scandal-Packed Spectacle of Vojislav Šešelj's Trial," *Balkan Transitional Justice,* March 30, 2016.

## 'Justice Delayed Is Justice Denied'

Once feckless appeals have been denied, lengthy prison sentences prove to be crueler than execution. Barred from pronouncing the death sentence, the ICTY resorted to unusually long prison terms that prove to be less humane than hanging. Advanced old age, sickness, and suicide behind bars are settling most scores.

The ICTY, ever devising new infrastructure and bureaucracy and setting precedents for UN tribunals, psychically re-invented itself to produce *The Mechanism for International Criminal Tribunals* (MICT) to tighten-up loose ends, cover-up judicial cracks, and fix the leaky pipes of injustice.

Ever vigilant for vulnerabilities in convictions that may cause later challenges, this sinister-sounding Mechanism functions as a "S.W.A.T. Team," on call to squelch surprises that might taint The Hague's principal "industry" — international "justice."

This Mechanism is wielded faster than Madame Dafarge, the legendary *tricoteuse,* knitted to keep pace with the executions by *guillotine* during the French Revolution.[7]

(*Caricature*! Remember?)

Of course, "Srebrenica" is the notorious Bosnian town that seized the starring role from dozens of neighboring hamlets that were once inhabited by Bosnian Serbs and Croats — who became "cleansed." The ICTY lexicon remains deliberately obfuscated, as it always was.

Srebrenica's celebrated *genicidalista* Naser Orić — the love-child of kangaroo courts in Bosnia and The Hague — was finally "sprung" from prison on technicalities in 2017 for his conviction

---

7    *Tricoteuse* is the fictional name for Thérèse Dafarge and her bloodthirsty French crones who knitted nonstop during hasty executions by guillotine in Dickens' *Tale of Two Cities.*

of loss of command and control of his thugs who torched over fifty non-Muslim villages and who kidnapped, molested, and killed more than 3,300 Serbs who got in his way in July 1995.[8]

Overall, Serbs got stiffer prison terms even though former UN Secretary-General Kofi Annan did take some blame: "[W]e made serious errors of judgement, rooted in a philosophy of impartiality and non-violence which, however admirable, was unsuited to the conflict in Bosnia... [T]he tragedy of Srebrenica will haunt our history forever."[9]

Orić, in his twenties when he became a Bosnian Army brigadier, was sentenced to a mere two years in prison. He sported a buzz-cut on exiting the UN court, and his T-shirted bodyguards led cheers of *Never forget Naser is a hero!* as his fans went wild. Orić still gives interviews, never misses photo-ops, basks in rock-star notoriety, and enjoys life (at 52) in his native Srebrenica and in his summer home at Kladanj. After the war, he dabbled with fitness salons. He maintains his bad-boy buff and is always ready for a TV appearance so he can show off his passable self-taught English.

Srebrenica remains sacrosanct with its internationally celebrated cemetery which holds several thousand Muslim grave-markers that multiply atop fewer and fewer corpses — or parts of them — transferred from...where? (No one knows how many Serbs and Croats are buried there — or Bosniaks either!)

Flawed claims that 10,000 Bosniaks perished in reprisal killings have preëmpted inquiries by prompting the question: *reprisal ... for what?*

---

8   *Media Cleansing, ibid*, p. 119; *TRIAL International* (Geneva, Switzerland), April 2018; *see also* https://www.britannica.com/event/Srebrenica-massacre.

9   July 11, 2005. Press conference announcing Annan's retirement.

But the number fell from 10,000 to 7,000 after many "missing" Bosnian Army soldiers and civilians showed up on new voter registration lists.[10]

Two decades later, without waiting for further guesses, the U.S. Congress was inspired to gavel-up and declare that over 8,000 Bosniaks at Srebrenica had been killed — officially.[11]

(More *caricature*.)

## What price? What costs?

If twentieth century history means anything, everything re-ignites. Then, indictments, jailings, and prosecutions by crusading judiciary re-treads and pack-journalists encamped at The Hague can be expected to continue indefinitely.

The ICTY's final 25-year scorecard boasts:[12]

- 161 persons indicted;
- 90 sentencings;
- 37 cases dropped;
- 19 acquitted;
- 13 referred;
- 2 pending.

One thing is certain: 100,000 lost lives in Balkan wars in the last three decades are just as obscene to contemplate and as indecent to debate.

Meanwhile, the financial backers of the UN are hardly blinking at disbursements for mandated court systems and associated costs that soar into the *BILLIONS!*[13]

---

10   http://www.icty.org/specials/srebrenica.

11   https://www.congress.gov/bill/114th-congress/house-resolution.

12   *http://www.icty.org/sites/icty.org/files/images/content/ Infographic_facts_figures_en.pdf.*

- ICTY expenditures mushroomed 500-fold after it started work in 1992–93, and it eventually began netting big fish and assorted small-fry after an outlay of $1 billion-plus in its first decade of existence.
- The ICTR (Rwanda Tribunal) matched with $1 billion for 91 suspects at a cost of $11 million each.
- The monstrous pay-out by the International Criminal Court (ICC) tops everyone at $1 billion for just two guilty verdicts in its first twelve years of existence![14] The ICC's budget is designed to top $200 million as it paves the way for future annual spending-sprees!

Indisputably, the ICC glitters atop The Hague's skyline, and it banks on the indefinite mandate it received to investigate crimes, apprehend suspects, and try cases of genocide, war crimes, crimes against humanity, and crimes of aggression.

True, the ICC's sticker-shock is mind-boggling:

> They say you can't put a price on justice, but $500 million per African warlord seems high by any standard. And what do judges do all day? You don't have to be a legal expert to figure that the preventive effect of convicting two warlords in 12 years doesn't exactly leave international war criminals shaking in their boots.[15]

---

(Footnote continued from previous page)

13  *See* http://djilp.org/1877/the-comparative-cost-of-justice-at-the-icc/ for various sources about the ICTY, ICTR (International Criminal Tribunal for Rwanda), ICC, International Court of Justice.

14  *Ten years, $900 Million, One verdict: Does the ICC cost too much?* University of Bedfordshire, March 14, 2012.

15  https://www.forbes.com/sites/daviddavenport/2014/03/12/international-criminal-court-12-years-1-billion-2-convictions.

## 'Out of Africa' by 'Moonlight'

Other UN judges busy themselves at The Hague's International Court of Justice (ICJ). They don't sit on either the Yugoslav or Rwandan tribunals, and they don't try ICC cases.

But several ICJ judges with flexible (*i.e.*, "slack") dockets are cashing in with hefty moonlighting fees for "arbitrations" — like the eye-popping $400,000 paid to the UK's Richard Greenwood for his work on two out of nine cases![16]

Originally, all ICJ judges were paid the same as other UN judges whose travel, hotels, and other expenses were also amply covered. They now receive about $230,000 annually with varying perks. ICC judges get about $200,000 annually.

But they want lots more: a 26% increase in annual salary PLUS retroactive compensation, pension increases, and damages that could run into the millions![17]

The president of the ICJ receives a special bonus of $15,000. And, judges at the ICJ sign on for nine years with subsequent eligibility for pensions worth 50% of their annual base salaries. Everything is tax free.[18]

Former ICTY judges and prosecutors populate the long lines of judicial exes who are waiting for "election" to various ICJ/ICC *ad hoc* benches.

---

16   https://www.dailyexcelsior.com/greenwood-and-several-icj-judges-worked-as-arbitrators-report"... Greenwood worked as an arbitrator in at least nine investment arbitration cases during his tenure at the ICJ. He was paid more than $400,000 in fees in two of those nine cases... A total of more than $1 Million in fees was paid to ICJ judges in nine of the 90 such cases that were compiled by the Canada-based International Institute for Sustainable Development.

17   *International Center for Transitional Justice Newsletter (online),* January 19, 2019.

18   https://www.forbes.com/sites/daviddavenport/2014/03/12/international-criminal-court-12-years-1-billion-2-convictions.

The ICC now has eighteen judges, a thousand employees, and an annual budget pushing $200 million which can only grow with its permanent mandate and with judgeships worth more than treasure chests full of *doubloons* dug up from Dutch beaches.

Here is a dubious assessment that comes from an ICC employee who is now facing a 10% ICC workforce reduction:

> Horrible management. People are not trained to manage others and generally don't know what they are doing. There's no real recourse if you're working with a mean or unsupportive colleague, and it's real easy for sub-par people to maintain their jobs, which encourages people (including excellent people) to become sub-par.[19]

All is overseen in-house by the ICC's Assembly of States Parties which meets annually.

After the completion two years ago of its new billion-dollar ten-story steel-and-glass "monument," the ICC categorized "situations" — not "investigations" or "cases" — in some African nations as well as in the country of Georgia on the east coast of the Black Sea.

A month ago, the Philippines became the latest country to leave the ICC. *Amnesty International* called the departure "cynical."[20]

Burundi was the first member to leave the ICC in 2017, which followed an investigation opened into its own human rights abuses. South Africa and Gambia are ready to follow amidst doubts arising in other countries on the Dark Continent.

---

19  *https://www.glassdoor.com/Reviews/International-Criminal-Court-ICC-Reviews.*

20  http://time.com/5553323/philippines-leaves-international-criminal-court/

Russia withdrew from the ICC in 2016 due to issues in The Crimea. The United States, China, and India are among other major nations that are not members.

The architectural illusion projected by the new, palatial ICC headquarters in The Hague is unmistakable: Justice at The Hague must be *transparent!* if not publicly accountable.

Certainly, justice at The Hague is not easy to get used to in Common Law countries.

The ICC's past focus on Africa and less-wealthy, less-sophisticated nations was more the honing of intentions to net bigger fish in the wealthy West, such as the U.S., UK and Western Europe where there are established judicial intricacies. Meanwhile, African countries are less patient, they are flexing more muscle, and they are energizing the exodus from the ICC.

How vulnerable are venerable Western institutions?

Chief Prosecutor Fatou Bensouda of Gambia claimed that a long-threatened ICC investigation into war crimes that American military personnel may have committed in Afghanistan was being obstructed.

The State Department revoked Gambian Bensouda's U.S. visa in April, and it added: "The United States will take the necessary steps to protect its sovereignty and to protect our people from unjust investigation and prosecution by the International Criminal Court."[21]

She countered that the ICC had "an independent and impartial mandate" under the court's founding Rome Statute of 1998, and that she would "continue to undertake that statutory duty with utmost commitment and professionalism, without fear or favor."

---

21 "Trump Administration revokes visa of International Criminal Court prosecutor"; https://www.latimes.com/world/la-fg-hague-icc-prosecutor-visa-revoked.

She was recently allowed entry into the U.S. but only to deliver a routine speech before the U.N. Security Council, provided, however, that she didn't push her investigation of alleged American "war crimes" during the Afghanistan war.

The ICC subsequently put an end to Bensouda's grandstanding by announcing that neither she nor the ICC would be making any official Afghanistan probes.

# POST SCRIPT

by

Jean Toschi Marazzani Visconti

When the first clashes began in Yugoslavia in the early 1990s, a group of people, each of whom was motivated by different reasons, gathered in Italy to create a communications network in order to provide accurate information to counter the violent anti-Serbian media campaign.

The members of this group were against the dissolution of the Yugoslav Federation, the separation of the invidual republics, and against the subsequent Western intervention in Yugoslavia, which was by then composed of only Serbia and Montenegro.

The group called itself Yugoslav Coordination. Later, it became an NGO. Thanks to a legacy bequeathed by Giuseppe Torre, the group's Secretary, Andrea Martocchia, was able to establish the eponymous Giuseppe Torre Award, which honors its generous benefactor.

The purpose of this award was to recognize the best essays on the subject of the International Criminal Tribunal for the former Yugoslavia (the "ICTY"). Invitations for submissions were extended to journalists, criminal lawyers, law students, and university professors; however, the substantial award failed to elicit a strong response from Europeans. Submissions did arrive from the U.S., Canada, and Italy.

In October 2018, the jury met in Rome. The three members, Aldo Bernardini (professor emeritus of Teramo University and essayist), Chiara Vitucci (Caserta University law professor) and I agreed to award the prize *ex aequo* to Stefan Karganović for his essay *The ICTY and Srebrenica* and to Jovan Milojevich for *When Justice Fails: Re-raising the Question of Ethnic Bias at the International Criminal Tribunal for the Former Yugoslavia* (ICTY). Karganović's text clearly explains the procedural inconsistencies that arose in the ICTY, even when it dealt with accusations of genocide for the events that took place in Srebrenica. His observations on the behavior of judges and prosecutors are particularly interesting, because the prosecutors presented and the judges likewise accepted photocopies of documents, which could have been falsified in order to support charges of Serbian guilt. In *When Justice Fails*, Jovan Milojevich performed a valuable statistical analysis on the severity and length of sentences meeted out by The Hague Tribunal in relation to the ethnicity of the defendants (Bosnian Serb and Bosnian Croatian) for crimes committed against Bosnian Muslims. The two essays complement each other and describe important aspects of the ICTY's system for the administration of justice in The Hague.

In May 1993, I was travelling from Pale to Belgrade by car. The chauffeur took a road that led to Bratunac, which lies on the Drina River in the Srebrenica region. The route our driver took led us through an incredible series of destroyed villages. Around twenty kilometers from the Drina, we were stopped by soldiers from the Drina Corps who were patrolling a village where some houses had been set on fire and whose inhabitants had been killed. They prudently asked us to wait until they were certain that the attackers, members of the 28th Muslim Division from the city of Srebrenica, had indeed left. A half an hour later, they allowed us to proceed, so we finally reached Bratunac. The town was covered with hundreds of small black and white mortuary announcements that had been pasted on walls, poles — everywhere. They bore the names of civilians who had been killed in the surrounding villages by attacks of the 28th Muslim Division. I was amazed. There was no official information about these persistent crimes against men and women of all ages as well as children. The international media was silent.

Perhaps because of my memories of that panorama of death, in 2006 I worked on the translation and editing of a book published in Banja Luka, *The Hidden Dossier of the "Genocide" of Srebrenica*. It was an extract from the report produced by the *Documentation Centre of the Republika Srpska for the Investigation of War Crimes* and the *Office of Relations with the ICTY*. The book was the result of seven years of research. It was based on forty-five thousand pages of documentation drawn from local as well as international documents from non-governmental organizations of different countries; statements made by the commanders of Muslim military units in Srebrenica; representatives of UNPROFOR forces; Dutch government documents as well as those of the International Red Cross; and articles by journalists from *The Guardian*, *The New York Times*, *The Times*, *The Globe & Mail*, *The Economist* and several news agencies. The book was printed in an edition of five hundred copies.

The conclusion of this report revealed a version of events that differed from the Western one, and above all it contradicted statements made by the ICTY in The Hague. It also named the 3,283 Serbian civilian victims who had been tortured and killed between 1992 and 1995 in the region surrounding the city of Srebrenica.

The original publication of the report provoked a furious reaction from High Commissioner Paddy Ashdown, who forbade its distribution. He then had a dossier compiled by a commission of his choosing that conformed to the official version. This took place in September 2004.

The book reported the ICTY judgement on the events that took place in Srebrenica from the trial of General Radislav Krstić, Commander of Drina Corp. Genocide (from the Greek word *génos* (lineage) and from the Latin verb *caedere* (to kill)) means the express will and action undertaken to destroy an entire population: men, women, and children. In order to validate its concept of genocide, the Court reasoned that genocide occurs when the members of an ethnic group are killed with the aim of one day diminishing its population, thus making the group in question no longer viable in that area. (Edward Herman, pp. 44, 55 and 60 in *Le dossier caché du "Genocide" de Srebrenica*, Editions le Verjus, Association Verité et Justice, Paris 2005 ; *Il dossier nascosto del genocidio di Srebrenica*, La citta del sole, Naples January 2007).

This ruling seemed to impose the notion that even the death of a small number of men could have either jeopardized the future of that ethnic group or destroyed it. It's a curious form of genocide!

There is no doubt that the Srebrenica problem of July 11, 1995 occurred as the logical conclusion of a long anti-Serbian disinformation campaign that began in the summer of 1992. I would like to call to mind the rising number of cases at that time in which Bosnian Serbs were charged with the cowardly murders of civilians in Sarajevo: the bread line massacre (May 27, 1992); the grenade attack during Douglas Hurd's visit (July 17, 1992); the shelling of the cemetery (August 4, 1992); and the killing of ABC TV producer David Kaplan (August 13, 1992). These events were followed by the discovery of the refugee camp in Trnopolje, where the image of a skeletal young Muslim man suggested the idea of a concentration camp. This fake news, along with the charge of the mass rape of Muslim women, renewed the media campaign against Bosnian Serbs. Finally, the shells that killed civilians at the Markale Street Market in Sarajevo (February 6, 1994 and August 28, 1995) were staged. Thus, the profile of the ideal Nazi criminals was created step by step. Everything took place in Sarajevo, where the world's attention was then focused. (See *Offensive in the Balkans* by

Yossef Bodansky, International Media Corporation Ltd. for ISSA, London, 1995)

James Harff, director of the American PR agency *Ruder & Finn Global Public Affairs*, whose client was the Sarajevo government, boasted of his great professional success in an interview with French journalist Jacques Merlino, who reported it in his book *Les vérités yougoslaves ne sont pas toutes bonnes à dire* (The Truths about Yugoslavia Aren't All Nice to Tell) (Albin Michel, Paris 1993). „He admitted that his ethics were not about verifying information, but about grabbing a good one for his client and taking full advantage of it," wrote Merlino. Harff had succeeded in branding the image of "Serbs = Nazis" in public opinion. He suggested the existence of death camps. He also challenged Merlino to prove the opposite of what was by then settled in public opinion.

Since Harff numbered the new Croatian Republic and the Albanians in Kosovo among his clients, a question spontaneously arises: who would benefit from the existence of new Nazis and a new genocide? Some parties in the Balkan Wars would undoubtedly benefit from it: Germany, marked by the Holocaust, could portray itself as a crusader against genocide; Turkey welcomed the opportunity to divert attention from the Armenian genocide they committed, a crime that was gaining official recognition throughout the world. It also benefitted Croatia, which was minimizing the number of victims of the Jasenovac extermination camp, where between 1941 to 1945 about one million Jews, Serbs and Roma were killed. Croatia could retrospectively claim to have been right all along.

During my travels along the front lines in Bosnia-Herzegovina and Krajina in 1992 and later, I noticed that the conduct of the Western powers towards the three warring parties was not impartial.

I would like to recall the attack on United Nations Protected Areas ("UNPA"), which were Serbian areas. In September 1993, the Croatian Army destroyed all the villages in the Medak Pocket. It killed 120 people, men and women over the age of sixty and 40 soldiers. The Croatian attack on the Kraijna by Operation Flash (May 1, 1995) and Operation Storm (August 4, 1995) resulted in 1,800 deaths and the flight of 230,000 refugees. Croatian General Ante Gotovina was responsible for these crimes against unarmed civilians. The Hague Tribunal sentenced him to twenty-four years in prison, but it later released him on appeal. Naser Orić, Commander of the 28th Muslim Division from Srebrenica, who was responsible for the killing of 3,283 Serbian inhabitants, was sentenced to only two years imprisonment, but was then also acquitted on appeal.

I always wondered about the inconsistency of U.S. policy in Bosnia-Herzegovina during the Bosnian War. Even today, I am amazed by the strong presence of Iranian and Saudi NGOs in Sarajevo. Turkey is acting as if Bosnia were its protectorate. I got answers for the first time when I read Michel Chossudovsky's article, which was published by Global Research in 2002: *NATO's War on Yugoslavia: Bill Clinton Worked Hand in Glove with Al Qaeda: "Helped Turn Bosnia into Militant Islamic Base".*[1]

> A 1997 Congressional document by the Republican Party Committee (RPC), while intent upon smearing President Bill Clinton, nonetheless sheds light on the Clinton administration's insidious role in recruiting and training jihadist mercenaries with a view to transforming Bosnia into a "Militant Islamic Base".

---

1   https://www.globalresearch.ca/bill-clinton-worked-hand-in-glove-with-al-qaeda-helped-turn-bosnia-into-militant-islamic-base/5474094

In many regards, Bosnia and Kosovo (1998–1999) were "dress rehearsals" for the destabilization of the Middle East (Iraq, Libya, Syria, Yemen).

(...)

The RCP report reveals how the US administration — under advice from Clinton's National Security Council headed by Anthony Lake — "helped turn Bosnia into a militant Islamic base" leading to the recruitment through the so-called "Militant Islamic Network," of thousands of Mujahideen from the Muslim world....

(...)

That policy, personally approved by Bill Clinton in April 1994 at the urging of CIA Director-designate (and then-NSC chief) Anthony Lake and the U.S. ambassador to Croatia Peter Galbraith, has, according to the *Los Angeles Times* (citing classified intelligence community sources), "played a central role in the dramatic increase in Iranian influence in Bosnia."

In closing, I would like to quote the extraordinary French geopolitical expert General Pierre-Marie Gallois, who declared during a discussion of American foreign policy in Bosnia in 1997: *"The United States opened the gates of Europe to Islam."*

**Ambassador James B. Bissett** joined the Canadian government in 1956, where he spent the next thirty-six years as a public servant in the Departments of Citizenship and Immigration and Foreign Affairs. During the early 1970s, he served at the Canadian High Commission in London, England. In 1980 he became the Assistant Undersecretary of State for Social Affairs in the Department of External Affairs. In 1990 he was appointed Canadian Ambassador to Yugoslavia, Bulgaria, and Albania, in which capacity he served until 1992. After leaving the government he became the Chief of Mission in Moscow for the International Organization for Migration (IOM), which helped Russia deal with the mass migration of ethnic Russians returning from other parts of the former Soviet Union. He returned to Canada in 1997 and continues to lecture and write articles related to foreign affairs and migration issues. (*Source*: Wikipedia)

**Christopher Black** is a Canadian international criminal lawyer and activist. He was a Vice-Chair of the International Committee for the Defense of Slobodan Milošević and Chair of its International Legal Committee.

He was also Lead Defense Counsel to General Augustine Ndindiliyimana, Chief of Staff, Rwanda Gendarmerie, in the Military II Trial at the International Criminal Tribunal for Rwanda. In 2014, he won General Ndindiliyimana's complete acquittal on numerous counts of genocide and crimes against humanity.

Mr. Black is also on the List of Counsel at the International Criminal Court and is an executive member of the Canadian Peace Council.

**Peter Brock** broke ranks with the American press in 1993 with his exposé about major Western news organizations trying to force the U.S. and European allies into the Balkan War against the Serbs. *His Dateline Yugoslavia: The Partisan Press*[1] rocked media giants like *The New York Times*, *The Washington Post*, *Associated Press* and others. He named names in his subsequent book, *Media Cleansing: Dirty Reporting* (2005/06).

**Stephen Karganović** played integral roles in the teams of defense attorneys at the ICTY in The Hague (2001–2008) that defended: Dragan Obrenović (Chief of Staff of the Zvornik Brigade in the Army of the Republika Srpska); Jovica Stanišić (the former Chief of the Serbian State Security Service); and Momčilo Krajišnik (co-founder of the Serbian Democratic Party (SDS) with Radovan Karadžić, Speaker of the National Assembly of the Republika Srpska, and member of the Presidency of the Republika Srpska).

Karganović has been the President of the non-governmental organization, The Srebrenica Historical Project, since it was founded in 2008. Its mission statement, in part, reads:

> The long-term goal of our project is to create a historical archive which would include testimony, documents, and the results of all relevant research that might shed useful light on Srebrenica, viewed not as an event but as a phenomenon.... We do not have a final word to offer, but we do suggest the following viewpoint which we believe is irreproachably correct: reducing Srebrenica to a couple of days in July 1995 does not simply trivialize the tragic events that took place during that brief period; it is a crude caricature

---

1     *Foreign Policy,* (Winter 1993/94), Carnegie Endowment for International Peace, Washington, D.C.

of broader historical reality. Any discussion of Sre-brenica outside its context (historical, political, cultural, and so forth) is meaningless.

**Višeslav Simić** has been professor at Tecnologico de Monterrey, Mexico City, since 2010. He is currently based at the International Relations Department, Campus Cuernavaca, Tecnológico de Monterrey, Cuernavaca, Morelos, México. He was Project Manager and Acting Director of an international humanitarian and development organization in Moscow and Tbilisi (1995–1997). He also served as a member of an ICTY investigative team for crimes committed at the Čelebići concentration camp in Bosnia-Herzegovina.

Mr. Simić holds a B.A. in International Relations from the University of Colorado at Boulder; a Master of Arts degree in International Cooperation from Ortega y Gasset Institute in Madrid, Spain; and he obtained a Ph.D. in Public Policy from EGAP Tec de Monterrey, in Mexico.

**Jovan Milojevich** recently received a Ph.D. in Political Science (specializing in International Relations, Methodologies, and Political Psychology) from the University of California, Irvine. He received a Master of Arts degree from the same institution in 2015 and a Bachelor of Arts degree from the University of California, Berkeley in 2011. From 2016–2017, he was a Visiting Researcher at the Sanford School of Public Policy at Duke University, where he worked as the Project Director of a National Institutes of Health (NIH) funded study on social connectedness. His work has been published in academic journals such as the International Journal of Press-Politics, International Journal of Communication, Journal of Balkan and Near Eastern Studies, and Serbian Studies. His paper, "When Justice Fails: Re-raising the Question of Ethnic Bias at the International Criminal Tribunal for the Former Yugoslavia (ICTY)," was recently awarded the prestigious Giuseppe Torre Award.

**Jean Toschi Marazzani Visconti** was born in Milan of an American mother and an Italian father. She began her career as an assistant director and casting director in the film industry. Later, she founded her own public relations and communications agency in 1980. In 1992, she organized a journey to Yugoslavia for the 1986 Nobel Peace Prize winner, Elie Wiesel. During the Balkan Wars, she visited the front lines from Croatia to Sarajevo, and from Krajina to Montenegro and Kosovo. She witnessed the NATO bombardment of Serbia in 1999, which she covered for *Il manifesto, Limes, Avvenimenti, Balkan Infos, Duga,* and *Maiz.* She translated into Italian *Monopoly* by Michel Collon and *Dossier Srebrenica.* She is the author of various books which include: *Le temps du réveil*; *The Corridor: Journey in the War of Yugoslavia*; and *The Gateway of Islam: Bosnia-Herzegovina, an Ungovernable Country.* She is currently working on collaborative projects with the Zambon Verlag publishing house. She is also the international spokesperson for Italian *CNGNN for a World without War.* She was also a jury member for the Giuseppe Torre Award, which is presented by the Italian *Coordinamento Jugoslavo* for the best essays on the ICTY.

# RETHINKING SREBRENICA

STEPHEN KARGANOVIĆ
LJUBIŠA SIMIĆ

*Rethinking Srebrenica* presents an irrefutable body of research that exposes the Srebrenica "narrative" as largely a legal and factual fiction that has been used to advance U.S. and E.U. political goals in Serbia and the Balkans, as well as to rationalize aggressive wars worldwide, using the pretext of "humanitarian intervention."

*Rethinking Srebrenica* is a holistic examination of the events that took place in Srebrenica during 1992–1995, which includes: the killing of more than 3,000 Serbian civilians in the Srebrenica area; the refusal of Muslim forces to honor disarmament agreements; and the UN's reluctance to enforce these agreements. Furthermore, *Rethinking Srebrenica* refutes the claim that "8,000 men and boys" were killed in Srebrenica by making a comprehensive review of The Hague Tribunal's (ICTY's) own evidence in the case. The authors conclude that about 950 Muslim soldiers were killed during the taking of Srebrenica, of which about 400 had been executed, as evidenced by ligatures and blindfolds found during exhumations. These executions were certainly a war crime, but by no means a "genocide."

*Rethinking Srebrenica* also demystifies the media manipulation that took place in creating the figure of "8,000" victims. For instance, the authors discovered that The International Commission for Missing Persons in the Former Yugoslavia (ICMP), the agency that performed the DNA testing to identify the alleged victims, had never been issued professional certification by Gednap, the international agency that regulates DNA testing laboratories. The authors also examine the contradictory and unreliable evidence presented by The Hague's star witness, Drazen Erdemovic. And the authors exposed the alleged satellite photos of the massacre to be a fraud, as well as the alleged radio intercepts that were used as evidence against the Bosnian Serbs.

US$19.95          ISBN: 978-09709198-3-0          368 pages

Available from: www.unwrittenhistory.com